LOGIC AND KNOWLEDGE

Logic and Knowledge

SELECTED PAPERS

Volume I

JOHN LESLIE

J. L. MACKIE

EDITED BY
JOAN MACKIE
AND
PENELOPE MACKIE

CLARENDON PRESS · OXFORD
1985

Oxford University Press, Walton Street, Oxford OX2 6DP

London New York Toronto
Delhi Bombay Calcutta Madras Karachi
Kuala Lumpur Singapore Hong Kong Tokyo
Nairobi Dar es Salaam Cape Town
Melbourne Auckland

and associated companies in
Beirut Berlin Ibadan Mexico City Nicosia

Oxford is a trade mark of Oxford University Press

Published in the United States
by Oxford University Press, New York

British Library Cataloguing in Publication Data
Mackie, J. L.
Logic and knowledge.——(Selected papers; v. 1)
1. Knowledge, Theory of
I. Title   II. Mackie, Joan
III. Mackie, Penelope   IV. Series
121   BD161
ISBN 0-19-824679-X

Library of Congress Cataloging in Publications Data
Mackie, J. L. (John Leslie)
Logic and knowledge.
Includes index.
1. Knowledge, Theory of——Addresses, essays, lectures.
2. Logic——Addresses, essays, lectures.
I. Mackie, Joan.   II. Mackie, Penelope.   III. Title
BD161.M22   1985   121   84-23101
ISBN 0-19-824679-X (v. 1)

Printed in Great Britain by
Butler & Tanner Ltd, Frome and London

PREFACE

J. L. MACKIE published over seventy articles between 1946 and his death in December 1981 at the age of sixty-four. The present volume contains a selection from his published papers on logic, epistemology, and metaphysics, together with four pieces on these subjects that have not appeared in print before. *Persons and Values*, a companion volume of papers on moral philosophy and related topics, is published simultaneously by Oxford University Press.

In September 1981 Mackie made a selection from his papers for publication by Oxford University Press in two volumes; Chapters I-XII of the present collection were chosen by him for a volume on logic, metaphysics, and epistemology. The diversity of John Mackie's philosophical interests will be well known to readers of his works, including the six books—on philosophical logic, causation, the philosophy of Locke, ethics, and the philosophy of religion—which appeared between 1973 and 1982. His selection of papers for the present volume gives some small indication of the range of his contributions, as well as exhibiting the characteristic features of his own brand of empiricism and his distinctive style of philosophical discussion.

The selection begins with a study of the philosophy of John Anderson, whose work is also reviewed in Chapter III, in the context of a discussion of the nature of empiricism and its relation to rationalism. Chapters II and V deal with topics that have been prominent in discussions of empiricism: in Chapter II, an examination of the epistemological status of sense-statements, Mackie gives a negative answer to the question whether such statements can possess incorrigibility in any philosophically important sense, while in Chapter V, 'Proof', Mackie seeks to undermine the basis of some arguments for the thesis that arithmetical propositions are non-empirical. Chapter IV, a logical study of the nature of self-refutation, includes remarks on the implications of this phenomenon for an empiricist philosophy, as well as an assessment of arguments employed by Descartes and Berkeley.

Two chapters deal with various problems involving causation:

Chapter XI, whose subject is Newcomb's Paradox, and Chapter X, where the main topic is the causal efficacy of mind (in particular, the question whether certain forms of non-reductive materialism can avoid commitment to epiphenomenalism), while Mackie's 'A Defence of Induction' is printed here as Chapter XII.

The collection also contains discussions of the nature of intentionality (Chapter VIII), of explanation in the social sciences (Chapter VII) and of problems in decision theory (the chapter on Newcomb's Paradox mentioned above), together with a previously unpublished paper on Karl Popper's 'third world' (Chapter IX), and a review article on the subject of Plato's Theory of Forms (Chapter VI). The first five chapters originally appeared between 1962 and 1966, and Chapter VI in 1952, while Chapters VII–XII belong to the period from 1975 to 1979. Full details of the provenance of the papers are given in the footnotes at the beginning of each chapter.

Mackie had undertaken to provide further unpublished material for the volume, and had also thought of writing an introduction to the collection, but he did not live to carry out these plans. In preparing the volume for publication we have added the papers printed as Chapters XIII–XVI. Chapter XIII ('Causation in Concept, Knowledge, and Reality') and Chapter XV ('Locke and Representative Perception'), both written in 1977 and published here for the first time, develop in greater detail arguments expressed in Mackie's *The Cement of the Universe: A Study of Causation* (Oxford, 1974) and his *Problems from Locke* (Oxford, 1976). Mackie wrote, but did not publish in his lifetime, a number of papers on absolute space and time; his latest thoughts on the subject are represented by Chapter XIV, a paper delivered at a conference in September 1981, and published after his death. Chapter XVI, the longer part of which is a paper read to the Oxford Philosophical Society in October 1980, is a contribution, printed here for the first time, to recent debates concerning the opposition between realism and anti-realism.

A complete bibliography of John Mackie's publications is to be found in *Morality and Objectivity*, the memorial volume edited by Ted Honderich (Routledge and Kegan Paul, 1985). Among Mackie's writings are many, besides those printed here, that might have been included in the present collection. However, we have thought it best to preserve Mackie's own selection, and space has not permitted the addition of more than three or four articles, which we have chosen from material still unpublished at the time of his death.

Oxford   P.M.
February 1985

ACKNOWLEDGEMENTS

FOR permission to include in this volume those papers that were originally published elsewhere we are very grateful to the various copyright holders and editors concerned, and express our thanks to the Aristotelian Society for permission to reprint 'Proof'; to *The Australasian Journal of Philosophy* for permission to reprint 'The Philosophy of John Anderson', 'Are There Any Incorrigible Empirical Statements?', 'Rationalism and Empiricism', and the critical notice of Sir David Ross's *Plato's Theory of Ideas*; to Basil Blackwell for permission to reprint 'Ideological Explanation' from *Explanation*, edited by Stephan Körner; to Cambridge University Press for permission to reprint 'Problems of Intentionality' from *Phenomenology and Philosophical Understanding*, edited by Edo Pivčević; to *The Canadian Journal of Philosophy* for permission to reprint 'Newcomb's Paradox and the Direction of Causation'; to The Macmillan Press for permission to reprint 'A Defence of Induction' from *Perception and Identity*, edited by G.F. Macdonald; to Peter A. French, Theodore Uehling Jr., and Howard K. Wettstein, editors of *Midwest Studies in Philosophy*, Vol. IV (*Studies in Metaphysics*), and the University of Minnesota Press for permission to reprint 'Mind, Brain, and Causation'; to *The Philosophical Quarterly* and Basil Blackwell for permission to reprint 'Self-Refutation—A Formal Analysis'; to D. Reidel Publishing Company, Dordrecht, Holland, for permission to reprint 'Three Steps Towards Absolutism' from *Space, Time, and Causality*, edited by Richard Swinburne.

CONTENTS

I

THE PHILOSOPHY OF
JOHN ANDERSON[1]

JOHN ANDERSON'S philosophy is at once so independent and so
systematic that it would be a mistake to assimilate either his position as a whole, or any of his main doctrines, to those of any
earlier or contemporary thinkers. He was prepared, in 1927, not
only to call his theory empiricism but also to speak of realism,
naturalism, materialism, pluralism, determinism, and positivism as
identical or closely related views;[2] and there are indeed similarities
and agreements between Anderson and other empiricists, realists
and so on; but these often mask fundamental disagreements and
differences in spirit or method. Nevertheless, it is not difficult to
state briefly the salient features of his philosophy.[3] His central
doctrine is that there is only one way of being, that of ordinary
things in space and time, and that every question is a simple issue
of truth or falsity, that there are no different degrees or kinds of
truth. His propositional view of reality implies that things are ir-
reducibly complex, that we can never arrive at simple elements in
any field. Anderson rejects systematically the notion of entities that
are constituted, wholly or partly, by their relations: there can be
no ideas or sensa whose nature it is to be known or perceived, no
consciousness whose nature it is to know, no values whose nature
it is to be ends or to direct action. Knowledge is a matter of finding
what is objectively the case; all knowledge depends on observation

Reprinted from the *Australasian Journal of Philosophy*, Vol. 40, No. 3 (December
1962). In Mackie's notes *'AJP'* stands for this journal and *'AJPP'* for the same
journal at an earlier period when it was known as the *Australasian Journal of
Psychology and Philosophy*.

[1] This article is based on a paper read at the Annual Congress of the Australasian
Association of Philosophy in Sydney, August 1962. References to Anderson's writings are given by pages in the recently published collection of his papers, entitled
Studies in Empirical Philosophy (Sydney, 1962)—hereafter abbreviated as *SEP*—
though most of the articles referred to appeared earlier in this or other journals.

[2] 'Empiricism', *SEP*, p. 3.

[3] The following summary repeats what I said in a brief note in the last (August
1962) number of this *Journal*.

and is fallible; we do not build up the knowledge of facts or laws out of any more immediate or more reliable items. Ethics is a study of the qualities of human activities; there can be no science of what is right or obligatory, and the study of moral judgements would belong to sociology, not to ethics. Similarly aesthetics can only be a study of the characteristics of beautiful things, not a study of feelings or judgements and not a source of directives for artists. Minds, like anything else, are complex spatio-temporal things: they are societies of motives or feelings, and there is no ultimate self to which the motives belong. Similarly a society is a complex of movements which both co-operate and compete; it has no inclusive social purpose, but neither is it reducible to its individual members. And all things have their regular causal ways of working.

But while it is easy thus to sum up Anderson's philosophical position, it is a more difficult and much more complicated task to show how these principles are established or supported, how they are worked out in detail, and how they would be defended against objections and criticisms.

A complete presentation of Anderson's system should start with a full account of his logic, and go on to show how his other theories are developed with its help. For Anderson holds that logic is also what we might call general ontology: it studies the formal features of facts, of what is objectively real. These general formal features do not in themselves determine what is the case in the other fields studied, for example, by epistemology or ethics or social theory, but they do determine a method of enquiry for all fields. Logic tells us what sorts of fact to look out for, and, what is even more important, it rules out as illogical certain views and certain ways of approaching special questions which inevitably result in confusion.

However, I cannot now present Anderson's system in this way. Even if it were otherwise possible, it would take too long. Also, Anderson did not publish any adequate statement of his logic, and one would have to rely at crucial points on unpublished material or hearsay evidence. And, finally, Anderson's philosophical system viewed in this way depends on a complete identification of logic with ontology which is, to say the least, very hard to defend and which , I shall argue below, cannot in the end be defended; but if it were rejected then his whole position, presented in the proposed way, would be undermined. But in fact much of Anderson's philosophy can be and was supported in other ways. It will be better to start, therefore, from what may be called his logic in use, his logic as revealed in the stock patterns of argument by which he criticizes views opposed to his own. His logic in use does provide a powerful battery of critical methods of which some are in fairly common use, but others are either peculiar to Anderson or are developed by him in a special way.

I QUALITIES AND RELATIONS

One of Anderson's most characteristic moves in controversy is to accuse an opponent of *relativism*, that is, the confusing of things or qualities with their relations. These can, of course, be distinguished: a quality is an intrinsic feature of a thing, it belongs to the thing itself, whereas a relation holds between two or more things. But the charge of confusing them seems to be directed against several distinct ways of thinking.

In the first place, we must not treat anything as being both a quality and a relation. This rule is broken, for example, by Bentham in that his theory presupposes that pleasure is a definite thing, and yet also treats it merely as that which we like or want,[4] that is to say, Bentham both takes being pleasant as a quality of certain states or conditions of human beings and also identifies being pleasant with being liked or wanted, which are relations. There are many other examples of this sort of confusion in ethics. Goodness is taken both to be a quality and to consist in a thing's being pursued;[5] and similarly rightness, wrongness, obligatoriness, and so on are both regarded as qualities of actions and also held to consist in the fact that the actions are permitted or forbidden or required by some authority; that is, in certain relations.

Applied thus, Anderson's criticism of relativism in ethics tells against views which would commonly be said to commit the 'naturalistic fallacy', by identifying ethical qualities with these natural relations. But Anderson's criticism is directed also against non-naturalist views. Besides the simple treatment of something as both a quality and an explicitly asserted relation, there is a more complex kind of view according to which the obligatory, for example, is 'that which is essentially demanded of us or that whose nature it is

---

[4] 'Utilitarianism', *SEP*, p. 229.
[5] 'Realism versus Relativism in Ethics', *SEP*, p. 240.

to command our obedience'.[6] There is no longer any definite authority that does the demanding. The relation 'is demanded by' has been shorn of its second term, so that it looks more like a quality, but the supposed feature of obligatoriness still has something of the relation in it, we are still expected to respond to it as to a demand. It is this more complex sort of confusion which Anderson takes to be most characteristic of relativism, describing this as 'the concept of something whose nature it is to have a certain relation'.[7] Another example of it is the notion of something's being intrinsically an end, or good as an end, that is, as something whose nature it is to be pursued, regardless of whether, as a matter of historical fact, anyone pursues it or not. It is clear that the supposed non-natural ethical qualities are unlike any natural qualities precisely because they involve such relations of requirement and pursuit, that is, because they are the outcome of this more complex sort of relativist confusion.

The Socratic or Platonic doctrine that an ordinary sensible thing can be described only by saying that it strives after or imitates certain Forms is an example of yet another variety of relativism: for all the qualities of such a thing are thus identified with relations to various Forms.[8] But here qualities are being explained away by being reduced to relations, and moreover to relations which are postulated for this purpose, for which we have no independent evidence. This example, indeed, also illustrates what Anderson regards as another basic type of philosophical error, the attempt to 'get behind the proposition'. A thing's being of a certain sort is the irreducible minimum of a fact or state of affairs, and if we try to analyse this further we encounter insurmountable difficulties. Any such analysis is circular, in that we cannot help introducing, in the analysis, *things of certain sorts*—that is, items of the kind that was to be analysed away—and this circularity can be emphasized by showing that the philosopher who attempts such an analysis is committed to a vicious infinite regress. For example, we may try to explain a thing's being of a certain sort by reference to a set of attributes and a substance which is distinct from all its attributes. But then the substance itself, to be a real entity, must have some features, and yet by the proposed analysis it has only some relation

---

[6] *Op. cit.*, p. 240.   [7] *Op. cit.*, p. 238.
[8] 'Realism and Some of its Critics', *SEP*, pp. 49–51.

of ownership to its various attributes, now regarded as distinct entities. Such a view is made plausible only by a confusion which enables us to treat the substance's relations to its attributes as being at the same time intrinsic qualities of the substance itself.

In these examples we find what amounts to a proposal to reduce all qualities to relations. Another mistake which Anderson includes under the heading of relativism is to treat as a quality what is really nothing but a relation. Thus consciousness has often been thought of as a quality of minds, indeed as the distinctive quality of mind or spirit, but, when we enquire what consciousness is, only two accounts seem to be possible, each of which treats consciousness as a relation. One is that to be conscious is to be aware of various things—that is, consciousness is a relation between a person and what he knows—the other is that to be conscious is to be a mental state or process of which its owner is aware, as when we distinguish conscious thoughts or wishes from unconscious ones—that is, consciousness is a relation between something mental and the owner who is aware of it. In fact the popular view of consciousness confuses these two converse relations with one another and treats the result as a quality.[9]

Anderson is also saying that any relation holds between two distinct and independent things. Realists commonly deny the idealist doctrine of 'constitutive relations', and Anderson generalizes this denial, saying that it cannot be part of anything's nature that it should have certain relations.[10] This point is to be combined with some well-known moves in the criticism of, for example, the notion of powers or agencies which explain why things behave as they do. It is a stock criticism that we cannot explain why fire warms us by saying that fire has a power to produce the sensation of warmth, because this explanation would be circular: to speak of this power is only to speak, in a somewhat misleading way, of the causal fact that fire does make us warm. But if someone denied this, and said that the power was an intrinsic feature of the fire, we could reply not only by making the stock objection that this power would be an unobservable entity and by criticizing the reasoning by which such purely inferential entities are introduced, but also by

[9] 'The Knower and the Known', *SEP*, pp. 29, 39; 'Mind as Feeling', *SEP*, pp. 69-70.
[10] 'The Knower and the Known', *SEP*, p. 29; 'Realism and Some of its Critics', *SEP*, pp. 42-6; 'The Cogito of Descartes', *SEP*, pp. 109-11.

making the characteristically Andersonian comment that such a
power would be something whose nature it is to have a certain
relation.[11] The presence of a power to produce warmth is supposed
logically to necessitate that warmth will (in the appropriate circumstances) be produced; and thus anyone who tried to defend the
notion of powers as entities distinct from the processes they explain
would be guilty of confusing quality with relation.

Similarly Anderson argues that there cannot be any such thing
as an idea or sensum or sense-datum, part of whose nature it is to
be known or perceived.[12] He develops this point especially in criticism of Berkeley, but if this principle is sound it has radical
consequences throughout epistemology and undermines views that
are still widely held.[13]

At times Anderson seems to argue that we cannot properly specify something by relations alone: 'we do recognise and speak of
minds and therefore we must already have recognised some mental
quality'.[14] This is more questionable, but what is clearly correct is
the point which he also makes, that if we did specify something
merely by its relations we would know nothing about the thing
itself. The fact that x has the relation R to b does not logically
imply anything intrinsic to x, and we can use this fact to infer
something about x only if we have independent information about
the sorts of thing that enter into this relation R, that is, if we have
sometimes observed directly both terms of this relation.

Since Anderson's condemnation of 'relativism' thus covers a
number of different ways of thinking, which he himself does not
distinguish clearly, we may well ask whether this line of criticism
is equally effective in all cases. Some of the views criticized are
simply inconsistent, and it is enough to point this out. But elsewhere we need arguments of other sorts. The philosopher who
speaks about consciousness is challenged to point out, empirically,

---

[11] 'Realism versus Relativism in Ethics', *SEP*, p. 238.

[12] 'The Knower and the Known', *SEP*, pp. 29, 32-3; 'Empiricism and Logic',
SEP, p. 163.

[13] Thus (as I shall argue in an article to be published in the May 1963 number
of this *Journal*) the view that our knowledge of our own present sensations is
infallible, and that statements about such sensations are (in one sense) incorrigible,
rests finally upon the identification of such a sensation with its owner's awareness
of *it*. [This article is reprinted as Chapter II below.—Edd.]

[14] 'Mind as Feeling', *SEP*, p. 75; cf. 'Realism and Some of its Critics', *SEP*,
p. 43.

any quality over and above the two relations; one who tries to reduce all qualities to relations is shown to be involved in a circularity or in an infinite regress. The non-naturalists' doctrine of intrinsic ends or duties is not, on the face of it, *inconsistent*, and to dismiss it Anderson has either to appeal to logic of a more informative sort, to the principle that there just cannot be qualities that are intrinsically prescriptive in the proposed way, or to argue on epistemological grounds in the traditional empiricist manner: 'an imperative quality is something we could never observe or study'.[15]

But although the accusation of relativism, by itself, is not equally effective in all cases, there is still some force in Anderson's bringing together, under this heading, of these different sorts of view. For he can plausibly explain the more complex confusions as having arisen from the simpler ones, and thus undermine any argument from a widespread tendency to speak and think in terms of, say, prescriptive qualities to the conclusion that we are right to do so.

2 OBJECTIVITY

Another of Anderson's characteristic methods is to insist on objectivity, on attending to *what is the case*. This, too, covers several distinct though related matters.

First, Anderson is maintaining that there are fully objective facts to be discovered; secondly, he is directing our attention, in any field of discussion or enquiry, to the facts, to what is the case, and re-formulating, if necessary, the questions under discussion so as to achieve this; and, thirdly, in examining what anyone says he asks what objective statement he is making, what he is asserting to be the case.

The third of these is a technique of clarification, and can also be a way of exposing 'fine phrases and mystification'. In Hume's *Dialogues*, Cleanthes speaks of 'the adjustment of means to ends' as a striking feature of the world, as a mark of design: but Anderson says that this 'signifies merely that when something happens to a thing it does something else'[16]—which, of course, is not very striking and could hardly be called a mark of anything. The reference to 'means' and 'ends' is not part of a description of what is there,

---

[15] 'The Meaning of Good', *SEP*, p. 260.   [16] 'Design', *SEP*, p. 93.

but represents someone's attitude to the matter: it is *we* who call an effect an end, and a cause a means, when we want to bring about that effect or are satisfied with it.

But, it may be objected, the speaker may fully intend to do something other than to describe what is the case: if he is expressing a feeling or attitude, giving an instruction or a piece of advice, and so on, why should we ignore or forbid this?

This objection brings us back to the second aspect of Anderson's insistence on objectivity. This looks like a particular scientific policy: it is as if he were saying, 'Let us ask and answer questions of this kind only'. But Anderson is doing more than this: he is saying that until a question has been framed in this factual way it is confused and misleading. If someone asks, in a context of moral choice, 'What am I to do?', no simple answer is possible because no clear question has been asked. Any answer of the form 'You ought to do such-and-such' would presuppose some interests, some purposes, and yet it suggests that the obligatoriness or rightness of the proposed course of action is a simple fact. Even if the answer satisfies the questioner, because he and the answerer are both thinking in terms of the same set of purposes, the position has still not been made clear.[17] To take such a question and answer at their face value is to think within a certain attitude, from a certain purposive point of view, and yet to treat what are mere reflections of our purposes as if they were features of the state of affairs being considered—an example of the relativist confusion examined above. The only satisfactory way of dealing with this situation is to make explicit the purposes that are implicit in the question, 'What am I to do?', and to ask what action will best fulfil these purposes. But we then have a question about a fully objective issue, not a problem of conduct.

Anderson, however, combines this criticism with a quite different one, that such a question of conduct presupposes that we can 'step out of the movement of things';[18] since the answer to such a question would be a directive for an *uncaused* act, this whole 'voluntarist' way of thinking is in conflict with Anderson's determinist view that 'all our actions, all our questionings and answerings, are part of the movement of things'.

These arguments are used against the view that ethics is a science

[17] 'Realism versus Relativism in Ethics', *SEP*, pp. 240-2.
[18] *Op. cit.*, p. 241.

of moral judgements.[19] To treat ethics in this way is to work within some practical system of thought, to fail to consider what simply is the case. To turn this into a genuine study we must take one of two courses: either we ask whether the moral judgements are true or false—and then we deal directly with ethical facts, whatever they may be, and the moral judgements are an irrelevant intrusion—or else we concern ourselves with the fact that these judgements are made—and then we are studying psychological or social facts: the judgements (that is, the judgings) are the objects of our study, not a contribution to the study itself. Whichever course we take, we achieve a genuine study only by considering *some* fully objective facts. If we work within the system of judgements we are confusing these two genuine studies to the detriment of both, and we are in danger of taking what are only discoveries about the judgements to be discoveries about ethical properties of the actions themselves.

While most of Anderson's important articles were written before linguistic philosophy became prominent, he would have applied a similar criticism to this approach. He spoke of 'linguistic' as 'one of the main sources of contemporary confusion, operating ... as a substitute at once for philosophy and for a real theory of language'.[20] The point is that to achieve a genuine study we must either investigate the facts that are talked about or study the fact that they are talked about in certain ways. If we concentrate on the uses of language we fall between these two stools, and we are in danger of taking our discoveries about manners of speaking as answers to questions about what is there. I do not think, however, that we can say any more on general grounds than that this is a *danger*; it is only by detailed discussion on specific points that one could show that linguistic philosophers have actually fallen into this trap.

The first aspect of Anderson's insistence on objectivity, that there are objective facts to be discovered, that some things simply are so, irrespective of anyone's attitude or point of view, and can be known to be so, might seem to be too obvious to need stressing. But Anderson thought it needed to be stressed, in opposition to idealists, to pragmatists, to Marxists, and to all those who in one way or another have taken up the dictum of Protagoras that man

[19] *Op. cit.;* also 'Determinism and Ethics', *SEP*, pp. 214–26. Parallel criticisms are made of the view that aesthetics is the science of aesthetic judgements.

[20] 'Ethics and Advocacy' (1944), *SEP*, p. 279.

is the measure of all things.[21] The basic point is quite clear: any thinker who alleges that all truth is in some way relative is either saying nothing at all or else cannot avoid committing himself to some assertions for which he claims simple and absolute truth. It may be alleged that everything exists only from a certain point of view; but (even if it made sense to speak of existing from a point of view) the fact that a certain thing exists from a certain point of view is itself a simple fact, it just is so, and not from any point of view. Even if we could not detach an object from someone's experiencing of it, the whole situation, the person's experiencing of this object, would itself just be there. A certain economic theory may be merely a part of bourgeois ideology, but if so the fact that it *is* a part of bourgeois ideology is not itself a part of any ideology, it just is the case. If some so-called truths are socially relative, then that they are so is a truth which is not socially relative. And once the relativist has acknowledged that he is himself claiming to know some absolute truths, he cannot consistently reject, *on general grounds*, all other claims to the knowledge of absolute truth: he would have to show in what way his own thinking and observation are more accurate than those of the people whose assertions embody merely relative truths.

These obvious points may be worth labouring because in popular discussion those who reject some of the absolutes that Anderson rejected (such as objective ethical norms, or objective values in general) are commonly called relativists. It would be particularly misleading to apply this term to Anderson, for he was very far indeed from accepting any theory of the relativity of knowledge or truth, and he held that it is misleading to speak of anything as existing relatively or subjectively. I would argue, however—in this partly against Anderson himself—that to say that certain supposed entities (e.g. values) are only relative or subjective is compatible with, and indeed is often an expression of, a concern for objectivity; what is traditionally called subjectivism in ethics is essentially the correct doctrine that the objective facts in this field do not include any (prescriptive) goodness or rightness of actions, that we have only the more complex relational situations that involve, as well as the actions, the attitudes of human beings to them. It is precisely because we want to distinguish what is simply and absolutely the

---

[21] 'Realism and Some of its Critics', *SEP*, pp. 47, 53-5; 'Propositions and Judgments', *SEP*, pp. 16-17; 'Marxist Philosophy', *SEP*, pp. 294-9.

case that we say, perhaps loosely, that values and obligations are merely relative or subjective.

Undoubtedly one of the most disputable—and more frequently disputed—parts of Anderson's philosophy is his own positive ethical theory, that there is an ethical quality, goodness, which characterizes certain human activities or social movements, but which is fully objective, natural, and non-prescriptive. Much of the opposition to this view is, no doubt, misguided. Anderson's positive ethics would be hopelessly implausible as an account of the bulk of moral talk and moral reasoning, or as a study of the ethical use of language; but it was never intended to be anything of the kind, and it would be an *ignoratio elenchi* to appeal against Anderson to the ordinary uses of the word 'good'. Anderson has argued that ordinary ethical thinking is radically confused: the question is, then, what remains of ethics after these confusions are removed.[22] In discussing this question, Anderson says at first that there are two possible consistent views, that we can either take good simply as a quality *or* say that 'X is good' asserts some genuine and explicit relation.[23] But he later rejects this second alternative, and maintains that the only satisfactory ethical position is the qualitative one.[24] However, it is clearly not the only consistent alternative: on this Anderson's first statement was correct. Admittedly the relational view will not be adequate, it will not cover the ground, if there really is a quality, goodness, which it ignores. And this is what Anderson maintains. He claims that he can detect a quality of the sort required; he argues, not very plausibly, that the confusions of traditional ethics are due to the mixing up of relations of demand with the very quality that he detects; and he says that if there were no such ethical quality there would be no separate subject, ethics: it would dissolve into psychology and social theory. However, the first two arguments have little force, and in the third Anderson is assuming far too readily, merely because there has been a traditional confused subject, ethics, that there must also be a corresponding genuine subject, a field for objective enquiry as separable from others as his notion of a 'subject' requires. It seems,

---

[22] Though Anderson rejects this way of putting it: 'Ethics and Advocacy', *SEP*, p. 280.

[23] 'The Meaning of Good' (1942), *SEP*, pp. 254, 262-3.

[24] 'The Nature of Ethics' (1943), *SEP*, p. 269; 'Ethics and Advocacy' (1944), *SEP*, p. 281; 'The One Good' (1945), *SEP*, p. 289.

then, that we can accept Anderson's criticism of normative ethics as involving 'relativist' confusions without adopting his own positive view, and without entering into the acrimonious controversy on the question whether in his own qualitative account he was covertly introducing relations of commendation or support.[25]

Anderson's insistence on objectivity has important corollaries in the peripheral branches of philosophy, such as educational, political and social theory: he constantly stresses a theoretical approach as contrasted with various forms of practicalism which mix up someone's purposes with the facts to be studied. In the same spirit he attacks indeterminism, or at least the approach of those who are indeterminists: 'The indeterminists are those with an axe to grind ... Theoretical concern with what is the case is, it seems to me, coextensive with determinism'.[26] But he also holds that a great deal of modern science, with its close bonds with technology, is equally infected with practicalism, and that mechanist and reductionist views improperly select the features that make things useful and ignore or deny those that are irrelevant to use.[27]

3 THE LIMITATIONS OF INFERENCE AND EXPLANATION

There cannot, Anderson holds, be any *sort* of thing of which we have purely inferential knowledge, and we cannot properly introduce any new *sort* of thing to explain those that are directly observed. No valid inference can introduce a new term: the most it can do is to put together terms that have occurred in the premisses. We can infer a cause from its effects, and use it to explain them, only after we have arrived at the causal law that connects them, and to do this we must have sometimes observed things of the sort to which we say the cause belongs. Explanations that are not of this empirical kind are unsound. When we postulate an explanatory entity of a 'higher' or more 'fundamental' sort to account for some ordinary things that are supposed to be in need of explanation, either the new entity is described in terms borrowed from the ordinary things, and then the explanation is circular and

[25] See the articles named in note 24 above, and the articles by A.D. Hope and A.N. Prior to which they were replies.

[26] 'Causality and Logic', *SEP*, p. 125.

[27] Review of *From Beast-Machine to Man-Machine*, *AJPP*, 1941, p. 285 (not reprinted in *SEP*).

may be shown up by an infinite regress argument; or it is not described at all, and the explanation is illusory; or else it is introduced as that whose nature it is to do such-and-such, and then the explanation is at first sight rationally satisfying, because it logically necessitates what was to be explained, but it is really empty and purely verbal.

It is perhaps unnecessary to describe this part of Anderson's logic in use, because arguments of these types are the familiar and constantly-employed weapons of empiricists of all varieties. But what is characteristic of Anderson is his very general and sweeping use of such arguments in all fields. He holds that they are equally efficacious for getting rid of a purely inferential 'matter' and a purely inferential 'mind' or 'spirit', that they bear equally against 'universals', 'ends', 'values', 'duties', 'powers', 'potentialities', 'essential natures', 'elements', and 'simple data' of all sorts.[28]

4 THE NARROWNESS OF ANDERSON'S LOGIC

One criticism which has been brought against Anderson's philosophy is that the logic on which it is based is far too exiguous.[29] To some extent this objection can be set aside as due to a misunderstanding. Ryle wants a much richer logic than Anderson's because he wants logic to do a quite different job. Where Anderson is concerned to describe whatever things, relations, facts, events, processes, situations, or states of affairs simply *are there*, e.g. when someone knows something, Ryle is concerned to describe the use of the word 'know'; such different questions will naturally call for different answers. It may be that a dispositional account is required of at least some uses of the word 'know', and therefore that we do not use the word 'know' (simply) for any mental process; but dispositions are not entities which are actually present in cases of knowledge. In general we may well need a more complicated 'logic' to describe our various ways of using language than we need to portray the structure of objective situations. And there is the further reply, mentioned above, that in so far as an account of the uses of language spills over into ontology it is liable to be a

[28] 'Design', *SEP*, esp. pp. 88–94; 'Empiricism', *SEP*, esp. p. 13; '"Universals" and Occurrences', *SEP*, pp. 115–21; etc.

[29] See Gilbert Ryle, 'Logic and Professor Anderson', *AJP*, 1950, pp. 137–53. Anderson replies to Ryle (at long last) in 'Empiricism and Logic', *SEP*, pp. 172–85.

confused mixture of what should be the two distinct investigations, the study of the facts about which the language is used and the study of the linguistic phenomena themselves. A straightforward study of the peculiar patterns of language as it is used is something for which Anderson's theory leaves ample room—though he would not call this study logic—just as his basic theory leaves ample room for the psychological and sociological and linguistic study of moral judgements, of the ways in which we deliberate about, recommend, justify, or condemn courses of action—though he would not call this study ethics. But at the same time it is clear that neither of these is a branch of enquiry that Anderson himself had much interest in pursuing.

There is another important contrast between Anderson's methods and those of linguistic philosophers. While Anderson and the linguists have in many respects similar 'deflationary' aims, as Ryle puts it, and are similarly opposed to many idealist, rationalist, or metaphysical doctrines, Anderson's method of criticism is in some ways more firmly based. There is a good deal of arbitrariness in the ontological claims made or presupposed in accounts of how words are used; and where the linguistic empiricists do argue (as opposed to merely reflecting empirical assumptions in their accounts) the arguments are often of a positivist sort; they rest implicitly on some Principle of Verification which their users are not prepared to embrace openly and consistently. But Anderson's empiricist conclusions are backed by arguments of types that he adopts *generally*, and some of these, I believe, are sound.

The charge that Anderson's logic is too exiguous can thus be rebutted with regard to such matters as prescriptive, normative, and performative utterances, causal statements, hypotheticals, modals, dispositional terms, and so on. In all such cases we can and should look for simply descriptive and categorical accounts which cover, perhaps separately, the situations talked about and our ways of talking about them. Anderson discusses these topics in a group of papers:[30] there may be dispute about the correctness of the actual accounts that he gives, but their general purpose can be defended. Nevertheless, I believe that Anderson's logic, even considered as a study of the structure of facts, is too exiguous in certain other respects. For example, there is a strong case for the

[30] 'Causality and Logic', 'The Problem of Causality', 'Hypotheticals', 'Relational Arguments', *SEP*, pp. 122–61.

recognition of singular propositions as distinct from the universals to which Anderson assimilates them; there are situations that involve multiple quantification; and, despite the importance of relations in his general position, relational propositions and the relational arguments that involve them are unfairly squeezed into the subject–predicate and syllogistic mould. If we think, alternatively, of a logical system as a formal calculus, there is a great variety of possible logical systems, with various possible interpretations and applications. In these Anderson was (perhaps perversely) uninterested: as we shall see, he had a reason—as I think, a bad reason—for dismissing them. But the sounder theoretical point which he could make is that the study he calls logic is not a calculus that can be constructed at will or chosen from a range of possible systems: there is a fundamental logic which is presupposed in, and cannot be reduced to, the development and the application of any calculus.

5 FACTS AND PROPOSITIONS

One of Anderson's distinctive doctrines is that things are propositional, that the propositional form gives a clue to the general character of what objectively exists. This doctrine links together his insistence on objectivity, on the one way of being, on plurality and complexity, and his rejection of necessary or self-explanatory entities, of universals and pure particulars. But it seems to me that while it may serve as a fruitful hypothesis, or as a summing-up of conclusions backed by other arguments, we cannot actually argue to the general character of reality in this way. To do so we should have to appeal to the principle of unspeakability, which is examined below, and also identify logic with ontology, propositions with facts; but this complete identification has always been a stumbling-block in his system.

Anderson has, indeed, a strong reason for this identification. He argues that there cannot be any entities that stand between the knower and the fully objective facts or states of affairs which he knows. If we were acquainted directly only with ideas or sensations, we could never infer an external reality from them. In the same way, propositions cannot be allowed to have any such intermediate status: 'When we assert the proposition "All men are mortal", *what* we are asserting is the actual mortality of men, and to call the assertion of the proposition merely a *means* to the asserting of the fact is to say that we have *no* way of asserting the fact, just as we have no way of specifying the "reality" with which certain ideas of ours are supposed to "agree" unless those "ideas" (what we know) *are* the reality'.[31] But against this it is clear that any logic that deals with false propositions, relations of contradiction and contrariety, entertained arguments, falsifications and *reductiones ad absurdum* must be something more than an account of propositions as what is there. This difficulty is an obvious one, but the solution is far from obvious. Anderson sometimes tries to minimize the problem by suggesting that logic can do without falsification and *reductio ad absurdum*,[32] but his real answer is that 'what is meant by the occurrence of a "false proposition" is explained ... as *someone's mistaking* X for Y', that is, there is a 'threefold relationship' which involves the assertor: there is no separable entity, the false proposition itself.[33]

It is, I think, along these lines that the problem is to be solved: but obviously what we *must* do for false propositions we equally *can* do for a great variety of other logical items—hypotheticals, modals, and formal calculi of all kinds. In dealing with these we are describing, incompletely, situations which actually involve 'threefold relationships' at least: but just as this does not prevent us from dealing formally with false propositions and neglecting their assertors, so the same incompleteness is no obstacle to a formal treatment of these further extensions of logic.

This argument also cuts the other way. While we protest against Anderson's dismissing of such extensions of logic merely because they go beyond formal ontology, we must likewise reject his assumption that a system which is satisfactory as logic is on that account alone authoritative with regard to what is there. And once the identification of logic with ontology is thus questioned, some of the arguments by which Anderson restricts his logical theory are undermined. In particular, the view that the 'four forms' cover between them every genuine proposition is defended on grounds that seem to belong less to the logic of facts than to the logic of discussion or debate.[34]

But there is nothing in these qualifications that in any way goes against what Anderson primarily and correctly maintains, that

[31] 'Empiricism and Logic', *SEP*, p. 169   [32] 'Hypotheticals', *SEP*, pp. 142–4.
[33] 'Empiricism and Logic', *SEP*, p. 170.   [34] 'Hypotheticals', *SEP*, pp. 138–9.

when we 'assert a true proposition' what we know and talk about is the objective state of affairs itself. Any *theory* of truth, whether a correspondence theory or coherence theory or any other, which attempts to explain the truth of what is asserted by reducing it to something other than its simply being so, can be rejected for the reasons that Anderson gives: unless at some point we arrive at something which is true just by being so we cannot even say that there is correspondence or coherence.[35]

Once we take account *both* of this point *and* of the fact that we can deal formally, neglecting the persons involved, with 'threefold situations' in which people make mistakes, entertain suppositions, and so on, there is no *further* question whether propositions are or are not facts: there is no set of entities, propositions, for which a home has to be found.

One of the most surprising aspects, to contemporary philosophers, of Anderson's system is his comparative lack of interest in questions about meaning. But he has, in one sense, a reason for not having any *theory* of meaning, just as he has a reason for not having any *theory* of truth. There must be some cases at least where no problem of meaning arises, where the speaker uses words simply to say that something is so, and his hearers are thus directly informed that it is so. The words assert and convey what is the case: that is all there is to it. No further *analysis* of meaning either can or need be given, though no doubt we can look for a *causal* account of how this has come about.[36] However, the fact that meaning is sometimes as simple as this does not show that it is always so, nor does it entail that detailed studies of different aspects or kinds of meaning are always mistaken. But Anderson sometimes suggests this, for example in his quite implausible attempt to reduce imperatives to indicatives.[37]

6 OTHER TYPES OF ARGUMENT

Anderson constantly makes use of the infinite regress form of argument, especially but not exclusively against attempts to 'get

---

[35] 'Mind as Feeling', *SEP*, p. 71.
[36] 'Propositions and Judgments', *SEP*, pp. 16–17; 'The Truth of Propositions', *SEP*, pp. 22–3.
[37] 'Empiricism and Logic', *SEP*, pp. 178–9.

behind the proposition'.[38] However, such regresses seem not to constitute a special sort of philosophical reasoning; they are only a dramatic way of bringing out a contradiction, or the circularity of an explanation or reduction, which could have been pointed out more directly.

He also uses as a fundamental form of criticism the charge that certain views are 'unspeakable', that they are at variance with the conditions of discourse.[39] But once we have distinguished between formal ontology and possible logics of discourse we must admit that something 'unspeakable' might nevertheless be real, though of course we should never be in a position to argue for it or even to assert it. The argument from unspeakability may serve as an *argumentum ad hominem*, but it is not a reliable instrument for ontological demolition or construction.

For similar reasons I am suspicious of what I would call Anderson's programmatic arguments. He will condemn a view on the ground that it could not be worked out, that its adherents will be forced into inconsistency, that they will have to give an account of such-and-such and will be unable to do so without making such-and-such admissions. This is an irritating method of controversy, because it gives us not a genuine argument but merely a sketch of an argument, and we still have to look into the matter in detail to see whether the sketch can be filled in. What sort of an account or working out is needed, and why? And could Anderson's opponents after all supply what is needed without incurring the disastrous consequences prophesied for them? Anderson uses this method partly out of impatience, out of haste to conclude a discussion, and partly because of his love of generalization. But at best it is only a challenge, and at worst it is a sophistic device which serves merely to frighten critics away.

Of these arguments the best-known is one closely connected with Anderson's central doctrine that there is only one way of being: if there were more than one level of reality, how could the different levels be related?[40] On its own, this argument is too vague to establish anything. It is not clear what differences would constitute different ways of being, or in what sense we are obliged to relate

---

[38] See, e.g., ' "Universals" and Occurrences', *SEP*, p. 116.

[39] 'Empiricism', *SEP*, pp. 4-6, 12-14.

[40] See, e.g., 'Causality and Logic', *SEP*, pp. 123-4; 'Empiricism and Logic', *SEP*, p. 179.

or connect them. Of course, if a dualist view is to be speakable we must say that there *are* things of both proposed sorts, but if we have abandoned the identification of logic with ontology it is not clear that things that are spoken of together must exist in the same way. In fact, this argument carries weight only as a summing-up of more detailed arguments—based, perhaps, on the limitations of inference or on the detection of 'relativist' confusions in the account of the things on one or other level, or both, and reinforced, perhaps, by infinite regress criticisms of whatever principle is supposed to authorize the postulating of an entity on a level other than that of empirical objects.

These comments may be illustrated by reference to Anderson's pluralism, his rejection of simple indivisible units (and equally of absolute totalities), whether in physics, in perception, in human society, or anywhere else.[41] There are good reasons for rejecting the rationalist argument that there must be simple units, either to make the world intelligible or because wholes are dependent on their parts, so that there must be ultimate parts for things to be ultimately dependent on. There are corresponding and equally good reasons for rejecting a similar argument that there must be an absolute totality. But Anderson seems to go beyond this to assert the contrary dogma that there *cannot be* ultimate parts or absolute wholes. But it seems to me that we should differentiate our problems. Atomism about perception can be criticized on the ground that the knowledge of a complex cannot be resolved into any collection of observations: observing A *and* observing B will never add up to knowing that A is B, or that A and B are connected in any way, so that unless we could observe complexes directly we should have no knowledge of them, and therefore no knowledge at all. Individualism in social theory is not essentially a doctrine of absolutely simple units: if individual selves are said to be indivisible units, this is a doctrine of philosophical psychology rather than of social theory. Individualism in social theory is the doctrine that societies are built up out of persons, that social phenomena can be adequately explained as the resultant of individual behaviour, and a meaning can be given to this such that we simply have to observe societies to see whether it is true or not; it cannot be ruled out on

---

[41] 'Empiricism', *SEP*, p. 14; 'Realism and Some of its Critics', *SEP*, p. 59; 'Empiricism and Logic', *SEP*, p. 163; 'The Nature of Ethics', *SEP*, p. 268; 'Psychological Moralism', *SEP*, p. 369; 'Classicism', *SEP*, p. 194.

general grounds. All that can be ruled out on general grounds is the argument that the complex *must* be explicable in terms of its components. *Mutatis mutandis*, the same comment applies to social solidarism. In philosophical physics, on the other hand, we do meet a doctrine of absolutely simple units. Now the suggestion that complexes could be built up out of such units is completely *obscure*; it gains plausibility from an improper analogy with observed buildings up of complexes out of smaller complexes. But I doubt whether even such absolute simples can be ruled out as unspeakable; the most we can say is that this suggestion is quite obscure, and that we could never have good grounds for making it. And the same applies to physical holism. That is, we should differentiate the perceptual, the social, and the physical issues, and in the latter two we should stop short of Anderson's extreme doctrine, being content to show that both atomism and holism are commonly adopted for bad reasons, and that we can accept as final, as not needing to be explained away, the observed plurality of complex interacting things.

Both the essential strength and the characteristic faults of Anderson's philosophy are bound up with his love of generality and system—features that he admires even in Hegel.[42] It is this that differentiates him most plainly from the majority of empirically-inclined philosophers of the present day. This tendency to generalize leads him to look for, and to think he has found, logical principles and critical methods that can dispose of false views of all sorts, in all fields, in a succinct and sweeping manner, and thus lay a firm foundation for enquiries that are free from the old confusions. He did in fact find common sources of error in superficially different theories, and he could detect, most penetratingly, the *spirit* of various ways of thinking. But he himself often relied on imperfectly worked out arguments, and impatience with what seemed to him to be obvious errors prevented him from showing in detail where his contemporaries went astray. Also, I have suggested that there were radical difficulties in the core of his system; his inability to surmount these difficulties and his unwillingness to resolve them may have obstructed any adequate presentation of his philosophy. Nevertheless, some of the natural protests against what seem to be his more outrageous doctrines rest on misunderstandings or on a

---

[42] 'The Place of Hegel in the History of Philosophy', *SEP*, p. 79.

sheer refusal to consider his case. And—though this claim needs to be defended not only in more detail than I have offered here, but with more care than Anderson himself was ever prepared to display—I believe that he was often right not only in those doctrines which he shared with other empiricists but also in his pressing of empiricist principles to more radical and surprising conclusions.

II

ARE THERE ANY INCORRIGIBLE EMPIRICAL STATEMENTS?[1]

I MERELY LINGUISTIC CORRIGIBILITY AND INCORRIGIBILITY

'ARE there any incorrigible empirical statements?' This is, I suggest, little more than an up-to-date way of asking the old-fashioned question, 'Are there any indubitable items of empirical knowledge?' The two questions are not exactly equivalent, and there are conceivable circumstances in which we should have to answer 'Yes' to one of them and 'No' to the other, but the latter seems to contain all that is of the greatest philosophical interest in the former: the reasons that we might have for answering the former in a different way from the latter are of comparatively little importance.

For example, suppose that there were no indubitable empirical knowledge, so that any statement that claimed to report an observation was open to the possibility of being false, it might yet be literally incorrigible if our language provided no device for correcting it, if we happened to have no way of saying 'I was wrong'. But this is surely not an answer to the question that really bothers anyone who asks whether there are any incorrigible empirical state-

Reprinted from the *Australasian Journal of Philosophy* Vol. 41, No. 1 (May 1963). References in Mackie's notes to *AJP* are to this journal.

[1] There is an excellent discussion of this question in A.J. Ayer's *The Problem of Knowledge*, Chapter 2, Sections (iv), (v), and (vi), which mentions almost all the relevant considerations. However, it seems to me to stress some of the less important points and merely to mention what I regard as the crucial argument. I refer to this discussion by the pages in the Pelican edition. The case against incorrigibility is argued also by J.L. Austin (against John Wisdom) in 'Other Minds', *Proceedings of the Aristotelian Society, Supplementary Volume XX*, reprinted in Austin's *Philosophical Papers*; I refer to the pages in the latter publication. The question is raised again by the controversy between J.J.C. Smart and Kurt Baier about the status of pains and other sensations in *AJP* Vol. 40, No. 1 (May 1962). [Mackie's references are, of course, to the first (1961) edition of Austin's *Philosophical Papers*; the corresponding pages in the later editions (1970 and 1979) have been added in square brackets to notes 2, 6 and 13.—Edd.]

ments. We are not interested in any incorrigibility that might lie only in a shortage of linguistic devices for the correction of error; we would be interested in an incorrigibility that lay in the absence of any possibility of there being an error to correct.

Again, suppose that there were indubitable items of empirical knowledge. Suppose, for example, that (sometimes at least) when I felt cold I knew, without any risk of error, that I did feel cold, that when I was in pain I knew, without any risk of error, that I was in pain. Nevertheless, my statements 'I feel cold', 'I am in pain' would be in one sense corrigible, because I might have an imperfect knowledge of the English language and I might have mixed up my terms. Although, on this supposition, I could not be wrong about what I felt, I could be wrong in my choice of words to describe it. I might at some time say, 'I'm afraid I've been misleading you. I have just realized that you, and everyone else who speaks English correctly, call "pain" the experience I have been calling "cold", so I shouldn't have said I felt cold, I should have said I was in pain'. It may well be that no statements that we make are entirely free from the risk of such verbal error. The most likely candidates for incorrigibility are statements about our own present sensations, and yet in making some of these we can hesitate and we can go wrong, for example, in deciding what is the right name for the exact shade of colour that we seem to see.[2] There are, no doubt, complex and subtle opportunities for such verbal error, and it may be far from easy in some cases to distinguish verbal from factual error. But to stress the genuine risk of verbal error is not to answer the most philosophically interesting question, and once we have classified something as a risk of merely verbal error we can set it aside as not part of our chief concern. Equally irrelevant is the obvious fact that any *statement* is corrigible in that the speaker may be lying; the question is whether there are any reports which *if* they are sincere are free from any risk of factual error.

Equally it is beside the point to insist that any statement I make about my experience at one time is 'corrigible' in the sense that I may later deny it:[3] if such subsequent 'correcting' were always erroneous, we should still want to say that the original statements were incorrigible in the important sense. Similarly it is true that since we are concerned with *empirical* statements, not logically

[2] Cf. Austin, *op. cit.*, p. 59. [91]   [3] Cf. Ayer, *op. cit.*, pp. 54-5.

necessary ones, it cannot be that *what is stated* is incorrigible; but this still leaves open the possibility that such a statement *made in certain circumstances* may be free from all risk of non-verbal mistake.[4]

2 THE RELEVANCE OF THIS PROBLEM TO WIDER ISSUES

The most plausible candidates for the role of incorrigible empirical statements are statements which report or describe the speaker's present experiences—for example, 'I am now feeling cold', 'I am in pain', 'Something looks red to me now', 'This note seems to me higher than that one', or 'I am angry'. It is, of course, only in so far as they are pure reports of present experiences that they have any chance of being absolutely incorrigible. 'I am in pain' may also convey something about my overt behaviour, present or future, it may strongly suggest that there is some appropriate cause of my present feeling (that something has hurt me) and perhaps also that I am in a certain physiological state: but in so far as it does any of these it is clearly not incorrigible. Similarly 'This note seems higher than that' must be taken, for our purpose, simply as a description of my present auditory sensations, not as even the most tentative judgement about objectively existing sounds. And perhaps 'I am angry' should be excluded altogether, on the ground that in saying that it is anger that I feel, and not some other violent emotion, I *must* be referring either to the sort of thing that has caused this disturbance in me or to the sort of actions in which it is likely to result. My strictly *present* experience when I am angry may be indistinguishable from my present experience of some other emotions. Similarly 'I am in an agony of indecision' would not be a suitable candidate: for my present experience is merely of agony, and to speak of indecision is to indicate what has caused this feeling or what would relieve it.

Once we have so restricted the meanings of these statements that they do no more than report or describe a present experience, we shall have to decide either that all of them are incorrigible or that none of them is: their claim to incorrigibility rests simply on features that are common to them all; of these the most obvious is that in these cases there is no distinction between evidence and conclusion, no question of going beyond one's evidence, and there-

[4] Cf. Ayer, *op. cit.*, pp. 55–6.

fore no room left for error,[5] but we shall encounter others as we go on. We may, then, group them all together and call them, say, *sense-statements*, whether the experiences they describe are fairly simple or extremely complex, and whether they are about what I seem to see, hear, etc., or about such feelings as pain or anger.

Apart from its intrinsic interest, this question has an important bearing on wider epistemological and metaphysical issues. To say that these sense-statements are incorrigible is to take the first step onto a slippery slide which lands you, in the end, in solipsism. This, view, as Austin says, 'is perhaps the original sin (Berkeley's apple, the tree in the quad) by which the philosopher casts himself out from the garden of the world we live in'.[6] Once you have said that there are indubitable items of empirical knowledge, and have admitted that empirical knowledge about material objects and other minds and even our own past is not indubitable, you may be led to say that our dubitable knowledge of these other things is reached through and based on our indubitable knowledge of our own experiences. From this in turn you may be led to say that our knowledge of other things is merely a construction out of our experiences, and thus to conclude that all we can really know and talk about is our own present experience. As this conclusion is intolerable, we should be very hesitant about taking the first step on the path that leads to it. Of course, it may be possible to escape after you have taken the first or even the second step on this path. It may be not a slippery slide but only a patch of scree, and with determination and circumspection you may be able to clamber out of it before you reach the bottom. You may be able to nibble Berkeley's apple and yet stay in the plain man's Eden; but not without some exercise of ingenuity.

This same view that what I am calling sense-statements are incorrigible also serves as a fundamental support of a dualism of mind and body. It is natural to argue that these introspective reports, being about something with regard to which the speaker has a peculiar epistemological authority—he cannot be wrong, whereas everyone else can—are about something necessarily private, and that such private psychic entities cannot be identical with public physical objects or processes.[7]

---

[5] Cf. Ayer, *op. cit.*, pp. 56–7.
[6] Austin, *op. cit.*, p. 58. [90]
[7] It is thus that Baier (*AJP*, Vol. 40, No. 1, especially pp. 59–62) argues against

3 THE PRIMA FACIE CASE FOR INCORRIGIBILITY

There is undoubtedly at least a *prima facie* case for the incorrigibility of sense-statements. If I say 'I feel cold', meaning it, not speaking in metaphor, not being misled by any ignorance of the English language, not intending to deceive myself or anyone else, speaking descriptively and not with any prescriptive or hortative purpose— not, for example, saying that I feel cold in order to keep up my morale at midday in a tropical desert—then how could this statement be corrected? How could it be in need of correction? If someone else has checked that I know English and mean what I am saying, that I am speaking descriptively and not either metaphorically or dishonestly, it would seem absurd for him to entertain any further doubt that I am feeling cold. Nothing except a rebuttal of one or other of these provisos would justify him in saying 'No, you aren't feeling cold'. My statement, it seems, is not corrigible by anyone else.

Nor does it seem to be corrigible by me. Of course I may find that the room I have been in all the time is not cold but very warm, but that will not show that I did not *feel* cold. My feeling cold may be due to some disorder or abnormality in me, but it is a genuine feeling for all that, and my statement, as a sense-statement, was true. Even if I feel differently the next minute, all I can say is '*Now* I feel warm'; however rapid the transition, I am not tempted to add 'so I didn't feel cold a minute ago, when I thought I did'. This stands even if nothing can be found in the circumstances to explain the change. However constant all the external conditions may have been it is perfectly possible that I should have felt cold a minute ago and yet should feel warm now. But what if nothing can be found even inside me, or in my relation to the environment, to

Smart's view that sensations are brain processes. It is true that Baier rejects the word 'incorrigibility', but only on the ground that a person may be mistaken in the *expectation* of further twinges, and therefore may wrongly believe that he still has an *intermittent* toothache; that is, Baier does hold that sincere reports of one's *present* sensations are incorrigible.

However, there seems to me to be little point in Baier's eagerness to establish, against Smart, that linguistic considerations tell against materialism, that the distinction between 'being about something physical' and 'being about something psychic or mental' is firmly embedded in the way we talk. Even if the rules of our language left no room for the materialist's 'metaphysical discovery', this might show only that these rules were in need of amendment. Ordinary language is not a final authority on any facts, even metaphysical ones.

explain the change? Suppose that physiologists make the most careful and detailed examination but find no sign that I am in a different state now from the one I was in a minute ago; will this make me doubt whether I felt cold a minute ago? Well, it may; but this is nothing to the purpose. It shows only that 'I felt cold a minute ago' is corrigible, but it is a memory-statement, and no one denies that memory-statements are corrigible. It does not cast even the shadow of corrigibility on the *present*-tense statement 'I am feeling cold'.

Let us try again. Suppose that I am under observation by a battery of linguists, psychologists, physicists, and physiologists. They check my knowledge of English, my sincerity, literalness, and so on. At 8.29 p.m. I say 'I am feeling warm', and this statement is recorded. At 8.30 p.m. I say, with equal sincerity, etc., 'I am feeling cold'. The observers find no trace of any change in the external conditions or in my physical or mental state, and they tell me so. I might then reason as follows: 'I know beyond reasonable doubt that I said I felt warm a minute ago, just as sincerely as I say I feel cold now. But my present state, internal and external, is just like my state a minute ago, so I cannot have been feeling differently then from now. Therefore one of these statements must be, or have been, false, and hence at least one of them is or was corrigible. But each is or was a statement of present experience, and there is nothing to choose between them. So both of them are corrigible, and hence my present statement "I am feeling cold" is so.'

However, I do not need to reason in this way. We have the following propositions:

A. At 8.29 I said I felt warm.

B. I feel the same at 8.30 as I felt at 8.29.

C. At 8.30 I say I feel cold.

D. The statements made at 8.29 and 8.30 are either both corrigible or both incorrigible.

E. The statement I made at 8.30 is incorrigible.

Now with a little logical manipulation we could show that A, B, C, D, and E cannot all be true. (They form an inconsistent pentad.) But we need not conclude that it is E that is false. The evidence for A, B, and D amounts at most to a very strong probability, and anyone who is inclined to regard sense-statements as incorrigible will say that this probability will not stand against my present certainty that I do feel cold. However careful the observers, however convincing the record, I might well conclude that there is something wrong with the evidence—even, at a pinch, that determinism has broken down and that there has been an uncaused change in my feelings—rather than that I do not really feel cold now. While, as Ayer says,[8] indirect evidence may have 'some tendency to show that I am making a mistake' about my present experience, such evidence can never be conclusive, and such considerations as these will not in themselves establish the corrigibility of sense-statements.

This *prima facie* case for the incorrigibility of these statements may be supplemented by three further arguments. First, as we have already noted, it may be said that, because there is no difference here between what is claimed and the evidence on which the claim is based, there is no room for error. Secondly, it may be argued that sense-statements are *basic* statements: they are used to test all other empirical statements, and so they must themselves be secure. As Ayer puts it,[9] 'it has been assumed that there must be some statements the recognition of whose truth or falsehood supplies the natural terminus to any process of empirical verification; and statements which are descriptive of the present contents of experiences are selected as the most worthy candidates'. Thirdly, it may be argued that if sense-statements were themselves corrigible we ought to say not 'It looks to me as if this is red now' but rather 'It looks as if it looks to me as if this is red' and not even this but rather 'It looks to me as if it looks to me as if etc. ...' where the infinite sequence of lookings can never be completed and so we shall never reach the final description 'is red'.

However, none of these arguments has much force. Against the first, we can point out that though a gap between evidence and what it supports is one thing that makes error possible, it need not be the only one. There could be error in direct as opposed to inferential cognition, we cannot assume that our immediate awareness is infallible for that reason alone. The most that the second argument could show is that we must have some items of empirical knowledge that are known directly, not indirectly by being verified by means of something else. But if our reply to the first argument

[8] *Op. cit.*, p. 66.   [9] *Op. cit.*, p. 54.

is correct, what is directly known may not be infallibly known. The third argument would be effective only if we assumed that we must put whatever we say into a perfectly guarded form. Unless we are trying to make our statements incorrigible, there is no reason why we should not say, as we do, simply 'This is red'. We *can* also say, for another purpose, 'It looks to me as if this is red', but we do not *need* to: so the infinite regress never gets going.

4   AN ARGUMENT AGAINST INCORRIGIBILITY BASED ON MEANING

If 'I am feeling cold' is a genuinely empirical and therefore contingent statement, it must have some positive content, it must say that my present experience is one of coldness and not, for example, one of warmth or of pain or of hearing a raucous noise. Since we are excluding from consideration any corrigibility that resides in the possibility that the speaker is misusing the word 'cold', we shall allow him to use this word for any sort of experience at all, even if it is what *we* call warmth or pain or seeming to see a herd of pink elephants. But if the statement is to have any positive content, the word 'cold' must have some definite meaning for him. So we might try to prove that the statement is corrigible by arguing as follows:

'The word "cold" has a meaning for the speaker, as applied to his present experience, only in so far as he is comparing this experience with others: he is saying that this experience is like such-and-such others, and unlike others again. Now all the experiences with which the present one is being compared are remembered, and since any memory-statement is corrigible, every such statement of comparison is corrigible too. "What I feel now is the same as what I felt last night" is not incorrigible, and since "I feel cold" is implicitly of this comparative form it is not incorrigible either'.[10]

This argument, however, rests on a nominalist account of meaning which I would reject. It is not true that the meaning of a statement which ascribes a quality to a subject consists wholly in its asserting of a resemblance between this subject and others. No doubt we learn to use quality words in a context of comparisons, but what we so learn is the link between the word and a quality

[10] Cf. Ayer's presentation of this argument and of the reply to it, *op. cit.*, pp. 63–4.

Logic and Knowledge

which is present independently in each subject, and once we have learned to use the word we use it to describe each subject on its own, not just to compare it with others. Thus although all comparison-statements are corrigible, sense-statements may none the less have a positive descriptive meaning and yet be incorrigible.

In any case, even if this argument had shown that all empirical *statements* were corrigible, it would not have established the more vital conclusion that all items of empirical knowledge are dubitable. Even if it had turned out that we could talk about our present experiences only by comparing them with others, it would not follow that we could be aware of their character only by literally knowing *what they are like*. The most that this argument could have established would have been another variety of merely linguistic corrigibility.

A similar comment could be made on any argument which purported to show that *because of the nature of language itself* there could not be a necessarily private language or even words with necessarily private meanings, and hence that there could not be statements possessing the kind of privacy that would go along with incorrigibility. Even if this were so[11] it would only establish linguistic corrigibility: it would show that no empirical statements are incorrigible, but not that there is no indubitable empirical knowledge. The impossibility of a necessarily private language would be relevant to the vital question here only if it were due not to the nature of language but to the lack of any necessarily private objects to which its meanings could be attached. That is, we should have to show *first* that there are no such private and indubitable objects, we cannot infer this from any considerations about language as such.

5 AN ARGUMENT AGAINST INCORRIGIBILITY FROM BRIEF EXPERIENCES

I have argued already that all sense-statements are corrigible, if any are; and there seem in fact to be some corrigible sense-statements. Suppose that I have a very brief, momentary experience—for example, I step into a bath and, receiving some sort of shock, step hastily out again. It can happen that I am not sure what I have experienced, whether it was extreme heat or extreme cold. Again,

[11] I agree with Ayer (*op. cit.*, pp. 59–61) that it is not in fact so.

I may have a very brief visual experience. I look into a room and just as I do so someone switches off the light: I have seen something, but I am not sure what I have seen. Or a psychologist gets me to look into a tachistoscope, a device in which he can display pictures or diagrams for a short and exactly controllable period, a tenth of a second, or two-tenths, and so on; he then asks me to draw what I have seen, and I am not sure what to draw. I am not merely doubtful about what is in the picture or diagram he displayed so briefly; I am doubtful even about the content of my own experience. And it seems that I can be blatantly wrong about it: I can sincerely believe that I have seen something that was not there at all, something to which, as it turns out, there could have been no counterpart in my retinal image, and yet I was wide awake and seeing with my eyes, not 'seeing' in a dream or vision.

Such examples seem to show that there are cases where I am not sure what experience I have had, and where I can be wrong in saying of what sort it was. Admittedly, these are examples of a special and unusual kind. But if I can be wrong about them, then the immediacy of an experience gives no guarantee against error, and reports even of longer experiences must be corrigible in principle. I may be *surer* about a longer experience, but I cannot be *absolutely* sure.

A possible reply to this argument is that the statements thus shown to be corrigible are all about past (though very recently past) experiences, not strictly present ones. I am uncertain, and perhaps wrong, about what I saw in the tachistoscope half a minute ago, not about what I am seeing now. It is my memory that is unreliable, not my awareness of my present experience. During the tenth of a second that the picture was illuminated I was in no doubt about what I was seeing, and in no danger of error, and if I could have made a statement within that tenth of a second it would have been incorrigible.

This reply is not very convincing: could I really have forgotten so soon? Unless we could develop this suggestion into a theory that memory, as it were, takes some time to record, and that the experience lasting only a tenth of a second was too brief to be remembered, it would seem arbitrary to ascribe all the blame for the corrigibility in these cases to memory, and none to doubt about the content of my experience while it is present. Again, if it is said that reports of such brief experiences are corrigible because there is a (very short) time lapse between the experience and the report, we may reply that a similar time lapse is concealed within what we ordinarily call present experience. It takes time to have an experience, not merely to record one, and 'I am feeling cold' is surely not a report of what I am feeling at the instant without duration when I begin to speak. So if any time lapse at all would introduce corrigibility, this will ensure that none of our empirical statements is incorrigible. Nevertheless, it would be possible, if not very plausible, to save in this way the doctrine of the infallibility of our knowledge of present experiences while they are present in a very strict sense.

There is, however, a better reply that could be made to this argument from brief experiences. I am not really in doubt about the content of my experience, but that content is itself faint, blurred, or indeterminate. In one sense, of course, the experience was quite determinate: it was exactly whatever it was. But I have no words with which to describe it in itself, and when I try to describe it in the way I normally describe visual experiences, by saying that it was like seeing such-and-such an object, there is no determinate object the seeing of which it was like. I knew at the time exactly what I was seeing, and I still remember it quite accurately, though I can describe it neither in words nor by drawing what I saw. It is only when I let the psychologist bully me into pretending that I saw something firm and determinate—which he does by asking me to draw what I have seen and handing me a sharp pencil—that I fall into error about what this something was. The right answer to the psychologist's request would be either 'I can't draw it, because it wasn't anything definite' or 'I can't draw it because I am not a clever enough artist: if I could do an impressionistic sketch I should be able to show just how it looked to me'. Similarly when I report what I felt on stepping into and hastily out of the bath I should not say either 'I felt cold' or 'I felt hot', but simply 'I felt a sudden shock'. There was, when I had it, no possible doubt for me about the sort of experience I was having, and there is still no practical doubt a moment later, but the sort of experience it was is just the sort you have when you encounter a violent change of temperature; it was *due* either to heat or to cold, but it was not in itself a feeling of either of these.

A similar reply might be made to other arguments that point to examples of present experiences about whose character we have some hesitation or doubt. Thus Ayer says that if two lines of approximately equal length are drawn and I am asked to say whether either of them looks to me to be the longer, I might be uncertain how to answer; I might not be sure whether either of the lines does look to me to be longer than the other; and he adds, 'But if I can be in doubt about this matter of fact, I can presumably also come to the wrong decision. I can judge that this line looks to me to be longer than that one, when in fact it does not'.[12] To this argument one might reply that I am letting myself be bullied by the questioner. The right answer is neither that this line looks longer than that nor that they look the same length. In my own observation of such a case, the comparative lengths seem to oscillate: first one looks longer, then the other, and sometimes they look equal. To ask 'Does either look longer?' is to ask me to give a stable report of my experience, and I hesitate over doing this because the experience itself is unstable.

Similarly Austin argues, 'Here, what I try to do is to *savour* the current experience, to *peer* at it, to sense it vividly. ... There is a lack of sharpness in what we actually sense, which is to be cured not, or not merely, by thinking, but by acuter discernment'.[13] But this argument will not shake the hardened incorrigibilist. There may, indeed, be this process of peering at a current experience, but it is too easy to reply that what we savour or peer at, what we scan over and over, is not the experience but the object experienced; we are not further examining the same taste sensation, but trying to get additional and more detailed taste sensations from the same dish.

It seems to me, therefore, that while we may in fact be uncertain about our present experiences in these ways, these arguments do not themselves establish this: alternative accounts could be given of such cases which would save the incorrigibilist thesis. To knock that thesis down, we need a more decisive argument.

6   A LOGICAL ARGUMENT AGAINST INCORRIGIBILITY

The strongest argument against incorrigibility, it seems to me, is this. It is one thing to have an experience and it is another to reflect on it, to notice what sort of an experience you are having. We have

---

[12] *Op. cit.*, p. 65.   [13] Austin, *op. cit.*, pp. 60-1. [92-3]

admitted (in §4) that to realize of what sort your experience is you need not compare it, even implicitly, with other experiences: you can be aware of its intrinsic character or content even while you are contemplating this one experience by itself. But you must contemplate it, not merely have it.[14] Once this is admitted, it follows that the result of this contemplation, the judgement that the experience is, say, of cold and not of warmth or pain, is open to the possibility of error and the corresponding statement is in principle corrigible. This is the crux of the matter. The reason why we are reluctant to admit corrigibility even in principle, to concede that there is any possibility of error about the judgement that I am now feeling cold, is that we tend to identify the having of the experience with the contemplating of its quality, we tend to imagine that just to feel cold is the same thing as to be aware that this experience is of the feeling-cold sort.[15]

An effort of introspection may help to show that this is an error. It is quite easy to feel cold: you need only immerse yourself in cold water or go out of doors without a coat in winter. But to notice what you are feeling requires something more, a distinct reflection over and above the feeling-cold itself. However, we need not rely on introspection here. As we shall see, there are logical objections to the view that one and the same item should both have a certain character and be an awareness of that character.

There are several reasons why this mistake is an easy one to make. Of these, one is linguistic: we commonly use the same words to express these two different things. The very same phrase, 'I feel cold', can be a mere expression of the experience of feeling cold,

---

[14] Cf. Ayer, *op. cit.*, pp. 67–8: 'In allowing that the descriptions which people give of their experiences may be factually mistaken, we are dissociating having an experience from knowing that one has it. To know that one is having whatever experience it may be, one must not only have it but also be able to identify it correctly, and there is no necessary transition from one to the other'.

But though Ayer mentions this point, he introduces it as a corollary, not as the main argument against incorrigibility.

[15] The core of this argument is the same as that in Smart's reply to Baier (*AJP* Vol. 40, No. 1, pp. 69–70). But I think that it is not enough to say, as Smart does, that 'the sincere reporting of a sensation is one thing and the sensation reported is another'. Though these are clearly different, it might be argued that the one logically requires the other, just as the sincere reporting of a belief logically requires that one should have the belief reported. The crucial point is that the *belief* that one has the sensation (which the sincerity of the report logically requires) is a distinct entity from the sensation itself, and this may not be so obvious that it can be laid down without such further argument as I have endeavoured to supply.

and it can also express a judgement that this experience is of the feeling-cold sort. What is called an *avowal* is, I suggest, a remark which combines these functions or hesitates between them. If I feel cold, I may shiver, I may say 'Brrr', or I may say 'I feel cold'; and each of these may perform the same function, each of them can serve as a mere expression of the feeling, a mere reaction to the feeling itself. Saying 'I feel cold' is no doubt a sophisticated, a learned reaction, whereas shivering is an unsophisticated and un-learned reaction, but it can be a reaction and nothing more. On the other hand, the remark 'I feel cold' can perform the very different task of stating an explicit judgement that my experience is of a certain sort, and it is only when it performs this function that it is an empirical statement, that it is capable of being true or false, or of conveying an item of knowledge. A shiver cannot be true or false, and no more can 'I feel cold' when it is merely a sophisticated substitute for a shiver. There is perhaps a difference in the intona-tion one would give to the phrase when it is used in these two different ways, but this is a fine distinction. By and large, it seems to be the same phrase, and this makes it easy to confuse the two uses and hence to identify the two things that they express.

But (as usual) the linguistic confusion is not the sole or indepen-dent source of the philosophical error. Behind it lies some such argument as this:

'When I am feeling cold the coldness just is the content of my experience: it is what I am aware of; and if I am aware of coldness, how could I be ignorant of it or in error about it? To be ignorant would be not to be aware of it, and to be in error would be to be aware of something other than coldness.'

But what is the force of this argument? Does it simply assert that when I am feeling cold it is cold that I am feeling—a tautology as harmlessly and uselessly true as the statement that when I am tying my shoelace it is my shoelace that I am tying? Or does it say that whenever I am feeling cold I know that it is cold that I am feeling? This seems to be a universal empirical proposition saying that of two quite distinct things the second always accompanies the first. But with this interpretation, what reason does the argument give for believing that this proposition is true?

It seems, then, that the force of the argument lies in some third interpretation, distinct from both of these. Feeling cold is taken to be a cognitive experience, an awareness of cold: it is not quite the same thing as knowing-that-the-experience-I-am-having-is-of-the-feeling-cold-sort, but it not quite different either. It is suggested that feeling cold is somehow an awareness of itself. It is clear that if anything were an awareness of itself it would, just by occurring, provide itself with an object, so that whenever this cognition occurred it would be true. But this suggestion contains the seeds of a paradox. If a cognition were either the whole or a part of its own object, it would have to be an infinite system of cognitions. If it were the whole of its own object it would be an awareness of an awareness of ... and so on to infinity. And if it were a part of its own object—the other part being, say, cold—it would be an awareness of both cold and ... etc.—as in the following diagram:

awareness of $\begin{cases} \text{cold} \\ \text{and} \\ \text{awareness of} \end{cases}$ $\begin{cases} \text{cold} \\ \text{and} \\ \text{awareness of} \end{cases}$ $\begin{cases} \text{...} \end{cases}$

It seems implausible to claim that each of our present experiences has this infinitely complex structure. However, if anyone is prepared to accept this, there is still a further difficulty. Each of our present experiences cannot be the *whole* of its own object, for if it were there could be nothing to differentiate one from another. We should not be able to distinguish feeling pain from feeling cold, for each would be just an awareness of ... etc. But if each is only a *part* of its own object, then this part and the other (distinguishing) part are not identical, and it would be a synthetic truth that the awareness of, say, cold and the awareness of this awareness itself went together.

It is questionable, therefore, whether we should call feeling cold a *cognitive* experience. It is not a knowing (or believing) *that* anything. (Obviously, too, it is not a knowing how.) Nor is it a recognition: to feel cold is not to meet anything again and recognize it, for the thing recognized could be nothing other than cold, but when you feel cold the first time you cannot be recognizing it, and yet feeling cold the first time is as genuine a case of feeling cold as feeling cold for the thousandth time. Moreover, within feeling cold itself (as opposed to judging that one feels cold) there is no room for error, there is no question of being wrong and equally no question of being right: the experience simply occurs. As an expression of this experience the utterance 'I feel cold' is incorrigible in the same way in which a shiver is incorrigible, but it is then not a statement, it does not express any item of empirical knowledge.

This might be conceded: it might be admitted that I can feel cold without reflecting on it, and therefore without realizing what sort of feeling it is, and yet it might be held that *if* I reflect I cannot judge wrongly: this would be sufficient to make the statement 'I am now feeling cold' incorrigible. Since the reflecting and that on which I reflect are different things, there is a logical possibility of error, but, it may be said, no practical empirical possibility of error.

But why should this be so? And if it were so, would it count as incorrigibility? If all that is being said is that as a matter of fact whenever anyone reflects on a present experience he states correctly what sort of experience it is, and that this itself is just a true universal empirical proposition, should we not rather say that sense-statements are in principle corrigible, but never actually in need of correction? It would be just as if we were all very accurate and careful estimators of length, so that no one ever said that a line was less than six inches long when it was not: but this would not make our length-statements incorrigible or show that there is any peculiar *privacy* about lengths. At least, if this is what is to be meant by incorrigibility, this should be made clear; this view should be sharply distinguished from the suggestion that there is some special guarantee against error in a judgement about one's present experience.

Besides, once it is conceded that there is no special guarantee against error, that having an experience is different from knowing that one has it, examples of the kind discussed in §5 above must be given some weight. They would not shake anyone who thought that there were *a priori* grounds for maintaining that sense-statements are incorrigible, but if it is said to be a purely empirical truth that such statements are never mistaken, these examples must be allowed to count against it.

7   ARE SENSE-STATEMENTS PRACTICALLY INCORRIGIBLE?

Even if it is argued that sense-statements are corrigible in principle, it must be admitted that it would be very difficult to correct them in practice. What would it be like to discover such a mistake? It is hard enough to imagine how I could feel cold, reflect on this experience, and in reflecting judge wrongly that I was feeling warmth or pain; but it would be impossible at the same time to detect this error, because to detect the error I would have to reflect correctly on the whole experience, that is, correctly to observe that I was feeling cold and that I was at the same time mis-observing this as a feeling of, say, pain. I could not do all this at once: the correct observation involved in detecting the error would destroy the error.

Alternatively, could I be in error at one time and subsequently observe that I had been in error? This is no doubt possible: I could now remember that I was feeling cold a minute ago but that a minute ago I was wrongly identifying this feeling as pain. Although this could happen, I do not know that it ever does happen. And even if it did happen I could never be sure that it had happened: there is always the alternative possibility that I might now be mis-remembering what I felt a minute ago, and (as we saw in §3 above) even in the most favourable circumstances we could not get a conclusive demonstration that a particular sense-statement was mistaken or even that it had a fifty–fifty chance of being mistaken.

It seems, then, that we can never make an observation or series of observations that will compel us to admit that a particular sense-statement is or was mistaken. It is not that such statements are incorrigible, but merely that we can never be forced to correct them. This is a guarantee not against error, but against the conclusive detection of error. If someone maintains, then, that sense-statements are never in fact wrong, I admit that I cannot dislodge him from this position. I cannot hope to produce an example of such a statement which he must admit to be false, or even of a pair of such statements about which he must admit that at least one of them is false. On the other hand, this is not to admit that the items of knowledge conveyed by these statements have any difference of status from other items of knowledge or belief.

8 INCORRIGIBILITY BY DEFINITION

One reason that might be given to explain why we are in fact unlikely to make mistakes about our present experience is simply that the reflection and that on which it is a reflection occur simultaneously in one conscious mind. No doubt exactly what this means needs further analysis, but whatever it means could plausibly be offered as an empirical explanation of the empirical fact that we seldom misjudge our present experiences. But we must not slip from this into saying that if I made a mistake about a present experience this would mean that I had a divided consciousness, so that the experience I made a mistake about was not really *mine*. To use the absence of such error as the test of whether an experience is mine would be, of course, to make true by definition, and therefore empty, the claim that my knowledge of all *my* present experiences is infallible.

This could come about also in another way. It has, I believe, been experimentally established that the following sequence of events may occur.[16] A person is hypnotized, and told by the hypnotist that he is insensitive to pain. A stimulus which normally produces pain—e.g. a small electric shock—is applied to his hand. He shows all the usual signs of being in pain: he grimaces, tends to pull his hand away, shows a galvanic skin response, etc. But both at the time and later he denies that he feels, or felt, any pain, and we can establish with reasonable certainty that he is not simply lying about this. Now two alternative accounts could be given of these admittedly abnormal occurrences. We could say that the subject felt pain, but that the hypnotist's influence prevented him from being aware of this. Or we could say that though the normal physiological causes, effects, and counterparts of pain were present, the hypnosis prevented him from feeling pain. I maintain that it is a real issue which of these accounts is correct. However, someone might rule out the former account by linguistic decision, by saying that a person cannot be said to feel pain unless he is aware at the time that he is feeling pain, and presumably also that he can properly be said to feel pain whenever he thinks he does. But if anyone makes or follows this rule, he has made it true merely by definition that a person has infallible knowledge about his own present pains. Such a linguistic decision cannot show that there is any class of real entities, pains, about which their owner has infallible knowledge.

Such a decision robs of empirical content not only the principle that sense-statements are incorrigible but also each of these statements themselves. For if to feel pain is defined explicitly or implicitly as to judge that one feels pain such judgements become self-certifying at the usual price of becoming empty. In fact a language

16 See J.P. Sutcliffe, ' "Credulous" and "Skeptical" Views of Hypnotic Phenomena', in *Journal of Abnormal and Social Psychology*, Vol. 62, No. 2 (March 1961), especially pp. 194–5.

that adhered consistently to this rule would contain no way of saying that one was simply in pain in the ordinary sense.

We must, then, distinguish carefully between two things: pointing to conditions in which it is most unlikely that a mistake will be made, and either laying it down by an explicit definition or implicitly ensuring by our linguistic practices that statements of a certain kind made in certain circumstances cannot be false. If we do only the former, then what we are indicating is not incorrigibility, but if we do the latter the statements we make incorrigible thereby cease to be empirical. Those who hold that there are incorrigible empirical statements must find a way between the horns of this dilemma, but I cannot see what it could be.

9 CONCLUSION

I conclude that in the philosophically important sense, the sense in which 'Are there any incorrigible empirical statements?' is another way of asking 'Are there any indubitable items of empirical knowledge?', there are none of these. The view that what I have called sense-statements are incorrigible, in so far as it provides either the first step onto the slippery slide to solipsism or the foundation of a dualism of mind and body, involves the claim that a present experience essentially *is* an awareness of its own character, and this cannot be so. Once this is established, the claim that such statements are incorrigible dissolves into the true but harmless assertions that we do not normally make mistakes about our experiences at the time that we have them and that it would be difficult conclusively to detect such mistakes if we did make them.

III

RATIONALISM AND EMPIRICISM

OUR purpose at this meeting is to commemorate the work of Professor John Anderson. The most appropriate way for me to do this, I believe, is not to speak in general about his views or achievements, but to examine one issue which he himself regarded as central in philosophy, the conflict between rationalism and empiricism. But before we can discuss this issue, it will be necessary to discuss what the issue is; for whereas the historians and systematizers of philosophy have interpreted it in one way, Anderson seems to have interpreted it rather differently. I shall therefore begin by contrasting Anderson's account of rationalism and empiricism with what I shall call the traditional account. Then I shall examine several ways in which the two accounts might be reconciled or brought into closer relation with one another. At the same time I shall be considering some arguments which have been employed by Anderson and by other empiricists against rationalism of one sort or another.

In one of his earliest articles, 'Empiricism' (1927), and in one of his latest, 'Empiricism and Logic' (1961), Anderson describes his philosophical position primarily as empiricist, and, by contrast, characterizes as rationalist all the various philosophical positions that he rejects. But his use of these terms is puzzling to anyone who comes upon it after a conventional training in the history of philosophy, for his classification both of philosophers and of doctrines fails to coincide with the traditional one. Locke, Berkeley, and Hume, who are traditionally grouped together as British Empiricists, are, according to Anderson, empiricists in only a slight degree; and some of their most characteristic doctrines are, he says, really rationalist ones. Sensationalism is 'a rationalist doctrine miscalled "empiricism".'[1] Similarly, many later philosophers who would call themselves empiricists, such as the logical positivists and

Written as the John Anderson Memorial Lecture for 1963 of the NSW Workers' Educational Association and the Sydney Philosophy Club and first published in the *Australasian Journal of Philosophy* Vol. 43, No. 1 (May 1965).

[1] *Studies in Empirical Philosophy* (hereafter abbreviated as *SEP*), p. 83.

many contemporary linguistic philosophers, would be said by Anderson to have adopted rationalistic views and methods. Some of these philosophers, moreover, would return the charge, and would say that Anderson's own procedure, when he tries to establish positive and far-reaching conclusions by sweeping and apparently *a priori* arguments, is more rationalist than empiricist in spirit.

It is true that disagreements in the classification of thinkers and doctrines as rationalist or empiricist need not reflect any differences in the meaning given to these terms. It might be that Anderson is using the terms 'rationalist' and 'empiricist' in their traditional senses, but is claiming to have detected, in the thought of many who are called empiricists, features or tendencies that are at variance with empiricism in the ordinary sense of that word, that sensationalists or logical positivists, for example, are, even by the traditional criteria, rationalists in disguise. But Anderson would appear, at least at first sight, to be saying more than this. Traditionally, empiricism is the doctrine that all our knowledge is derived from experience or from observation, and rationalism is the doctrine that to some extent at least our knowledge, or some part of it, is not derived from experience but is established by reason—either that 'the intellect is a source of significant knowledge in its own right', or that 'it necessarily co-operates with the senses in the production of knowledge'.[2]

But Anderson lays down quite different criteria. 'Rationalistic theories of all sorts', he says, 'are distinguished from empiricism by the contention that there are different kinds or degrees of truth and reality. The distinguishing-mark of empiricism as a philosophy is that it denies this, that it maintains that there is only one way of being'.[3] He goes on to say: 'The issue has been confused in the past by a reference to knowledge. It was quite naturally maintained, by those who postulated different ways of being, that in relation to them different ways of knowing are required. Hence empiricism has been connected, in the history of philosophy, with the view that there is only one way of knowing, and particularly that that way is what was called "sense" in contrast to "reason"; or, rather differently, that sense is the only *originator* of knowledge. But fundamentally the issue is logical; the dispute is about ways of being or

---

[2] W.H. Walsh, *Reason and Experience* (Oxford, 1947), pp. 106-7.   [3] *SEP*, p. 3.

of truth, not about ways of knowing truth. It is only after it has been assumed that there are other truths than matters of fact, or that there are objects which "transcend" existence, that a special faculty has to be invented to know them.'[4]

There is, here, a striking divergence between Anderson's account and the traditional one. On the traditional view, the dispute between rationalists and empiricists is essentially a dispute about how we know what we know, but on Anderson's view the question whether there is more than one way of being is prior, both logically and historically, to the question about knowledge.

Taken literally as an historical assertion, Anderson's view may seem implausible; yet there is evidence that gives it at least partial support. A sharp distinction between ways of knowing was first drawn by Empedocles about 450 BC; in advising us to 'consider everything in the way it is clear,'[5] he meant that we should accept both the rational arguments of Parmenides and the everyday evidence of our senses: the chief aim of Empedocles' own theory was to reconcile these two. But these Parmenidean arguments are concerned with 'what *is*', with 'substance' (*physis*) as opposed to perishable things, and Anderson would therefore contend that these arguments presuppose an entity, or entities, that exist in a special way. But even this illustration does not support Anderson's claim that a special faculty 'has to be invented' to know the things that exist in a special way. This, rather, is the order of events: the Milesians and the Pythagoreans developed theories of entities more real or more fundamental than ordinary changing things, and something implicit in these theories enabled Parmenides and his successors to construct *a priori* arguments about these entities, to present what are at least initially plausible examples of rational knowledge.

With regard to other supposed fields of rational knowledge Anderson's historical claim is even more open to question. It was surely the success of the early geometers in constructing proofs whose force was not impaired by the inaccuracy of the figures drawn to illustrate them that suggested to Plato that the mind had here a source of knowledge independent of sensory observation. Similarly it was because mathematics in general—but arithmetic

---

[4] *SEP*, pp. 3–4.
[5] See Fragment 4 in J. Burnet, *Early Greek Philosophy*, 4th edition (London, 1930), p. 205.

and algebra even more clearly than geometry—appeared to provide demonstrative knowledge that not only 'rationalists' like Descartes and Leibniz but also 'empiricists' like Locke and Hume were led to distinguish what Leibniz calls 'truths of reason' from 'truths of fact', or what Hume calls 'relations of ideas' from 'matters of fact and existence': it was not that the distinction between the two ways of being was drawn first and that *a priori* demonstration had to be 'invented' to explain our knowledge of the truths of reason.

It would be wiser, therefore, to withdraw any claim that Anderson may be making that the question about ways of being is *historically* prior to that about ways of knowing, and to consider only his claim that the former is *logically* prior to the latter—in other words, that distinctions between ways of knowing turn out, on criticism, to rest upon and require distinctions between ways of being. For this, indeed, we shall find considerable support.

One of the initially surprising features of Anderson's account is that he brings together, under the heading of rationalism, so many varied philosophical views. What is commonly called idealism, 'the conception of a total truth to which all "merely particular" truths contribute', is a variety of rationalism, because this total truth is supposed to be a truth somehow higher than any matter of fact.[6] 'The "unitary" view of mind, the conception of it as having only one character and being self-contained in that character', is another rationalistic view.[7] The Pythagorean dualism, the view that behind ordinary things are ultimate units of which they are made, and the Eleatic monism, the view that there is only one ultimately real thing, in contrast to which all else is merely appearance, are, according to Anderson, only variants of the same rationalist approach. Descartes is always called a rationalist, but Anderson characterizes Descartes's rationalism as 'a philosophy of essences and identities', arguing that Descartes reduces inference to identity, and that on his view the knower is always known as a knower, 'known by the inner or identical knowledge of the *cogito*'.[8] Anderson finds rationalism likewise in the Marxist 'conception of a *true* state or outcome of things, with the connected conception of reality, society, humanity advancing as a *whole*',[9] and in Freud's simplification of mental structure, his 'setting up of *units*' and 'identification of things which

---

[6] *SEP*, p. 5.   [7] *SEP*, p. 14.   [8] *SEP*, pp. 101, 109.
[9] *SEP*, p. 324.

are merely connected'—for example, 'unifying [sexual and alimentary] tendencies under the heading of a "libido" '.[10]

But these characterizations are made in too impressionistic a manner. In his published writings at least, Anderson does not develop or explain adequately this notion of ways of being. Just what sort of difference between things would constitute a difference in their ways of being?[11] Again, he does not show exactly what is wrong with doctrines of 'units' or 'wholes'; even the purest empiricist will presumably have some use for such terms as 'unit', 'whole', 'separation', 'distinction', 'identity' and so on, but how does his defensible use of these terms differ from the objectionable use that the various kinds of rationalists make of them? What is called for, then, is a closer examination of all these notions—a task which can, of course, be only begun but not completed in this lecture.

Let us start by working out some of the implications of rationalism as it is traditionally understood, the doctrine that at least some of our knowledge, in some respects at least, is not derived from experience but established by reason, that the intellect makes some positive contribution to knowledge. This may mean that we have a power of intellectual intuition, that there are certain objects or facts which can be 'seen' by the mind in a way that is analogous to the way in which ordinary things are perceived by the senses. Alternatively it may mean that the mind supplies certain *a priori* concepts, that the senses give us only isolated and disordered data, which the mind builds into complex and orderly structures in accordance with categories of its own.[12] Now there are overwhelming objections to the theory of intellectual intuition, if this means that the mind can respond to and derive information from objects that belong peculiarly to it, that it has, as it were, intellectual senses in addition to the ordinary senses. But if intellectual intuition is understood not so literally as a further kind of sensation, but as a matter of seeing, in a more metaphorical sense, that certain principles hold, then the rationalist is faced with the problem of justifying the claim that the principles framed by the intellect hold for

[10] *SEP*, pp. 350, 346.

[11] I have mentioned this problem in an article. 'The Philosophy of John Anderson', *Australasian Journal of Philosophy*, Vol. 40, No. 3 (December 1962), pp. 280-2. [Now reprinted as Chapter I above—Edd.]

[12] Cf. W. H. Walsh, *Reason and Experience, passim*, and especially pp. 106-7.

an independent reality. Similarly, even if he says only that the intellect co-operates with the senses, supplying *a priori* concepts or categories in which sensory data are ordered, he faces the fundamental criticism that what such intellectual construction gave us would be not knowledge but fantasy. If order and structure are *imposed* arbitrarily on sense-data, not *derived* from an order possessed by independent objects themselves, then what we call knowledge really is knowledge not in respect of its structure, but only in respect of the data it contains: in adopting this view the rationalist is abandoning the claim that our so-called knowledge depicts how things objectively are, and that it would be different if things themselves were ordered differently. In either case, then, the rationalist will be forced, if he is to defend the objective validity of these intellectual principles or concepts, to claim that these principles or concepts are *necessary* ones. The principles framed by the intellect, or the structure which it imposes on the data of sense, constitute a necessary order, an order that is not only subjectively necessary, because our minds impose it, but objectively necessary, because anything at all must conform to it. If the rationalist says that reason sets the data of sense in order, he will have to say that although it is not deriving that order from a corresponding order in the things by way of any sort of perception, it is none the less creating an order which agrees with an objective order: we *know* that it is an objective order not because we 'see' it, that is, respond to it, but because we reason that it must be so; and equally it *is* so because it must be so.

What is traditionally called rationalism is, therefore, committed to the claim that there are synthetic necessary items of some sort both in our knowledge and in objective reality. They must be synthetic, otherwise reason would not be making any positive contribution to our knowledge, and they must be objectively necessary, or else what reason thus gave us would be, in this respect, not knowledge but fantasy. Rationalism in the traditional sense, therefore, is committed to the assertion that there are synthetic necessary features of reality, and this is one of the things that Anderson would count as a special way of being: what *must be* is contrasted with what merely *is* the case. This is at least a step towards a reconciliation of Anderson's account of rationalism with the traditional one.

A *prima facie* obstacle to such a reconciliation is Anderson's claim that there is a great deal of rationalism even in the central and characteristic doctrines of the British Empiricists. Of course, it is generally recognized that even in the traditional sense of the term Locke is far from being a consistent empiricist.[13] But it is worth while to see just how rationalism invades his theories. He defines knowledge as 'the perception of the connection and agreement, or disagreement and repugnancy, of any of our ideas',[14] and he thinks that we have certain knowledge of synthetic truths in mathematics and in ethics, and that though we do not in fact have knowledge of necessary coexistences of the qualities of material substances, such knowledge is not impossible in principle. Also, from the in- tuitive knowledge which he says that we have of our own existence, he thinks that we can with certainty infer the existence of God. In each of these cases such knowledge depends, or would depend, upon synthetic but necessary connections between our ideas and between any things that agree with them: they must be synthetic, since such knowledge would be expressed in 'instructive', not 'tri- fling', propositions, and Locke repeatedly says that they are neces- sary, clearly linking this with the certainty which he takes to be a requirement for genuine knowledge.

Again, in discussing the 'reality' of knowledge, Locke claims to know that our simple ideas are the 'regular productions of things without us' and have some 'conformity' with those things:[15] since this knowledge could not itself be derived from experience Locke is here committed to claiming that he has *a priori* knowledge of a synthetic connection. This would have to be a necessary connec- tion, because by considering only one term of the relation, the simple ideas, we are supposed to be able both to infer that there are some external things producing them and to infer at least that these external things correspond in some systematic way with the ideas they produce.

In these two respects, then, Locke is explicitly or implicitly com- mitted to saying that there are synthetic necessary connections among ideas and things, and these remain rationalist elements in his theory despite his insistence that the ideas themselves are de- rived from experience, from sensation and reflection.

Berkeley leaves less scope for reason than Locke does, and of

13 Cf. R.I. Aaron, *John Locke* (Oxford, 1955), pp. 10, 88, etc.
14 *Essay Concerning Human Understanding*, Book IV, Chapter I.
15 *Essay Concerning Human Understanding*, Book IV, Chapter IV.

course he was the first to expose the unempirical character of Locke's account of material substance and its qualities; but he too relies on inference beyond experience for our knowledge of God and of other spirits, and perhaps of our own minds as active spiritual substances. Also, Berkeley's famous attempt to prove that trees and books cannot exist unperceived or independently of minds is an attempt to establish a synthetic necessary truth by *a priori* reasoning: his procedure is just as rationalistic as the very similar procedure followed by Descartes in his *cogito*.[16]

Even Hume, according to Anderson, 'went back to an acceptance of "rational science" in his doctrine of relations of ideas'.[17] However, I am not sure whether this charge could be sustained. The crucial question is whether Hume thought that these relations between ideas are synthetic as well as necessary, or whether his account of relations between ideas is to be understood as an anticipation of Kant's account of analytic judgements. Only in the former case would he be accepting rational science in an important sense.

A charge which Anderson makes against these philosophers in general is that 'they took a view of sense'—that is, of empirical observation—'which was dependent on its having been regarded as an *inferior* way of knowing. It was supposed to provide isolated data, materials which reason had to shape into ... the coherent system of knowledge which we call science.'[18] Anderson's view here is that these thinkers started from the rationalist doctrine that sense and reason are alike sources of or contributors to our knowledge; that Hume in particular argued against this, criticizing the account of the supposed work of reason, but that having excluded reason he was left saying either that the whole of our knowledge consists in the mere possession of isolated data, or that any organization of these is the work of imagination and therefore does not amount to knowledge. This sceptical conclusion offers a standing invitation to the rationalist to re-enter the field. The Humean account of what

---

[16] Berkeley, *Principles of Human Knowledge*, § 23. I have examined both these arguments in an article, 'Self-Refutation—A Formal Analysis', *Philosophical Quarterly*, Vol. 14, No. 56 (July 1964), pp. 193–203. It is a curious fact that Locke accepts the argument of Descartes's *cogito*, blending it with his own claim that our knowledge of our own existence is intuitive (*Essay*, Book IV, Chapter IX). [The article referred to by Mackie in this note is reprinted as Chapter IV below.—Edd.]

[17] *SEP*, p. 81.

[18] *SEP*, p. 12.

we can know falls short of the organized knowledge that we seem to have, and we are therefore constantly tempted to help it out by adding some synthetic necessary principles. As long as we take sensation to provide merely isolated data, we shall be tempted to postulate a cognitive factor radically different from sensation. As we have seen, the claim that what such a factor gives us is knowledge and not fantasy involves the claim that it works in accordance with necessary but synthetic concepts or principles.

This is, I believe, a sound criticism of the Humean view, and it shows that empiricism can be plausible and stable only if it recognizes that observation itself gives us complex, organized information, not isolated materials. But what it shows is not that Hume's position is a disguised rationalism, but that it contains a rationalist gap, a vacuum which is constantly asking to be filled by fresh rationalist postulates.

There is another way in which Anderson would have developed the charge that many so-called empiricists are close to the rationalists in spirit. Cartesian doubts provoke both parties to look for a basis of knowledge that cannot be doubted. Both are searching for certainty, though the rationalists think that they find it in one or more rationally necessary and therefore indubitable truths, while the empiricists think that certainty resides in our immediate and therefore infallible awareness of ideas or phenomena or sense-data. But such similarities of aim and spirit, however psychologically revealing or historically instructive, would not in themselves undermine the distinction between the two schools.

However, as I have argued elsewhere,[19] the view that our immediate awarenesses are infallible rests in the end on an identification of the awareness with that of which it is an awareness. When someone feels cold, what he feels, on this view, is just his own feeling-cold and that is why he cannot be mistaken about this. I have argued that there cannot be any such entity, any experience which is its own object. But what matters for our present purpose is that if there were such an entity our certainty about it would be rational and not merely empirical. If someone tried to doubt whether he was feeling cold, then (on the view under discussion) this doubt would be ruled out by *a priori* reasoning: his seeming to

---

[19] Are There Any Incorrigible Empirical Statements?' *Australasian Journal of Philosophy*, Vol. 41, No. 1 (May 1963), especially pp. 24-5. [See Chapter II above, especially pp. 35-6.—Edd.]

feel cold would *by definition* be a genuine feeling-cold. This *a priori* reasoning in support of a so-called empirical certainty is closely related to the admittedly rationalistic argument behind Descartes's *cogito ergo sum*. In both cases an appeal to immediate experience is combined with an appeal to a rational necessity. There is, therefore, a basis for Anderson's view that all those 'empiricists' who rest their theories of knowledge on data of which we are said to be infallibly aware are rationalists at least with regard to their starting-point.

We can put this in another way. If there were an experience which was its own object, there would be not even a logical gap, in this case, between the knowing and what was known, so there would be no logical possibility of error. This would constitute rational certainty. But, someone might object, why could there not be empirical certainty distinct from this, and constituted by the fact that though there was a logical gap between the knowing and what was known, these being 'distinct existences', there was no spatio-temporal gap and so no room for a practical possibility of error to creep in? That is to say, why should not literally direct observation be infallible, but only empirically so? To this, we may concede that there could be kinds of direct observation which never actually go wrong, and we can, if we wish, call observations of these kinds empirically infallible. But since it would be merely a matter of fact that such observations never go wrong, to know this would be to know an empirical universal proposition. Consequently, even when we were using such an empirically infallible kind of observation, we would not know infallibly that it was infallible. In this respect empirical certainty would always fall short of absolute certainty, and anyone who persistently pursues the goal of absolute certainty, even about the data of experience, will have to resort in the end to a typically rationalist device.

We have already seen that a plausible and stable empiricism, one without a 'rationalist gap', can be reached only be abandoning the assumption that experience gives us isolated data. But the main reason for making this assumption is the belief that it is about isolated data, and about these alone, that we can have infallible empirical knowledge. And we have now seen that the search for certainty, even about empirical data, will in the end drive us into rationalism. The search for certainty thus has two results: on the one hand it tempts the would-be empiricist to use rationalist devices to support his claim that the basic data are known infallibly, and on the other it leads him to treat those data as isolated in such a way as to leave a 'rationalist gap' in his theory. Conversely, a consistent empiricist would not look for infallible knowledge anywhere, he would therefore be free to recognize that observation gives us complex and organized information, and would be able to develop a stable and plausible empiricism, which would not need to introduce the suggestion that the mind works in accordance with necessary but synthetic principles to explain our systematic knowledge.

Another of Anderson's dicta is that 'rationalism is a philosophy of essences or identities'.[20] Taken on its own, this is obscure: to understand it, we need to be told what an 'essence' is, and to what special sort of identity rationalism is addicted, as opposed to the harmless identities that any philosophy would have to recognize, for example, the identity of the Morning Star with the Evening Star. Presumably what Anderson is referring to is the sort of identity that was asserted by his idealist teachers, when they said that distinctions are not ultimately real. As Anderson expresses this idealist view, distinctions are only ' "distinctions within identities", and any relation is a "form of identity". If a thing is *really* related in a certain way, the relation in question belongs to its "nature", and since that to which it is related is thus not essentially separate from it, a certain "identity of nature" holds between the two'.[21] It is with this 'theory of natures or essences' that Anderson is equating rationalism, and he says that 'the treatment of relations as forms of identity was definitely exploded by Hume, whose argument on causality is applicable to any other case'.[22] I think, however, that Anderson is here conflating two points that should be made separately. One thing that Hume showed, quite conclusively, is that since a cause and its effect are distinct existences, the one cannot logically necessitate the other. Putting it the other way round, if we took 'A causes B' to be analytic, then B could not be a new event different from A. Analogously, if we took any other relation to be literally a form of identity, we would make analytic the proposition which asserts that this relation holds. Of course, a genuine relation can be described by an analytic proposition, as when we say that a husband is married to his wife; that is, we may use, to describe the terms between which the relation holds, words or phrases which presuppose that relation. But in this case there is

[20] *SEP*, p. 101.   [21] *SEP*, pp. 27-8.   [22] *SEP*, p. 45.

still the synthetic fact, describable by the synthetic statement that this man is married to this woman, whereas to take a relation to be literally a form of identity would be to suppose that there is no such synthetic fact, and that every possible description of the relational situation would be analytic.

But Hume also argued, not quite so conclusively, that a cause is not connected with its effect even by some tie which falls short of logical necessity, but of which we could have synthetic *a priori* knowledge, and so be able to infer the effect from the cause alone, or vice versa. Hume criticized not only a notion of *power* such that the cause's having the power to produce the effect would make the effect part of the cause, but also one such that if only we could see this power in the cause we could infer the effect, distinct though it is from the cause, independently of any observation of the effect. Power in the second sense would constitute not a sheer identity between the effect and (part of) the cause—which would go with analytic statements—but rather synthetic but necessary connections which would lead us, with *a priori* certainty, from one thing or event to another.

I believe that rationalism takes sometimes one of these forms, and sometimes the other. We have already seen how the theory of infallible sensations relies upon a literal identification of an awareness with its own object. Similarly an explanatory entity is sometimes postulated in such a way that it is by definition that which produces such-and-such a result, and the explanation is consequently tautological and empty. But an explanatory entity is also sometimes treated as operating in the required manner, and as constituting certain resultant features, or producing the effects to be explained, by some kind of synthetic necessity: this treatment makes more plausible the claim that the hypothetical presence of such an entity renders intelligible the observed behaviour of ordinary things. Similarly, when it is suggested that rational inference will carry us beyond the observed entities to some that are never observed, that the things which we directly encounter somehow point beyond themselves, it is a synthetic necessary connection that is being propounded. But in every such case it is open to the empiricist to reply that no examples of synthetic *a priori* connections can be found, and that what appear to be such examples result from the confusion of synthetic connections with analytic formulae.

In conclusion, let me sum up what I have tried to show. Although Anderson's account of the distinction between rationalism and empiricism is at first sight very different from the traditional one, they can be related to one another. The so-called empiricists whom Anderson classes as partly rationalist did embrace views which are at least implicitly rationalist even in the traditional sense. What is traditionally called rationalism, the attempt to show that the intellect is either a source of knowledge on its own or contributes in a positive way to the construction of knowledge, is committed explicitly or implicitly to a doctrine of synthetic necessary existences or relations. This doctrine of what not merely is so but must be so—*must* in some sense that is not merely logical or linguistic or subjective—is a typical example of the introduction of what Anderson would call a second way of being. And indeed if we examine the various theories which, on Anderson's view, involve distinctions between ways of being, we shall in general find that they are committed in one way or another to the claim that there are synthetic necessary truths. Perhaps it may be possible to use this principle to clarify Anderson's initially obscure notion of ways of being. If so, then Anderson's description of rationalism as 'the contention that there are different kinds or degrees of truth and reality', and the traditional description of it as the doctrine that the intellect contributes in some positive and independent way to knowledge, will turn out to be equivalent. For each will be equivalent to the doctrine that there are necessary but synthetic features of reality, and by contrast a consistent and thorough-going empiricism will be built upon a systematic rejection of all variants of this doctrine.

IV

SELF-REFUTATION—
A FORMAL ANALYSIS

THE attempt is sometimes made to establish philosophical conclusions by arguing that certain contrary views are self-refuting.
To determine how much, or how little, this method can achieve,
I suggest that we should begin with a formal analysis of several
distinct elementary types of self-refutation, and then apply this to
the classification and evaluation of some of the arguments that
have actually been used.[1]

I   ELEMENTARY TYPES OF SELF-REFUTATION

We have *pragmatic* self-refutation when the way in which something is presented conflicts with what is presented. For example, if
I say that I am not saying anything, what I say is false; it is falsified
by the very way in which I put it forward. Similarly, if I write that
I am not writing, what I write must be false. To all simple cases of
this kind the following formal analysis can be applied.

Let d stand for any proposition-forming operator upon propositions—for example, it can represent 'I am saying that', or 'I am
writing that', or again 'It can be proved that', 'I sometimes think
that', 'Smith believes that', and so on.[2] Then in the symbolism of
Łukasiewicz, using N for 'not', and Σp for the quantifier 'for some
p', we can take the formula $d(N\Sigma pdp)$[3] to represent 'I am saying that
it is not the case that for some p I am saying that p'—or, more
briefly, 'I say that I am not saying anything'—and equally to represent any other statement of the same form, such as 'I write that

Reprinted from *The Philosophical Quarterly*, Vol. 14, No. 56 (July 1964).

[1] This kind of argument has been examined, less formally, by J.A. Passmore in
Chapter 4 of *Philosophical Reasoning* (London, 1961); he distinguishes absolute
from pragmatic (and also from *ad hominem*) self-refutation, but my account of how
these come about differs from his.

[2] This technique is borrowed from A. N. Prior, 'On a Family of Paradoxes',
Notre Dame Journal of Formal Logic, II (1961), pp. 16–32.

[3] The brackets are not essential; they are inserted at times only to show more
clearly the structure of the formulae.

I am not writing', 'It can be proved that nothing can be proved', 'Smith believes that he believes nothing', and so on.

It can be shown as follows that whatever d stands for, $Cd(N\Sigma pdp)N(N\Sigma pdp)$ is a logical law:

1. $d(N\Sigma pdp)$
2. Σpdp from 1 by existential generalization
3. $NN\Sigma pdp$ from 2 by double negation
4. $Cd(N\Sigma pdp)N(N\Sigma pdp)$ from 1–3 by conditional proof.

That is, if the antecedent of this conditional is supposed, the consequent can be deduced from it, and therefore the conditional itself is a logical law.[4] But this law has as its interpretations, for different values of the variable d, such statements as these:

'If I say that I am not saying anything, then it is not the case that I am not saying anything'.

'If Smith believes that he believes nothing, then it is not the case that he believes nothing'.

And so on.

This law, therefore, provides a formal and hence general account of the basic type of pragmatic self-refutation. Whenever an item occurs which can be symbolized by $d(N\Sigma pdp)$, it is self-refuting in the sense that what this d here operates on, what is represented by $N\Sigma pdp$, must be false. The occurrence of the operation symbolized by $d(N\Sigma pdp)$ makes false what is symbolized by $N\Sigma pdp$, that is, what is asserted in the noun clause in each example.

Where we have such pragmatic self-refutation, it is not the *proposition* symbolized by $d(N\Sigma pdp)$ that we should call self-refuting, but rather the actual operation which it describes, such as my writing that I am not writing. And even this is self-refuting only in that its occurrence refutes its content, its noun clause. There is no bar to the actual occurrence of this operation; I can perfectly well write that I am not writing, and the corresponding proposition $d(N\Sigma pdp)$ will then be true. And equally what is asserted in the noun clause could, by itself, be true; at another time I may well not be writing.

This pragmatic self-refutation gives rise, in two ways, to what can be called *absolute* self-refutation.

---

[4] Though this law is here stated only as a material implication, it holds also as an entailment, as the proof shows. This fact is used in one of the following proofs.

First, we note that among the operators that can be represented by our d are some which we may call *truth-entailing*, that is, ones for which if dp is true, p itself must be true also. That is, $Cdpp$ is a law for this sub-class of operators. To this sub-class belong, for example, 'It is true that', 'I know that', and 'It can be proved that'. The following proof shows that $Nd(N\Sigma pdp)$ is also a law for this sub-class of d's:

1. $Cdpp$
2. $Cd(N\Sigma pdp)(N\Sigma pdp)$ from 1 by uniform substitution
3. $Cd(N\Sigma pdp)N(N\Sigma pdp)$ the already-established law of pragmatic self-refutation
4. $Nd(N\Sigma pdp)$ from 2 and 3 by simple destructive dilemma.

For example, if it can be proved that nothing can be proved, then nothing can be proved; but equally if it can be proved that nothing can be proved, it is not the case that nothing can be proved; therefore it cannot be the case that it can be proved that nothing can be proved.

This last conclusion is the interpretation of our new law $Nd(N\Sigma pdp)$ where d stands for 'It can be proved that'; other interpretations, for other truth-entailing d's, are 'It is not the case that it is true that nothing is true', It is not the case that I know that I know nothing', and so on.

With absolute self-refutation of this sort, an item that would be symbolized by $d(N\Sigma pdp)$, such as my knowing that I know nothing, simply cannot occur. Here we can say that each *proposition* of this form is self-refuting. It must be false; given that d is truth-entailing, its form guarantees its falsehood.

But, secondly, we note that among the operators that could be represented by our d are some which we may call *prefixable*, that is, ones for which if p itself is true, dp must also be true. Obviously, 'It is true that' is such an operator, and so is 'It is possible that', in various senses of 'possible'. The former of these is truth-entailing, but not the latter: but whether d is truth-entailing or not, another sort of absolute self-refutation arises if d is prefixable. We can argue as follows:

1. $Cpdp$
2. $C(N\Sigma pdp)d(N\Sigma pdp)$ from 1 by uniform substitution
3. $Cd(N\Sigma pdp)N(N\Sigma pdp)$ the law of pragmatic self-refutation

4. $C(N\Sigma pdp)N(N\Sigma pdp)$ from 2 and 3 by hypothetical syllogism

5. $N(N\Sigma pdp)$ from 4 by the law $CCpNpNp$.

That is to say, for any prefixable d, the proposition symbolized by $N\Sigma pdp$ requires its own falsehood, and so it must be false. For example, 'It is not the case that something is possible' is in this way absolutely self-refuting. In these cases, where d is prefixable, it is the proposition symbolized by $N\Sigma pdp$ which refutes itself and must therefore be rejected, whereas where d is truth-entailing what refutes itself is the proposition symbolized by $d(N\Sigma pdp)$.[5]

There seem to be very few operators that are prefixable in the strict sense that the law $Cpdp$ holds for them. But there may be operators that are prefixable in a weaker sense. It can be argued that if someone puts forward any factual claim or makes any assertion, say that p, then he is implicitly committing himself also to making the claim that he knows that p. If so, then if I assert that I know nothing, I am implicitly committing myself to the claim that I know that I know nothing, and hence to a denial of what I originally asserted. From this it would follow that 'I know nothing' cannot be coherently asserted. Yet it may well be true, in that someone else may be able to say truthfully about me, 'He knows nothing'.

Similarly it could be argued that anyone who asserts that p is implicitly committing himself also to asserting that he believes that p (in the sense in which 'I believe' is entailed by, and does not exclude, 'I know').[6] If so, anyone who asserts that he believes nothing implicitly commits himself to asserting that he believes that he believes nothing, and hence to denying his original assertion, to admitting that there is something that he believes. Thus 'I believe nothing' would be another item which could not be coherently asserted, though there is a clear sense in which it could be true.[7]

---

[5] Passmore unduly restricts his discussion by assuming that the only absolutely self-refuting form is the explicit self-contradiction, *p and not-p*. There are, as we see, more complex forms which are self-refuting because of special features of the operators they contain.

[6] Cf. Passmore, *op. cit.*, pp. 74

[7] This shows how a statement may be absurd and yet not self-contradictory, and even true. Passmore criticizes Moore for saying this about 'I believe he has gone out, but he has not', but Moore is right about this. This statement is absurd because asserting 'he has not' commits the speaker to denying 'I believe he has gone out'; yet the whole statement may be true: the speaker may believe, falsely, that a certain person has gone out.

In order to state formally reasoning of this kind, let us introduce another variable operator *a*, to be read as '*x* coherently asserts that'. Its meaning is to be such that one cannot coherently assert a self-contradiction and that if *x* coherently asserts that *p*, and *x*'s asserting that *p* would implicitly commit *x* to asserting that *q*, then we may say that *x* coherently asserts that *q*. Of course we still have to decide in what circumstances someone is implicitly committed to asserting something. We may start by laying it down that anyone who asserts something is thereby implicitly committed to asserting at least whatever is entailed by what he asserts, but we shall have to add further rules later. From what we have said it follows that *a* will obey these rules: (i) Not both *ap* and *aNp*; (ii) If *p* entails *q*, then *Capaq*.

The reasoning given above about 'I know nothing' and 'I believe nothing' can now be put into a form analogous to that of our last formal proof. For any *d* that is prefixable in the weaker sense, the law *Capadp* holds, and we can argue as follows:

1.	*Capadp*	
2.	*Ca(NΣpdp)ad(NΣpdp)*	from 1 by uniform substitution
3.	*Cad(NΣpdp)aN(NΣpdp)*	from the law of pragmatic self-refutation and rule (ii)—see footnote 4
4.	*Ca(NΣpdp)aN(NΣpdp)*	from 2 and 3 by hypothetical syllogism
5.	*Na(NΣpdp)*	from 4 by the law *CCpqCpKpq* and rule (i).

This constitutes a general proof that for any *d* that is prefixable in the weaker sense, *NΣpdp* cannot be coherently asserted. Nevertheless, for a *d* that is only weakly prefixable *NΣpdp* may be true, and *Σpdp* may be false, whereas for a *d* that is strictly prefixable in the sense that *Cpdp* is a law, *NΣpdp* must be false and *Σpdp* is necessarily true.

If the phrase 'pragmatically self-refuting' had not been pre-empted for another use, we might have applied it to examples of this type; but since it has already been used in a different sense we may perhaps say that in examples of the present sort the proposition symbolized by *NΣpdp* is *operationally* self-refuting. This is something stronger than pragmatic (though weaker than absolute) self-refutation. In pragmatic self-refutation the way in which an item happens to be presented conflicts with the item itself. But where we find operational self-refutation there is no other way in which this precise item can be presented. The only possible way of presenting the item is to 'coherently assert' it, and since this involves asserting something that conflicts with the item itself, this precise item cannot be presented at all. And yet what is in a sense an equivalent item can be presented (say by another speaker) and may be true.

This formal survey, then, has brought to light four distinct basic types of self-refutation, which may be summed up as follows:

(i) For any d, $Cd(N\Sigma pdp)N(N\Sigma pdp)$ is a logical law, and hence the operation symbolized by $d(N\Sigma pdp)$ is pragmatically self-refuting; if it occurs, what is symbolized by $N\Sigma pdp$ is false. For example, if I write that I am not writing, then what I write is false.

(ii) For any d that is truth-entailing, $Nd(N\Sigma pdp)$ is a logical law, and hence the proposition symbolized by $d(N\Sigma pdp)$ is absolutely self-refuting. For example, the proposition 'It can be proved that nothing can be proved' must be false.

(iii) For any d that is strictly prefixable, $N(N\Sigma pdp)$ is a logical law; hence the proposition symbolized by $N\Sigma pdp$ is absolutely self-refuting and that symbolized by Σpdp is necessarily true. For example, 'There are no truths' is absolutely self-refuting and 'There are some truths' is necessarily true.

(iv) For any d that is prefixable in the weaker sense that asserting that p would implicitly commit one to asserting that dp, $Na(N\Sigma pdp)$ is a logical law, that is, the proposition symbolized by $N\Sigma pdp$ cannot be coherently asserted, and hence this proposition is operationally self-refuting. For example, 'I believe nothing' seems to be operationally self-refuting; I may in fact believe nothing, but I cannot myself coherently assert that this is so.

2 APPLICATIONS AND EXTENSIONS

I believe that Passmore is right in ascribing a self-refutation argument to Descartes,[8] though we have to read between the lines in either the *Discourse* or the *Meditations* to find it. The suggestion is that I can establish beyond all doubt that I am thinking (and hence that I exist) because if I were to doubt that I am thinking I should

[8] *Op. cit.*, pp. 60-4.

be thinking that I am not thinking, and if I think that I am not thinking I must be wrong. Passmore takes this as an example of merely pragmatic self-refutation. However, it is plausible to claim that 'I think that' is prefixable in the weaker sense, and hence that 'I am not thinking' is *operationally* self-refuting. It seems that it cannot be coherently asserted, that there is no way of presenting it which would not conflict with what is presented. Of course it may be true; I, or anyone else, may at any moment not be thinking, and 'I am not thinking' is not absolutely self-refuting, because 'I think that' is not strictly prefixable. In this respect Descartes's implied argument is wrong, for he drew the conclusion that he was essentially a thinking being; that is, he argued as if 'I am not thinking' were, in our terminology, absolutely self-refuting. Equally, I may well think that I do not think; such a belief, however misguided, may actually occur: 'I think that I am not thinking' is not absolutely self-refuting either, because 'I think that' is not a truth-entailing operator. But while Descartes is wrong (as Passmore points out) in thinking that there is any absolute self-refutation here, Passmore is wrong in concluding on this account that we have here only pragmatic self-refutation. His account omits the intermediate possibility, revealed by our formal treatment, of operational self-refutation. It is this logical feature, combined and confused with the direct *empirical* awareness of one's own thinking, that makes the *cogito* appear at once indubitable and informative.

In order to determine which propositions are operationally self-refuting we must decide which operators are weakly prefixable, that is, we must decide in what circumstances asserting one thing commits us to asserting something else. We have already said that one who asserts that p is implicitly committed to asserting anything entailed by p. We may now add that if x asserts that p, then x is committed to asserting anything entailed by 'x asserts that p'. It is by this principle that we can defend our claim that 'I believe that' and 'I think that' are weakly prefixable. For 'I assert that p', in the ordinary sense of 'assert', entails 'I believe that p'.

We may examine, in the light of these rules, the suggestion that scepticism is self-refuting. If knowledge were defined simply as true belief, 'I know that' would be weakly prefixable. For if I assert that p, I am implicitly committed (by the second rule) to asserting that I believe that p and (by the first) to asserting that this belief is true, and hence I am committed to asserting that I know that p. For this sense of 'know', therefore, 'I know nothing' is operationally self-refuting. With a stronger sense of 'know', such that 'x knows that p' entails not only that x truly believes that p but also that x has reason to believe that p, 'I know that' will be weakly prefixable only if we can add the further rule that in asserting that p one is implicitly committed to claiming that one has reason to believe that p. A case can, indeed, be made out for this view; for if anyone makes an assertion, and yet admits that he has no reason to believe what he asserts, we may well say that his position is incoherent. If we adopt this third rule, then we can say that 'I know that' in this sense—which is at least close to the ordinary sense of the word 'know'—is weakly prefixable, and hence that for this sense also 'I know nothing' is operationally self-refuting. On the other hand, where 'know' has the still stronger sense of 'know for certain', 'I know that' is not even weakly prefixable, and consequently 'I know nothing' in this sense ('I know nothing for certain') is not even operationally self-refuting. But because 'I know that' is truth-entailing, 'I know that I know nothing' is absolutely self-refuting for any of these senses of 'know'.

Similar considerations apply to scepticism with regard to proof. As we have seen, 'It can be proved that nothing can be proved' is absolutely self-refuting, because 'It can be proved that' is truth-entailing. But this operator is not even weakly prefixable, so 'Nothing can be proved' is not even operationally self-refuting; this sceptical view can be coherently presented without any difficulty. All we can say, then, is that while scepticism with regard to proof is in itself a coherent doctrine, the sceptic *may* fall into the trap of pretending to prove that nothing can be proved, and then we shall have him.

Again 'scepticism with regard to the senses' is not self-refuting, either absolutely or operationally, on its own. But if the claim that the senses are totally misleading is put forward with the support of an argument whose premises include the results of certain sensory observations, then this procedure is pragmatically self-refuting.

Passmore draws attention (p. 78) to another way in which a sceptical position may be criticized as self-refuting. G.E. Moore has argued that to say that the commonsense view of the world is false is to presume that there is a commonsense view of the world, and this itself presupposes the truth of some of the main parts of the commonsense view. But if the statement 'The commonsense view of the world is false' did conflict with one of its own presuppositions in the alleged way, this would not show that its formal contradictory, 'The commonsense view of the world is true', which shares this presupposition, is correct. It is still possible that the common presupposition is mistaken, and then it would not be the case that the commonsense view of the world is true, though this could not be expressed by saying that the commonsense view of the world is false. In fact, what we have here is only a pragmatic self-refutation. The man who says that the commonsense view of the world is false is presenting something in a way which conflicts with what is presented; but this does not show that what is presented is false, or even that it cannot be coherently presented in some other way—here, by explicitly denying the particular parts of the commonsense view which the speaker rejects. As Passmore says (p. 79), this sort of appeal to self-refutation is uncomfortably reminiscent of the ontological argument; we cannot establish positive conclusions in this manner.

The modest statement 'There are truths which I do not know' is not self-refuting in any way. But as soon as I try to specify explicitly one of these truths, describing it as the truth that x, I am in difficulty. If I say 'That-x is a truth which I do not know', then by calling this a truth I have committed myself to saying also that I believe that x and have reason to do so, and hence that I know that x. Thus 'That-x is a truth which I do not know' is operationally self-refuting. This difficulty arises with any attempt to set limits to our knowledge in this way, by actually presenting items that lie beyond the limits. But there is no such difficulty if the items are indicated less explicitly. I can refer to, say, the binomial theorem as a truth which I do not know, for I may have reason to believe that something called the binomial theorem is a truth of mathematics without being able to state it and therefore without knowing this truth or being even implicitly committed to claiming that I know it.

Passmore discusses at length (pp. 67–9) the Protagorean doctrine that truths are always relative. Since anything that simply is the case is an absolute and not merely relative truth, 'It is an absolute truth that' is strictly prefixable, and 'There are no absolute truths' is absolutely self-refuting. Passmore rightly comes to this conclusion; but when he says also (p. 71) that with 'No sentences are intelligible' it is not 'just a question of pragmatic self-refutation', this comment, though literally true, is misleading; for as he allows nothing between pragmatic and absolute self-refutation he must mean that 'No sentences are intelligible' is absolutely self-refuting, and this is not so. This cannot be absolutely self-refuting, for it is clearly a contingent matter whether there are intelligible sentences or not. The most that can be claimed here is that 'No sentences are intelligible' is operationally self-refuting. One can put it forward only by using a sentence which one is thereby committed to claiming to be intelligible, and therefore although it is clearly possible that there should be no intelligible sentences, one cannot coherently assert that this possibility is fulfilled.[9]

More explicitly than Descartes, Berkeley uses a self-refutation argument (in §23 of the *Principles* and in the corresponding passage of the first of the *Three Dialogues*) against the view that material objects can exist outside minds. One who believes in such independent existence is challenged, in effect, to say 'I conceive a tree existing unconceived', and Berkeley then points out that this is a contradiction. Let us examine this argument formally, letting Ixp stand for 'x imagines that p', $I'xp$ for 'x imagines truly that p', and Ty for 'y is thought of' or 'y is conceived'. We have the rules that $I'xp$ entails both Ixp and p, and also that if anyone imaginatively predicates something of y, y is thought of, so that $Ix\phi y$ entails Ty.[10] Now because $I'x$ is a truth-entailing operator, these rules enable us to show that $I'xNTy$ is absolutely self-refuting; that is, it is logically impossible that x should truly imagine that y is not thought of[11]. This holds where x and y stand for definite indivi-

---

[9] To bring this matter under our formal treatment, we have to say that 'It is an intelligible sentence that' is weakly prefixable; there are complications here, because we have so far defined d as an operator upon propositions, not sentences. But the analysis could be extended to cover such cases as this, and certainly 'x asserts that p' could be held to entail '"p" is an intelligible sentence'.

[10] This treatment is based on that of A.N. Prior, *Theoria*, Vol. XXI (1955), pp. 117–22.

[11] The proof may be set out as follows:

1.	$CI'xpp$	because $I'x$ is truth-entailing
2.	$I'xNTy$	
3.	$CI'xNTyNTy$	from 1 by uniform substitution
4.	NTy	from 2 and 3 by *modus ponens*
5.	$IxNTy$	from 2 by the rules stated
6.	Ty	from 5 by the rules stated
7.	$KTyNTy$	from 4 and 6
8.	$NI'xNTy$	from 2–7 by indirect proof

We obtain the quantified form by universally generalizing 8 to give $\prod x \prod y NI'xNTy$ which is equivalent to $N\Sigma x\Sigma yI'xNTy$.

duals, and equally if these are treated as variables and existentially quantified: $\Sigma x \Sigma y \Gamma x N T y$ is also absolutely self-refuting, and $N \Sigma x \Sigma y \Gamma x N T y$ must be true. However, as Prior points out, what Berkeley needs to prove is not this, but the statement which would be symbolized by $N \Sigma x \Gamma x \Sigma y N T y$, that is, 'No one truly imagines that there exists a thing which is not thought of'. But the latter is not a necessary truth; it cannot be derived validly from the preceding formula; and if Berkeley is so deriving it he has fallen into the fallacy of mixing up two possible orders of his operators, that is, into a variant of the fallacy of composition.

However, this is not the whole of the story. Suppose that I try to put forward the suggestion that a certain thing, y, is not thought of, that NTy. 'I imagine that', which we may symbolize here by Ix, is weakly prefixable, so that asserting that NTy implicitly commits me to asserting that $IxNTy$, and hence (by the rule that $Ix\phi y$ entails Ty) to asserting that Ty. Thus NTy is operationally self-refuting: no one can ever coherently assert that a certain thing exists unconceived. This, I think, is the point that Berkeley was initially making, and making quite correctly. This is analogous to the point noted above, that one can never specify explicitly an unknown truth.

But having conceded this, we can proceed to show how Berkeley goes astray in trying to use this point. He argues as if NTy were not operationally but absolutely self-refuting, indeed as if it were internally self-contradictory. He thinks he has shown, for example, that 'a tree existing unconceived' is a self-contradictory concept; that is, he has confused operational self-refutation with outright logical impossibility. Also, from the fact that NTy is operationally self-refuting, it does not follow that $\Sigma y N T y$ is so too, and indeed it is not so; anyone can coherently assert that some things exist unconceived, and even that some trees do so. Besides, there is a confusion in the phrase 'exist unconceived'; although Berkeley has shown that I cannot coherently assert that y exists and y is not conceived, and therefore that if I say that y exists I must admit *also* that y is conceived, it does not follow that I must admit that y exists *by being conceived*, that y exists 'in someone's mind'. 'Exist unconceived' should contrast with 'exist *and* be conceived', not, as Berkeley intends, with 'exist *by being conceived*'. And finally, as Prior points out, if Berkeley had shown that trees, houses, and so on cannot exist unconceived he would have shown also that minds and spirits are equally unable to exist unconceived; the argument, being formal and therefore quite general, would prove far too much.

Passmore repeatedly says that absolute self-refutation occurs when we violate 'the invariant conditions of discourse' (p. 80), the 'presuppositions of proposing' (p. 68). There may indeed be conditions of discourse,[12] but they seem to be of more than one type. The doctrine that all truths are relative is absolutely self-refuting, because the condition of discourse which it violates is the fact that 'It is an absolute truth that' is a strictly prefixable operator. But in general what could be called a condition of discourse sets limits only to what can be coherently asserted, it is concerned with the way in which saying one thing implicitly commits us to being prepared to say something else as well, and it therefore gives rise only to what we have called operational self-refutation.

3 CONCLUSIONS

The main effect of this discussion has been to establish both the formal possibility of what we have called operational self-refutation and its importance for a critical history of philosophical argument. As our formal study shows, this is something intermediate between merely pragmatic and either kind of absolute self-refutation. Lack of this category has led Passmore into mistakes in classification: seeing that Descartes's argument yields something less than absolute self-refutation, he has set it down as a merely pragmatic case, but in some other examples which are really similar to this he has seen something more than pragmatic self-refutation, and so has classified them as 'absolute'. We have found that Descartes and Berkeley both begin by drawing attention to items which really are operationally self-refuting, but that the errors which creep into their subsequent arguments are due, at least in part, to their mistaking these operational self-refutations for absolute logical impos-

---

[12] Passmore takes over this view from Professor John Anderson. See John Anderson, *Studies in Empirical Philosophy* (Sydney, 1962), pp. 4, 11, 116, 123, etc. Anderson uses this notion especially in arguing that any entities whose existence we can intelligibly assert must be propositional in form, and therefore that we cannot 'get behind the proposition', we cannot analyse propositional facts into any simpler components such as 'universals' and 'pure particulars'. But even if this is correct, all it shows is that non-propositional entities cannot be coherently asserted. It would require a further step to show that there could not *be* such entities.

sibilities, and so coming to regard certain contrary propositions as necessary truths.

Another result of our formal study is that it enables us to undertake in a more systematic way the task of deciding what arguments of the various types are available, and what we can expect to establish in philosophy by using them.

There is, clearly, an indefinitely wide range of possible examples of pragmatic self-refutation, but in themselves they are of only limited importance. Nothing much follows from such facts as that if I write that I do not write then what I write is false, and even in more complicated cases the most that is shown is that a certain way of presenting a certain view is unsatisfactory, that a proposed supporting argument will not support the view that it is intended to support; but the view itself is not thereby refuted, and it may well be presented and supported in other ways.

Again there are plenty of truth-entailing operators—indeed they can be constructed at will—and consequently there are plenty of absolutely self-refuting propositions of the form $d(N\Sigma pdp)$. But these tell us only such things as 'It cannot be proved that nothing can be proved'. Such points may be useful in philosophical debate, for example with a sceptic who abandons the security of his entrenched position and lapses into dogmatism; but they do not in themselves establish important positive conclusions.

There seem to be very few strictly prefixable operators, and consequently very few absolutely self-refuting propositions of the form $N(\Sigma pdp)$. The main problem, then, is to discover which operators are prefixable in the weaker sense, and thus to discover propositions that are operationally self-refuting, that cannot be coherently asserted.

Our enquiry has another philosophically important consequence. We might be tempted to believe that there is a special form of philosophical argument which enables us to establish positive conclusions by showing that certain contrary statements would be self-refuting. This would go against empiricism, for if any view would literally refute *itself*, its denial would be a necessary truth. However, our analysis shows that this challenge to empiricism evaporates on closer inspection. Pragmatic self-refutation, it is clear, creates no such problems. Nor does absolute self-refutation of the first kind; in rejecting such claims as 'It can be proved that nothing can be proved', we are merely avoiding logical contradictions. The second kind of absolute self-refutation yields, as positive conclusions, only such purely formal items as 'There are some (absolute) truths' and 'Something is possible'. The items that would have been troublesome are those that we have now classified under operational self-refutation. Empiricism would have been seriously undermined if they had enabled us to establish as necessary truths such propositions as 'I am (essentially) a thinking being', 'I know something', or 'Material objects do not exist unconceived'. But since the items opposed to these are at most operationally self-refuting, the detection of them does not lead to any such necessary truths. On the contrary, we are now in a better position to understand why these propositions have seemed to be necessary and to criticize the arguments by which philosophers have tried to establish them.

V

PROOF

WE sometimes think of proof as a source of knowledge which is independent of and perhaps superior to observation. What has been proved must be so, and we need not wait for experience to tell us that it is so. It is widely believed that many propositions of arithmetic can be proved in some way that shows them to be something other than empirically known matters of fact. That is, it would appear that there are kinds of proof which have an important bearing on the question whether arithmetical propositions are analytic, or synthetic but *a priori*, or empirical. This is the contention which I shall examine.

1 The problem of the epistemological status of arithmetic may be clarified by first sketching an answer to the corresponding—but, I hope, less controversial—question about the status of geometry.

Before we can answer the question 'Are geometrical propositions analytic or synthetic, and are they empirical or *a priori*?' we must draw a number of distinctions.

Suppose that we have a formal deductive system for, say, Euclidean geometry, with the usual apparatus of primitive symbols, formation rules, axioms, derivation rules, and theorems, and suppose that we regard it initially as uninterpreted, though its primitive symbols include what in other contexts are ordinary English words and logical constants. We must distinguish sharply between each theorem and what I shall call the corresponding theorem-conditional, that is, the statement of the form 'If (the conjunction of the axioms) then (this theorem)', and we must also distinguish stages of interpretation as follows:

(i) When the symbols are completely uninterpreted, each thesis (axiom or theorem) is a mere string of marks, or a type of which actual strings of marks are the tokens. It is not a proposition or even a propositional form. At this stage no thesis is either true or false, and *a fortiori* none is analytic or synthetic, empirical or *a priori*. Even a theorem-conditional is not yet a proposition (since the items indicated by the words in brackets above are not yet

Reprinted from *Aristotelian Society Supplementary Volume XL* (1966).

propositions or propositional forms), and cannot therefore be a logical truth. The theorems are proved only in the sense that they result from successive transformations of the axioms which are in accordance with the derivation rules.

(ii) When the logical words and symbols in the system are given their ordinary logical interpretation, but the specifically geometrical expressions are left uninterpreted, the axioms and theorems become (in general) propositional forms. We may assume that the derivations licensed by the derivation rules become, on this interpretation, logically valid argument-forms. The theorem-conditionals are now logically true; but at this stage the axioms and theorems are (in general) still neither true nor false, and *a fortiori* are not analytic or synthetic *a priori* or empirical.

(iii) An interpretation of the specifically geometrical items may now be added. For example, plane surfaces may be defined in terms of contact between the surfaces of movable but rigid solid bodies, straight lines by intersections of plane surfaces, equalities by co-incidences, and so on: thus meanings which approximate to at least part of the ordinary meanings of 'point', 'line', 'straight', 'equal', and so on may be given to these terms as they occur within the system. On this interpretation of their geometrical constituents, the axioms and theorems become (in general) synthetic statements. Also, it is now an empirical question whether each of them is true or false. The theorem-conditionals are still logically true, and hence *if* the axioms are true, so are the theorems, but the separate axioms and theorems are at most empirical truths. Their status is not affected by the fact that the proofs of the theorems from the axioms are formally rigorous and, we have assumed, logically valid. Or, putting the same point in another way, it is a strictly empirical question whether this formal deductive system as a whole fits the empirical material to which the given interpretation applies it.

(A thorough account of geometry along these lines is given by Nagel in Chapter 8 of *The Structure of Science*.)†

This situation is complicated by the fact that the propositions of any consistent system may be made *analytic by resolution*, that is, we may so handle them that they are permanently protected from all possible falsification or disconfirmation. This can easily happen with Euclidean geometry. Although the axioms were originally

† E. Nagel, *The Structure of Science: Problems in the Logic of Scientific Explanation* (London, 1961).

adopted because (with the ordinary meanings of the terms) both the axioms themselves and the theorems derived from them were observed to be true or at least approximately true, it is possible now to treat the truth of the axioms (and, consequently, of the theorems) as restricting the range of permitted interpretations. We might now be so wedded to the system that if certain lines which were straight by our present tests were found not to obey the Euclidean propositions about straight lines, we would say that they were not straight, modifying our tests so as to exclude them. This treatment is not strictly compatible with that sketched in (iii) above: once a definite empirical interpretation has been given to the term 'straight line', it is a matter of hard fact whether certain lines are straight, and hence whether certain propositions are true of all straight lines. Nevertheless, the two treatments can in a sense peacefully coexist, so long as the propositions we want to protect from falsification are true, or appear to be true, on the given interpretation. We can go on using the terms with the given meanings, while at the same time being prepared to protect the propositions from falsification, if necessary, by changing those meanings. But we can combine these treatments only so long as the necessity does not actually arise. Our meaning-policies are then inconsistent, but the inconsistency may escape exposure. However, such coexistence does not and cannot entail that the propositions *with the given meanings of their terms* are analytic.

2 An analogous account of the epistemological status of arithmetic is at least worth consideration. This would run as follows. Suppose that we have a formal deductive system for arithmetic— or for part of arithmetic: we can leave aside any questions about completeness. The axioms are formulae some of whose constituents will eventually be interpreted as logical constants, but others will eventually be interpreted as specifically arithmetical terms, as standing for numbers, addition, equality, and so on. Once the logical items have been interpreted and given ordinary logical meanings, the theorems follow from the axioms, whether the arithmetical items are interpreted or not. The theorem-conditionals will then be logically true, but this leaves the status of the separate axioms and theorems quite undetermined. Until the arithmetical items are interpreted, the separate axioms and theorems are (in general) only propositional forms: they are neither true nor false and *a fortiori*

they are neither analytic nor synthetic, and neither empirical nor *a priori*. Finally the arithmetical items are interpreted, so that some expressions in the system are given the meanings which words and symbols like 'one', 'two', '1', '2', '+', '=', and so on ordinarily have, or at least part of their ordinary meanings. On this interpretation the separate theses become (in general) synthetic statements. But at the same time—though their being synthetic does not *entail* their being empirical—they also become at most empirically true. Though the theorems can be proved from the axioms, the axioms themselves are empirical: we have to rely on experience to check the truth either of the theorems themselves or of the axioms from which they are deduced. Or in other words, it is an empirical question whether the formal system as a whole fits the empirical material to which the proposed interpretation applies it. We can, of course, make the theses of the system (provided that it is consistent) analytic by resolution. We can resolve so to restrict the interpretation of the arithmetical items that the theses always remain true. But this means that we are prepared to change the meanings of the arithmetical items if necessary: it is not strictly compatible with the giving of a definite interpretation to the arithmetical items. For example, once a certain interpretation has been given, one of the theorems will state that a group of two things and another, non-overlapping, group of two things always together form a group of four things, and with ordinary meanings for 'two', 'four', and so on it is a question of hard fact whether they do or not. Admittedly, so long as the theses which we resolve to protect from falsification are, on the chosen interpretation, in fact true, the two treatments can coexist peacefully. We can use arithmetical terms with an interpretation that makes the theses synthetic, while being prepared to change the interpretation, if necessary, to protect the theses from falsification, so long as the necessity does not arise. But this possibility of coexistence does not entail that the theses as interpreted are analytic. So, despite our tendency to make the corresponding formulae analytic by resolution, the propositions of interpreted arithmetic are synthetic just as the propositions of interpreted geometry are; this being so, it is plausible to suggest that they are likewise empirical.

There is a great variety of possible and indeed actually used interpretations of arithmetic. I think that what I want to say will hold for all of them, but it will make the discussion more concrete if I specify one very simple interpretation, and confine myself to it. Similarly I shall consider only the most elementary numerical propositions.

We have an empirical concept of a discrete individual thing, persisting for at least the period of time that it is under consideration; we know what it is for this thing not to come into existence or pass out of existence, not to divide up into more than one thing and not to coalesce with another thing during this period. Similarly, we have an empirical concept of a group of such things. Also, we know the conventionally established sequence of number words in English, 'one, two, three, four, ...', and we know what it is to count correctly a group of things—that is, to set up a one–one correlation between the things and the number words in their standard order, and if, say, 'four' was the last word used in this correlation to say that there are four things in the group. Again, we have an empirical concept of adding two such groups with no common members and of counting correctly the resulting group.

With this account of what it means to say that there is a certain number of things in a group, it is, I think, a synthetic and indeed empirical truth that any given group contains a unique number of things, that counting correctly a group as described above yields the same number in whatever order its members are counted. But I need not insist on this point. Granting that every group has in this sense a unique number—whatever sort of truth this may be— let us call a group which when it is counted correctly is found to contain four things a four-group, and so on. Then '$2 + 2 = 4$', considered as a theorem of arithmetic as thus interpreted, asserts that the result of adding any two-group to any two-group, where the groups have no common members, is always a four-group.

This interpreted theorem seems to be universally true; it states a fact which we cannot change at will. We cannot make this expression state something false without varying some of our previous specifications of groups of things and of correct counting and adding. Apparent falsifications with raindrops, amoebas, rabbits, queer counting procedures, or mistakes in counting are all beside the point. The theorem, as here interpreted, simply is not about any of these. In particular, what it asserts is not any regularity of behaviour; it does not state that an occurrence of one sort is regularly followed by an occurrence of another sort, so it cannot be used on its own to license predictions. It states what Mill calls a uniformity of coexistence. This, of course, does not show that it is non-empirical: it is a mistake to suppose that every empirical universal must directly license predictions. We cannot validly convert Hume's principle that all statements connecting temporally distinct events are empirical.

On the other hand, this theorem on this interpretation is not analytic by resolution. We have not laid it down that it is to be universally true and resolved to call incorrect any procedures of adding and counting that yield results that conflict with it. Correct counting has been described in terms of one–one correlation between the members of a group and the standard sequence of number words, not by reference to the actual results of adding and counting.

Nor is the theorem thus interpreted analytic in any more direct way. A four-group has not been *defined* as the result of adding a two-group to a distinct two-group, but separately by reference to the counting procedure. Nor have we included among the criteria for calling certain things two-groups that the result of adding two such distinct things should be a four-group. (True, we *might* have defined a four-group as the result of adding a pair of distinct two-groups; but then it would have been a synthetic statement that a four-group gives the result 'four' when counted correctly: the synthetic content breaks out somewhere.)

But if this statement is synthetic, there is at least a *prima facie* case for its being empirical. To say that it is synthetic but *a priori*, we should have to maintain either that the entities for which it holds are partly dependent on our minds or that our thinking is authoritative about a world of independent things, and there are well-known objections to both these views. It will be generally admitted that when we learn numerical truths like this theorem for ourselves, and do not merely accept them on the authority of our teachers, we do so empirically: we check them by counting specimen groups of things. I grant that this historical fact does not in itself settle the issue: something that is knowable *a priori*, that *could* be learned independently of experience, may none the less be learned and checked by observations. But I think that this interpreted theorem asserts something that we can establish only by experience, for example by observing specimen instances, or by imagining instances on the basis of what we have previously observed, or by deducing it from premises which incorporate the results of similar observations.

3 I suspect, however, that many philosophers will reject this suggestion, and will say that the theorems even of interpreted arithmetic are analytic, unless the interpretation makes them refer to processes or behaviour, to what *happens* when raindrops or rabbits get together or when fallible human beings actually count groups of things—and then, of course, the theorems are not merely empirical but false. I think they will say this for a variety of reasons that are not always distinguished from one another with sufficient care. First, they may be mixing up the theorems with the theorem-conditionals. Secondly, they may be referring to our tendency to make the theorems analytic by resolution; but this cannot entail that the theorems as interpreted are analytic. Thirdly, they may be noting that some numerical statements are 'true by definition', indeed that any one numerical formula may be true by definition; but only a limited number can be so at once. If '2' and '+' have been interpreted as above, '4' can be given an arithmetical interpretation by being defined as '2 + 2', and the interpreted formula '2 + 2 = 4' will then be 'true by definition'; but we cannot simultaneously make '3 + 1 = 4' 'true by definition', if '3' has been defined already. Fourthly, these philosophers may be claiming that the theorems even of interpreted arithmetic can be proved without the use of empirical premisses. Of these four kinds of reason for saying that the theorems of interpreted arithmetic are analytic, the first three are palpably bad reasons; but the fourth deserves careful examination.

This is the logicist argument that a numerical proposition, such as '2 + 2 = 4' as interpreted above, can be proved, using no premisses that are not logically valid. This argument would be combined with a criticism of the account sketched in §2 above, that whereas we can distinguish geometrical items from logical items, we cannot similarly distinguish arithmetical items from logical items, and therefore that the two stages in the interpretation of a formal system for arithmetic cannot be distinguished. Arithmetical expressions like 'two' in its ordinary sense can be defined in terms of logical constants alone, so that once the logical items have been given a logical interpretation there is no need to add an arithmetical interpretation, and indeed no opportunity to do so. Some formulae constructed out of logical items alone will automatically have the meanings that would be assigned to them by (for example) the above-stated interpretation of arithmetical theorems.

Whatever may be said about the wider claims of the logicist theory, this objection with regard to elementary numerical propositions can be made highly plausible. Consider, for example, this proof of '$2 + 2 = 4$'.

1. $(\exists r)(\exists s)[r\varepsilon K.\ s\varepsilon K.\ r \neq s.\ (w)\{w\varepsilon K \supset (w = r\ v\ w = s)\}].$
   $(\exists t)(\exists u)[t\varepsilon L.\ u\varepsilon L.\ t \neq u.\ (x)\{x\varepsilon L \supset (x = t\ v\ x = u)\}].$
   $(y)[\,y\varepsilon K \supset\ \sim y\ \varepsilon L].\ (z)[z\varepsilon M \equiv (z\varepsilon K\ v\ z\varepsilon L)]$—supposition.
2. $a\varepsilon K.\ b\varepsilon K.\ a \neq b.\ (w)[w\varepsilon K \supset (w = a\ v\ w = b)]$—from 1, by simplification and EI.
3. $c\varepsilon L.\ d\varepsilon L.\ c \neq d.\ (x)[x\varepsilon L \supset (x = c\ v\ x = d)]$—from 1, by simplification and EI.
4. $a\varepsilon M.\ b\varepsilon M.\ c\varepsilon M.\ d\varepsilon M$—from 1, 2, and 3, using UI etc.
5. $a \neq c.\ a \neq d.\ b \neq c.\ b \neq d$—from 1, 2, and 3, using UI, Id., etc.
6. $e\varepsilon M$—supposition.
7. $e\varepsilon K\ v\ e\varepsilon L$—from 1 and 6.
8. $e = a\ v\ e = b\ v\ e = c\ v\ e = d$—from 2, 3, and 7.
9. $(x)[x\varepsilon M \supset (x = a\ v\ x = b\ v\ x = c\ v\ x = d)]$—from 6-8 by CP and UG.
10. $a\varepsilon M.\ b\varepsilon M.\ c\varepsilon M.\ d\varepsilon M.\ a \neq b.\ a \neq c.\ a \neq d.\ b \neq c.\ b \neq d.\ c \neq d.$
    $(x)[\chi\varepsilon M \supset\ (x = a\ v\ x = b\ v\ x = c\ v\ x = d)]$—from 2, 3, 4, 5, and 9.
11. $(\exists r)(\exists s)(\exists t)(\exists u)[r\varepsilon M.\ s\varepsilon M.\ t\varepsilon M.\ u\varepsilon M.\ r \neq s.\ r \neq t.\ r \neq u.\ s \neq t.$
    $s \neq u.\ t \neq u.\ (x)\{x\varepsilon M \supset (x = r\ v\ x = s\ v\ x = t\ v\ x = u)\}]$— from 10 by EG.
12. $(K)(L)(M)[(1) \supset (11)]$—from 1-11 by CP and UG.

How this proof works can be explained briefly and non-technically. It begins with the supposition (1), a formulation of the statement 'K is a two-group and L is a two-group and K and L have no common members and M is the group that results from adding K and L'. From this it derives (basically by existential instantiation, some inferences about the instances thus introduced and some regrouping of information, followed by existential generalization) an expression (11) which is a formulation of the statement 'M is a four-group'. Finally, using conditional proof and universal generalization (which is valid because the derivation of (11) from (1) is a specimen derivation, that uses only information that could be applied to any such group as K, L, and M) it draws the conclusion (12) which is a formulation of the statement 'For all

K, L, and M, if K is a two-group and L is a two-group and K and L have no common members and M is the group that results from adding K and L, then M is a four-group'. And this, it is claimed, is synonymous with '$2 + 2 = 4$' in our interpreted arithmetic.

The proof as set out above is somewhat condensed, and not all the transformations used have been made explicit. But it could easily be expanded so that every move was an instance of a logically valid procedure, and the conclusion (12) would then have been proved as depending only on those procedures, not on any premisses at all. This seems to substantiate the claim that a theorem of interpreted arithmetic, with the interpretation sketched in §2, can be proved by logical procedures alone, and is thus a logical truth.

Before commenting on this, let us consider two other ways in which someone might profess to prove the interpreted arithmetical statement that the result of adding any pair of distinct two-groups is always a four-group.

4 'Here is a group of two apples. Over there is another group of two apples. Now count the apples in the group we get by taking these two groups together: one, two, three, four. And I could do the same in every other case where I had a group of two things and another, non-overlapping, group of two things. So the result of adding any two-group to any distinct two-group is always a four-group.'

It would be generally agreed that this would not be a proof of '$2 + 2 = 4$' in the sense required. The fact that a demonstration of this sort can be given does not tell against the suggestion that such theorems of interpreted arithmetic are empirical. This demonstration consists in checking one instance of the universal proposition which is the theorem in question, and then generalizing the result of this check. The first of these steps is obviously empirical: we simply try out the counting procedure on the group that results from the adding of the two original groups. Consequently no demonstration of this sort can show that the theorem is anything more than an empirical generalization.

5 We might try to improve on this by constructing the following proof:

1. For all x, x is a two-group iff the members of x can be one-one-correlated with the number-word sequence 'one, two'.

2. For all x, x is a four-group, iff the members of x can be one-one-correlated with the number-word sequence 'one, two, three, four'.

3. Suppose that K is a two-group and L is a two-group and K and L have no common members and M is the result of adding K and L.

4. The members of K can be one-one-correlated with the number-word sequence 'one, two'—from 1 and 3.

5. The members of L can be one-one-correlated with the number-word sequence 'one, two'—from 1 and 3.

6. The members of K and L together can be one-one-correlated with the number-word sequence 'one, two, one, two'—from 3, 4, and 5.

7. The members of M can be one-one-correlated with the number-word sequence 'one, two, one, two'—from 3 and 6.

8. The number-word sequence 'one, two, one, two' can be one-one-correlated with the number-word sequence 'one, two, three, four'.

9. The members of M can be one-one-correlated with the number-word sequence 'one, two, three, four'—from 7 and 8.

10. M is a four-group—from 2 and 9.

11. The result of adding any two-group to any distinct two-group is a four-group—from steps 3 to 10 by conditional proof and universal generalization.

This seems to be an improvement on the 'proof' of §4. Here (1) and (2) express the account given in §2 of what it is to be a two-group or a four-group, (4) and (5) are logical consequences of (1) and (3), and similarly (10) is a logical consequence of (2) and (9). The final generalization at (11) is now *logically* legitimate, because the derivation of (10) from (3) is a specimen derivation in the sense required by logic: everything said in it about K, L, and M has been deduced from the definitions (1) and (2) and the supposition (3), and could therefore be said about any three groups which obeyed a statement of the same form as (3). This proof does not involve any observation of the groups K, L, and M. These groups, therefore, are being used in a way quite different from that in which the groups of apples were used in the 'proof' of §4.

But this does not mean that the job that was done by the apples is not now being done at all. It is still being done, but this time by the number-word sequences 'one, two', 'one, two', and 'one, two, one, two'. Step (8) is not logically deduced from any previous steps: we simply have to try it and see that it is so. This, therefore, is an empirical premiss, and since it is an essential one the proof as a whole fails as an attempt to establish the conclusion as an *a priori* truth. In fact, (8) presents what is really one instance of the theorem we are trying to prove: the two successive occurrences of the number-word sequence 'one, two' are distinct two-groups which taken together constitute a four-group.

If (8) were the only empirical step, we should have the surprising result that the general theorem (11) was conclusively verified by the singular observation (8). If this were so, we should have to say that (11), despite its formal universality, had the epistemological status of a singular empirical statement. (A view of this sort has been defended by Erik Stenius in the *Philosophical Review* for July 1965.) However, there are two other moves in this proof which are not purely logical, and which, occurring within what is treated as a specimen derivation, require general principles to validate them, if the final generalization is to be valid. These are the moves from (3), (4), and (5) to (6), and from (7) and (8) to (9). The general principle required to validate the former is difficult to state briefly, that required for the latter is the principle that one–one-correlation is transitive. I do not see how either of them can be anything more than an empirical generalization. If one–one-correlation is introduced ostensively, we cannot also make its transitivity analytic by resolution. Each of these two principles can be demonstrated by a procedure analogous to the apple 'proof' of §4, but this will not give them any more than an empirical status.

This proof as a whole, then, leaves the conclusion (11) as a consequence of a singular empirical observation and two empirical generalizations. The latter allow us to generalize from (8) to a conclusion about all pairs of distinct two-groups, but the status they give to that conclusion is only that of an empirical generalization. This proof, then, resembles that of §4 in an essential feature: it too presents an instance of the theorem we are trying to prove, and generalizes from that instance to the theorem.

6 We can now return to the proof of which a condensed version was given in §3. Comparing this with those given in §4 and §5, is it not clear that the job which was done by the apples in §4 and by the number-word sequences in §5 is being done here by the symbols '*a*', '*b*', '*c*', and '*d*'? The logical techniques used here to formulate '*K* is a two-group' and '*L* is a two-group' enable us to introduce '*a*' and '*b*' as names of the members of *K*, and '*c*' and '*d*' as names of the members of *L*; this ensures that the names of the members of *M* will be '*a*', '*b*', '*c*', and '*d*'; and the fact that there are just four names here ensures that *M* will be described by the expression which is a formulation of '*M* is a four-group'. The proof goes through, and it yields the desired result; but it does so precisely because the theorem which we are trying to prove is true of the groups of symbols which play a vital role in this proof.

There is, indeed, another objection to the claims made for this proof in §3. It was there suggested that the logical formulations given in (1) for '*K* is a two-group' and '*L* is a two-group' and that in (11) which was read as '*M* is a four-group' were, once the symbols were given their ordinary logical interpretation, synonymous with the statements '*K* is a two-group' etc. in our interpretation of arithmetic. But they are plainly not *synonymous*. To say that there is an *r* such that there is an *s* such that *r* is a member of *K*, and so on, is not to *say* that when *K* is counted correctly its members will be one–one-correlated with the number-word sequence 'one, two'. We may, however, argue that the expressions are *equivalent*, as follows:

From '$(\exists r)(\exists s)[r\varepsilon K.\ s\varepsilon K.\ r \neq s.\ (w)\{w\varepsilon K \supset (w = r\ v\ w = s)\}]$', logically interpreted, we can infer by EI a formula which says that *a* and *b* are the only members of *K*, and then by correlating *a* with 'one' and *b* with 'two' we can show that *K* is, by the criteria of §2, a two-group. Conversely, if *K* is, by those criteria, a two-group, we can give the names '*a*' and '*b*' to the members correlated respectively with 'one' and 'two', so that *a* and *b* are the only members of *K*, and after giving this its logical formulation we can infer from it, by EG, the above quantified formula.

The equivalence of '*L* is a two-group' and '*M* is a four-group' with the respective logical formulae could be established in the same way. Using these equivalences, we could add steps to the proof given in §3 so as to derive from (12) the conclusion 'For all *K*, *L*, and *M*, if *K* is a two-group, etc.' with the meanings assigned in §2 to '*K* is a two-group', etc.

But these steps would introduce transitions that are not logically guaranteed. For in the above argument for the equivalence of the logical formula with our statement '*K* is a two-group', we were forced actually to count the members *a* and *b*. The proof in §3 then, is not a proof from logic alone of '2 + 2 = 4' in our interpretation of arithmetic, nor can it be extended into such a proof.

This is, perhaps, a minor point, for it could be replied that though (12) does not state '2 + 2 = 4' in *our* interpretation, it does state '2 + 2 = 4' in *an* interpretation of arithmetic, so that we have here a theorem of interpreted arithmetic which has been proved from logic alone. But the major point is that made at the beginning of §6: the proof in §3, no less than those in §§4 and 5, rests upon the truth of one particular instance of the theorem which is being proved.

Of course this does not show that the proof is circular or that the theorem is false or unfounded. Quite the reverse: it is because the theorem is true as a matter of fact that it can be proved in this way. And it is true in a peculiarly pervasive manner. We can run through the proof as a sequence of spoken sounds instead of a sequence of marks on paper, and we shall get the same result, because the theorem is equally true of groups of sounds; or an electrical computer could run through a counterpart of this proof and get the same result, because the theorem is equally true of groups of electric impulses. But the point is that this proof was put forward in an attempt to show that the interpreted theorem is something more than a truth of fact, and it is in this respect, and this respect only, that it fails.

A crude statement of this criticism would be that this proof is essentially equivalent to demonstrating the truth of '2 + 2 = 4' with apples or pennies or any such material instances: it differs only in that it wraps up the factual instance in a blanket of logical symbols. But this is not quite fair. It ignores the fact that this proof, up to (12), is—unlike the others—logically valid, and that what (12) states when it is logically interpreted is therefore a logical truth. We seem, then, to have a paradox on our hands, that the same expression, on the same interpretation of its symbols, states what is both a logical truth and a merely empirical matter of fact.

7   As an aid to resolving this paradox, let us consider yet another proof, which is stated initially in an uninterpreted formal system, but one which could subsequently be interpreted into a small part of arithmetic.

This system is set out formally as follows:

Primitive symbols: .*†~ (The first three of these will be called number-symbols.)

Formation rules: There are two kinds of well-formed formulae, numbers and equations. Any sequence of one or more number-symbols is a number. Where α and β are numbers, $\alpha \sim \beta$ is an equation.

Axiom Schema: $\alpha \sim \alpha$ (Where α is any number.)

Definitions: $* \sim$ ..

$\dagger \sim$ ....

Derivation rule: If $\alpha \sim \beta$ is a definition, and A is a thesis, and B results from the substitution of α for β or of β for α anywhere in A, then B is a thesis.

In this system, the following sequence of formulae is a proof:

$$.... \sim ....$$
$$*.. \sim ....$$
$$** \sim ....$$
$$** \sim \dagger$$

This is a proof in the most rigorous sense. The first line is an instance of the axiom-schema, the second line is derived from the first by the derivation rule and the first definition, the third line is similarly derived from the second, and the fourth line is derived from the third by the derivation rule and the second definition.

This sytem could be interpreted directly into a part of interpreted arithmetic. We could take '.' as standing for 1, '*' for 2, '†' for 4, juxtaposition of number-symbols for addition, and '$\sim$' for $=$ in the sense of arithmetical equality. This turns the axiom-schema into the tautology that any number is equal to itself, the definitions into possible definitions of '2' and '4' in interpreted arithmetic and the conclusion of the proof into the theorem '$2+2=4$'. (It may look as if the derivation rule is turned into a logical truth, but it is not really so innocent. For example, it includes an associative rule, as a comparison of the following formal proof with its interpretation will show.

Proof	Interpretation
$\dagger* \sim \dagger*$	$4+2=4+2$
$....* \sim \dagger*$	$1+1+1+1+2=4+2$
$...... \sim \dagger*$	$1+1+1+1+1+1=4+2$
$*.... \sim \dagger*$	$2+1+1+1+1=4+2$
$*\dagger \sim \dagger*$	$2+4=4+2$

What this reveals is that since juxtaposition is associative—i.e., if γ is juxtaposed to the juxtaposition of α and β, then α is juxtaposed to the juxtaposition of β and γ—this derivation rule, in connection with the interpretation of juxtaposition as addition, asserts that addition is associative.)

Although the proof of '$** \sim \dagger$' given above is a purely formal proof, there is no doubt that it yields the result it does, a result which can be interpreted into '$2 + 2 = 4$', because '$2 + 2 = 4$' as a statement in interpreted arithmetic is true of each of the rows of dots in the first line of that proof—that is, because each array of four dots is also a group of two dots followed by another distinct group of two dots. Thus the conclusion reached even by a purely formal uninterpreted proof may depend upon arithmetical features of the groups of symbols that enter into that proof. If this is true even of an uninterpreted formal proof, it is equally true of a proof which contains symbols that have been given a logical interpretation, even if the derivation rules, on this interpretation, are all logically valid. This resolves the paradox mentioned at the end of §6: it shows how something which is a logical truth in the sense that it can be proved, without premisses, by means of logically valid procedures may nevertheless incorporate empirical information.

8 It has been correctly pointed out (for example by Stenius in the article referred to in §5) that to check that a certain sequence of formulae really constitutes a formal proof is to make an empirical observation. But the point that I am making is different; it is that a formal proof depends on certain kinds of truths about the symbols it uses in such a way that its conclusion, when it is interpreted, may incorporate those truths. Normally, of course, this is not so: a formally rigorous proof about, say, chemistry will not feed into its conclusion any chemical information that was not in the premisses or derivation rules; but such an intrusion is harder either to prevent or to detect when the proof has arithmetic as its subject-matter.

My general conclusion, then, is that the objection put forward in §3 does not after all refute the suggestion outlined in §2. If we are willing to consider the hypothesis that interpreted arithmetical propositions are empirical, we find that it cannot be rebutted even by the possibilities of logical proof, for we can explain, in terms of this hypothesis, just why such proofs work as they do. And although our detailed discussion has been confined to an almost trivially elementary example, it is reasonable to expect that the same conclusion will hold *a fortiori* for all more complicated arithmetical propositions and for all the more abstruse interpretations of arithmetic.

Two further corollaries, however, are suggested by points made in the course of this discussion. If even a formal proof is infected by arithmetical truths about its symbols we should reconsider what we usually say about pure, formal, uninterpreted arithmetic; there are limits to what we exclude by denying meaning to the symbols. And if, as I have argued, what counts as a truth of logic may also incorporate empirical information, we should re-examine the epistemological status of various kinds of logical truths. In such an examination, it will not do to define 'analytic', as we often do, so as to make truths of logic analytic by definition. This device does not answer the important question; it merely prevents if from being asked.

VI

CRITICAL NOTICE:
PLATO'S THEORY OF IDEAS

BY SIR DAVID ROSS (OXFORD, CLARENDON PRESS, 1951)

AFTER laying down the approximate order of the composition of the dialogues (determined mainly by stylometry), Sir David Ross traces the theory of Ideas (or Forms) through the dialogues in this order, and then gives an account of Plato's latest views. Some of his most interesting discussions are those of the passages in Aristotle which throw light on such topics as the Ideal Numbers and 'the population of the world of Ideas'. Ross assumes that the thought that is expressed in the dialogues is that of *Plato* throughout: he completely rejects the Burnet-Taylor theory, taking it to have been already refuted by other scholars and by himself in other writings. Though I cannot argue the points here, I think that this rejection is too complete, and also that in some of the later dialogues Plato at least hints at a new theory, distinct from the theory of Forms.

The value of this book cannot be denied; Ross brings together in a remarkable way the evidence of the Greek texts and the arguments of modern scholars on each problem of interpretation as it arises, and while his own conclusion at each point is clearly stated the rival views are given a very fair hearing.

Of course, a great many detailed questions could be discussed further, but the main points I wish to take up are two very general ones, closely connected with each other, about the precise nature and origin of the theory of Forms.

In his summing up (p. 225), and in many places throughout the book, Ross takes the theory of Forms to be essentially the assertion that there are universals, 'a class of entities ... entirely different from sensible things'—and he believes that this assertion is true.

Reprinted from the *Australasian Journal of Philosophy* Vol. 30, No. 3 (December 1952). Although Mackie intended to use this article in his *Selected Papers*, he contemplated rewriting it in the style of a note on the Theory of Forms. He did not carry out these alterations, and the paper is reprinted in the form in which it was originally published.

Whether the Forms are immanent in sensible things, or transcendent, is a further and quite minor question, to which Plato gives no single clear answer. Ross repeatedly suggests that the consistent view which Plato *approaches* is that there is a Form for every 'common name'. Correspondingly, he finds the origin of the theory in the question how a number of things may all be called by the same common name—this question arising out of Socrates' search for definitions of temperance, courage, and so on.

Now I suggest that this is a one-sided account, that while these elements are present more emphasis should be given to other aspects of the theory and to other influences that helped to produce it.

In addition to their role as universals, the Forms have other roles to play. Ross recognizes their importance as the field of eternal truths, which are 'relations between universals', but he underemphasizes their role as ideals and standards. And whereas he says that his object is 'to trace the history of Plato's views rather than to assess their value' (p. 165) it seems that an adequate account would have to bring out the difficulties in those views, in particular the tension between these various roles—the very point at which Aristotle is hinting in the passage (*Met.* 990b8–17) that Ross has quoted on p. 165: not everything that receives a common name, nor every object of science, is an ideal. Ross's arguments in Chapter XI do not really show that Plato regularly took a very broad view of 'the population of the world of Ideas'. Ross makes it quite plain elsewhere that it is the moral and mathematical Forms of whose existence Plato was most fully convinced. And there seem to be at least two instances of a limit to this population. (i) Plato did not recognize an Idea of number in general (pp. 181–2)—yet 'number' is a common name. (ii) There is a serious problem whether Plato recognized Forms of artefacts, such as Bed (pp. 171–5). They are mentioned in several dialogues, but Aristotle (apparently supported by a fragment from Xenocrates) says that Plato did not admit them. After discussing several unsatisfactory solutions of this problem, Ross accepts that of Robin (the rather makeshift one that Plato rejected only 'Forms of the products of the imitative arts'), but he does not mention the most likely solution, that Plato was drawn in different directions by the different aspects of his theory. 'Bed' is a common name, and there is also an ideal or standard to which the craftsman looks, but (in spite of what Ross says on pp. 174-5) it is hardly a subject of eternal truths, hardly something which God had to take as given when He made the sensible world. Along these lines we can understand an admitted inconsistency, that in the *Republic* Socrates speaks of God as the maker of the Form of Bed, while in the *Timaeus* and elsewhere the Forms are independent of any maker; for once you admit Forms of what are essentially artefacts you are practically compelled to introduce an artificer for them, if you are also treating the Forms as 'perfect particulars'.[1]

This is, indeed, another role that the Forms normally play, though in the end it seems to have been taken from them and assigned to the 'mathematicals'. It is incompatible with their role as universals, but it obviously controlled a great deal of Plato's thought, as well as his language, and cannot be set aside as a mere mistake, as Ross suggests (p. 88). The treatment of the Forms as distinct entities even seems to necessitate this 'mistake': we can think of Beauty as a distinct thing only if we think of it as a purified and perfected *beautiful*.

In line with his interpretation of the Forms simply as universals, Ross says (p. 24) that 'it is not by despising the senses and turning to pure contemplation, but by using the senses and finding out what they suggest to us, that (in Plato's view) we arrive at a knowledge of the Ideas'. Now this is a fair account of Plato's description of anamnesis, but it is utterly at variance with what is said elsewhere in the *Phaedo* (e.g., 65e-66a: μήτε τιν' ὄψιν παρατιθέμενος ἐν τῷ διανοεῖσθαι μήτε ἄλλην αἴσθησιν ἐφέλκων μηδεμίαν). And the latter view, that thought can operate entirely by itself, is essential for the argument: on it rest both the description of philosophy as a 'practising to die', and the very possibility of giving a description (in terms we can understand in this life) of the life after death. This reveals another conflict within Plato's theory: the Forms both enter into ordinary observation and are objects of pure thought.

It must be remembered that this plurality of roles is the strength, as well as the weakness, of the theory of Forms; an implication of the theory which has appealed to many later Platonists (such as Galileo) is that *the objects of science are in some way ideals*.

Similarly, the theory seems to have had its source not just in 'common names', but particularly in situations where there is some *difficulty* about a common name. Admitting that it starts from

[1] I owe this phrase to Professor John Anderson.

Socrates' search for definitions, we must remember that Socrates looked for definitions not of terms like 'stone' (where one could say without hesitation, 'This is a stone') but of moral and aesthetic terms, where it is hard to see that a number of acts are all, say, *intrinsically* courageous in the same sense (while other, somewhat similar, ones are not) and where relational or partly relational accounts of these terms, such as those advanced by the sophists, have a good deal of plausibility.

Indeed, while Plato's defenders and critics alike have usually treated the theory of Forms as a theory of predication, it might be at least as accurate to describe it as a theory of the apparent failures of predication; it is precisely where there is some obstacle to simple unequivocal predication that the Forms are introduced.

Plato, indeed, lumps together a great variety of obstacles which ought to be overcome in different ways. Forms are brought in where there are relative or, as we might say, scalar terms ('hot', 'tall', 'strong', 'like', etc., where we cannot say simply 'Simmias is tall' or 'Simmias is like'); also where the particulars are inexact (equality and geometrical terms generally are the clearest cases, but moral and aesthetic terms also come under this head); also where the particulars 'appear' variously (now beautiful, now ugly, equal to one man, unequal to another); and where the particulars are inconstant. Examples of the introduction of Forms on these grounds are found in *Phaedo* 74-9 and 102, and *Parmenides* 129. Ross notes it as an inconsistency in Plato that in the *Phaedo* he fails to recognize that 'things which seem to some person unequal may nevertheless be ... perfect examples of equality', but this is at any rate one important line of thought in Plato, exemplified again in the argument (*Republic* 476-9, especially 479a) that the object of opinion must be between being and not-being.

In the *Republic* (523-4), while discussing the studies which 'draw the soul towards reality (οὐσία)', Socrates makes the very point that I am suggesting. The mind is not roused to reflection by perceptions which are 'judged adequately by sense', but by those with regard to which 'sense does nothing sound'. That each finger is a finger does not excite thought, but the difficulties of deciding whether a finger is large or small, and of dealing with the sense perceptions that the same thing is both hard and soft, etc., do excite thought which leads ultimately to the Forms.

This treatment throws light on the passage (130b–e) in the

Parmenides where Socrates is sure that there are Forms of the just, the beautiful, the good, and 'everything like that', doubtful whether there are Forms of man, fire, and water, and almost certain that there are not Forms of mud, hair, and dirt, since 'in these cases the things are just as we see them' (ταῦτα μέν γε ἅπερ ὁρῶμεν, ταῦτα καὶ εἶναι). The point is not only that muddiness is not an ideal,[2] but also that mud just *is* mud, that there is no difficulty about so describing the perceived object and so no need to introduce a Form. The cases of man, fire, and water are doubtful, because on the one hand Socrates, etc., just *are* men, and yet there is some question of a distinction between those who are more or less perfect as men, and similarly fire or water can be more or less pure.

It is implausible to say that the theory of Forms was developed simply to explain predication. For what need would there have been to *explain* it, to go beyond the fact of predication itself, if it had not seemed to be in some way faulty? We must here reject the now-popular view (not, of course, shared by Ross) that the theory originates from a misunderstanding of the use of abstract nouns, from an attempt to find things of which 'beauty', 'unity', etc., are names; for such nouns were not much used before Plato, and he had to coin many of them, and use awkward circumlocutions instead of abstract nouns as names of the Forms—a clear case of the philosophical theory *preceding* the linguistic forms from which it is supposed to have arisen!

In his final chapter Ross discusses Plato's views on the question whether the Forms are immanent or transcendent. He divides (p. 228) the words used to express the relation between Forms and particulars into 'a group ... implying or suggesting the immanence of the Forms, and a group implying or suggesting their transcendence', lists the occurrences of these in the dialogues in order of composition, and draws the conclusion that 'there is a general movement away from immanence towards transcendence. In the early period almost everything speaks of immanence'. However, the contrast between immanence and transcendence misses the vital

---

[2] Cf. Anderson's criticism of the Socratic view in 'Realism and Some of its Critics', *AJPP*, Vol. 8, No. 2, pp. 124-5: '... the ridiculousness of saying ... that a particular piece of mud is striving after the ideal of perfect muddiness'. Yet 'whether we take the case of mud or any other ... we have to admit that they are just something'. [Mackie's reference to the *AJPP* is to the *Australasian Journal of Psychology and Philosophy*—the same journal in which he was himself writing under its earlier name.—Edd.]

point, that even on the 'immanent' view the Forms are not merely 'different from sensible things' (p. 227) but distinct from the whole observable situation: the fact that beauty is present in the man is distinct from (and explains, or explains away) the fact that the man is beautiful. But besides this, Ross's study of the words used is misleading, for several reasons. (i) This 'relation' is rather rarely mentioned in any way in the later dialogues (except the *Timaeus*), and in the later dialogues other than the *Timaeus* there is a big majority of 'words suggesting immanence'. (ii) The 'words suggesting immanence' (*in, possess, receive, participate*, etc.) only suggest that a Form *can* be present in a particular: they leave it open that the Form may also exist separately, and indeed in the *Phaedo* (103b5) Socrates speaks at once of the Form 'in us' and 'in nature'. On the other hand the 'words suggesting transcendence' (*pattern*, αὐτὸ καθ' αὐτό, *strive after, imitate*, etc.) suggest that the Forms *must* be transcendent. (iii) The choice of words is really determined by Plato's purpose from time to time rather than by any change in his views; thus in *Phaedo* 100-6, apart from one αὐτὸ καθ'αὑτό, there are only 'words suggesting immanence', because Socrates is there discussing the effect of the Forms on the particulars—a thing is beautiful because it participates in Beauty, etc.—whereas in the same dialogue in 74-8 there is nothing but 'words suggesting transcendence', because the subject there is the nature of the Forms themselves and their distinctness from particulars. Thus the context itself would suffice to explain the occurrence only of 'words suggesting immanence' in the earliest dialogues, even if Plato already held a 'transcendent' view.

Ross's conclusion (p. 231) is that while Plato was not satisfied with either 'participation' or 'imitation' as an account of the relation between particulars and Forms, 'he saw no way of getting nearer to the truth than by using both expressions'; they were 'complementary metaphors', and he 'may even have had an inkling of the fact that the relation is completely unique and indefinable'. Ross is intending to reduce this relation simply to predication, but while we might say that one of the lessons of the *Parmenides* is that predication is not a *relation* at all, the essential point for the interpretation of Plato is that the Form is always something more than a predicate.

There are two minor points concerned with the 'mathematicals'. (i) Ross's suggestion (pp. 223-4) that Plato finally rejected these as mathematical fictions, and that this might even be part of the meaning of the statement in the *Republic* that dialectic annuls the hypotheses of mathematics, will not harmonize with his earlier statement (p. 62) that 'it was not till very near the end of his life that Plato formulated the doctrine, though he had long been on the point of formulating it'. In any case there is no need to suppose, as Ross does, that Plato's rejection of points is part of a general rejection of mathematicals; the paradoxes of Zeno, to which Plato adopted the 'indivisible lines' solution, would be a sufficient reason for his rejection of points by themselves. (ii) Ross seems to be wrong in taking αὐτὰ τὰ ἴσα (*Phaedo*, 74c1) as a foreshadowing of the mathematicals (p. 60). This phrase, though αὐτὸ τὸ ἴσον is commoner, is just another parallel to αὐτὸ τὸ δίκαιον, not to a possible αὐτὰ τὰ δίκαια; the plural refers not to a plurality of perfect instances of equality, but to the fact that equality, even perfect equality, requires a situation with at least two components. So this phrase is no more than another illustration of the frequent treatment of the Form as a perfect particular.

My general impression, then, is that Sir David Ross is too much of an Aristotelian in spirit to be quite fair to Plato; his estimate of the broad character of the theory of Forms is less balanced than his discussion of detailed points. He defends Plato, indeed, against Aristotle's criticisms (pp. 226, 233), but at the price of minimizing the differences between them.

VII

IDEOLOGICAL EXPLANATION

AN ideology is a system of concepts, beliefs, and values which is characteristic of some social class (or perhaps of some other social group, perhaps even of a whole society), and in terms of which the members of that class (etc.) see and understand their own position in and relation to their social environment and the world as a whole, and explain, evaluate, and justify their actions, and especially the activities and policies characteristic of their class (etc.). Thinking in terms of this system unites and strengthens that class and helps to maintain it and to advance its interests. This system is determined by the social existence of the class (etc.) of which it is characteristic. It is not in general deliberately invented or adopted (though it may be deliberately fostered and propagated). At least some of the beliefs and concepts in the system are false, distorted, or slanted, and at least some of the activities sustained and guided by the ideology have a real function different from that which, in the ideology, they are seen as having.

This notion of an ideology is, I think, fairly widely employed. It is due primarily to Marx, but similar notions, sometimes under different names, have been developed by Pareto, Sorel, and Mannheim. But I shall not be concerned with scholarly questions about the ascription of such a notion to this or that thinker. Nor am I primarily concerned with the empirical question how widely applicable or how useful the notion is. Rather I shall discuss certain difficulties and problems that the notion involves or might be thought to involve and consider what bearing the notion has upon the question, 'What kinds of explanation are possible in the social field?'

The phrase 'ideological explanation' which I have taken as my title is, of course, radically ambiguous. (1) An ideological explanation might be an explanation given within and in terms of an ideology by some of those whose ideology it is—for example, an explanation of inflation given by bourgeois economists using concepts and beliefs that belong distinctively to the bourgeois ideology.

Reprinted from *Explanation*, edited by Stephan Körner (Basil Blackwell, 1975).

(2) An ideological explanation might be one given by someone who refers, as from the outside, to an ideology. We could further distinguish, within this, between (a) an explanation of the ideology itself or of some part of it—perhaps showing how, in Marx's famous phrase, it is determined by social existence—and (b) an explanation of something else that occurs, for example some actions or behaviour of some of those who have a certain ideology (or of some further social phenomena to which such actions contribute) by reference to the fact that they have this ideology.

These three varieties of ideological explanation give rise to three main groups of problems.

(i) Must an ideology be false or distorted? If this feature is included—as I have included it above—in the definition of ideology, we can still ask whether this feature necessarily accompanies the other features that have been mentioned in the definition. And if an ideology is false or distorted (whether or not it is necessarily so), must this vitiate any explanation of kind (1), that is, any explanation given within the ideology? An associated question is whether it can be coherently maintained that all thinking about society is ideological, in particular whether the doctrine of the general 'sociology of knowledge' is defensible or self-refuting.

(ii) One problem in the first group was whether explanation of kind (1) is radically faulty because it is irretrievably biased. A similar problem in the second group is whether explanation of kind (2b) is radically faulty because it explains something other than what it purports to explain. It purports to explain actions and social behaviour: but the ideology of the relevant class is a constituent of those actions and behaviour—they are essentially however the agents see them to be—so any explanation from outside, which treats the ideology merely as a fact, causally related to actions and behaviour described in other terms, will inevitably neglect something essential. This point and the previous one together set up a dilemma: if you try to explain social phenomena from inside the relevant ideology, your explanation is hopelessly biased and distorted, but if you try to explain them from outside the ideology you are ignoring something essential to those phenomena. If this dilemma can be evaded or overcome, there is the further question whether any explanation of actions by ideology can be a causal one, or whether actions and ideology are too intimately related to be such distinct existences as cause and effect, at least on anything like a Humean view of causation, are required to be. This is obviously a variant of the old issue about reasons and causes.

(iii) There is a similar problem about explanation of kind (2*a*): just how can social existence determine consciousness? If this is supposed to be a causal relation, can we find a 'social existence' which is logically separate enough from the ideology to cause it? Does not anything that we can call social existence already incorporate the associated ideology? Also, is it at all plausible to suggest that this is a case of one-way causation, that social existence determines consciousness whereas consciousness does not determine social existence, as Marx and Marxists have frequently maintained—though they have also frequently maintained the opposite, that mental and material factors interact. Are ideologies epiphenomenal or not?

Taking this last question first, I would insist that any strict doctrine of one-way causation would be utterly implausible. As Popper points out (*The Open Society and its Enemies* (London, 1945), vol. II, p. 108) the changes made in Russia by Lenin and his successors are a clear example of ideas revolutionizing economic conditions. And in any case we can understand the evolution of ideologies only on the assumption that they perform some function—in my original definition of an ideology I said that it unites and strengthens the class and helps to maintain it and to advance its interests. An ideology would have no survival value if it did not react on social existence at least in these ways. If Marx's thesis is to have any truth or even plausibility it must be taken in some different sense. It could be taken first as a denial of one-way causation in the other direction, as saying that ideas do not spring either from nowhere or only from other ideas and then control social policies and social structure, but are themselves affected by the other, for example economic, aspects of society. It could be taken secondly as saying that aspirations and schemes for social betterment are powerless if other conditions are not ripe for their implementation, for example as condemning 'utopian socialism'. Both these points are now truisms, but perhaps only because Marx has made them so. But a third and now more interesting interpretation of Marx's dictum would be this. Although 'social existence' and 'consciousness' interact, we can still ask in which of them major changes typically originate, whether the material or the mental is the leading edge of social change, and we might answer that it is the material. It is, however, very doubtful whether this answer can be true. We must, of course, distinguish as Marx did between the forces of production—that is, resources and technology—and the relations of production—that is, economic structures, as well as contrasting these two together with political and legal superstructure and consciousness or ideology. But then it seems plausible to say that sometimes new resources and technology initiate social change, sometimes new relations of production do so, and at least sometimes ideology takes the lead, particularly where economic structures that already exist in some countries are introduced into others from which they have been absent—Russia after Lenin, as mentioned above, is a case in point. We have a genuine form of question here, but not one that admits of a universal answer.

The other problem in this group was whether we can find a 'social existence' which is sufficiently distinct from consciousness or ideology to be even a possible cause of the latter. (This question seems to worry Plamenatz in Chapters 2 and 3 of *Ideology* (London, 1970).) Now of course there never is or can be a social existence as a concrete whole, an actual collection of goings on, which does not involve ideas and ideology. Concrete social existence always involves, among other things, conventions, established patterns of behaviour supported by various sorts of pressure. Any concrete relations of production will thus have an ideological aspect or component. Equally resources are resources only in so far as they are recognized as being such—or, more strictly, potential resources become actual resources only when they are recognized as being potential resources—and technology obviously includes an intellectual component, both knowing that and knowing how. So neither the forces of production nor the relations of production nor any social existence that includes the two can fail to involve quite a number of forms of consciousness, and none of these can cause whatever forms of consciousness are involved in it. However, this difficulty disappears as soon as we explicitly introduce the time dimension. Social existence, in all its aspects, at one time t_1 is a distinct occurrence from all forms of consciousness at any later time t_2, and may well be causally related to it. If the forms of consciousness are the same at t_2 as at t_1, we can say that social existence is a sustaining cause of them: if they change, then it can be a cause of those changes.

Though this resolves the problem of getting logically distinct causes and effects, there may be another objection. In so far as consciousness is a component of social existence at t_1, consciousness at t_2 will be just a later phase of the same thing or activity, and we do not commonly say that a persisting thing *causes* its own later existence, or that an earlier phase of a continuous process *causes* a later phase of that same process. Hence it might be argued that if C_2 is a later phase or continuation of C_1, we should not say that a whole consisting of C_1 and other things causes C_2. Admittedly we do not speak in the ways mentioned. But I think we might well extend the concept of causing to include these, since in all important respects the relations between earlier and later phases of a thing or process are just like the relations that we unhesitatingly accept as causal. But in any case nothing turns upon the use or non-use of the word 'cause'. Marx's word, after all, was 'determine', and it will be no great loss if we say that this determining is not exactly causal, but is just like causal determining in all important respects.

We encountered another form of the logical connection problem with regard to explanations of the second group. If we explain the actions of people of a certain class by reference to a class ideology in which they share, this is not a causal explanation of what is commonly taken to be the typical Humean form. It is not a purely contingent regularity of succession, discovered by observation of a number of particular sequences that instantiate it, that people's having a certain ideology leads to their acting in such-and-such a way. Rather their having this ideology makes their acting in this way (relatively) rational, and rationally intelligible; we should expect that if they have this ideology they will act accordingly; and we should expect this independently of any particular observations. Typically, this will be because the ideology shows the actions in question in some kind of favourable light, as being natural, or part of the divine plan and order, or as being necessary for some end which is itself also shown as desirable, or perhaps as historically required and inevitable. The ideology may in some such way as one of these itself motivate actions, or it may merely remove inhibitions that the agents might otherwise feel, as the ideology of *laissez-faire* removes inhibitions about cut-throat competition and the driving of hard bargains, and a revolutionary ideology may remove inhibitions about killing and destruction.

There are several points to be made here. First, the fact that ideology-action is not a non-expected regularity of succession is irrelevant. It might be expectable and expected because it exemplified a well-known general pattern of human behaviour, but it could for all that be a purely contingent regularity satisfying the most extreme Humean demands. Secondly, we seem to have here a variant of the standard 'logical connection argument' which purports to show that intentions cannot be causes. The simple version of this is that A's intending to do B can be adequately described only as his intending to do B, that is, in a way that logically involves the notion of A's doing B. So A's intending to do B and A's doing B are logically connected, so that the one cannot be even a partial cause of the other. But a logical connection of this sort will not prevent A's intending to do B and A's doing B from being distinct existences in Hume's sense—they can even be separated in time— so that this is no obstacle to their being cause and effect one of another. But some who have recognized this (notably von Wright and Stoutland*) suggest that there is another sort of logical connection which makes a purposive explanation of action non-causal. Thus von Wright sees a purposive explanation as simply turning upside-down a practical inference which when fully formulated is logically binding. Essentially, a person who fully intends to do something and believes that the time for doing it has come logically cannot fail to set himself to do it: if he fails to do so, it will show that he either does not fully intend this or does not believe that the time has come.

Any force that this argument has lies in its claim that A's fully intending to do B now and his now setting himself to do B are not distinct occurrences, that they are just the same thing described in slightly different ways. But if so, not only can the one not be the cause of the other, it cannot explain the occurrence of the other in any way at all. If we go beyond the bare report 'A fully intends to do B now' and put in A's further reasons we might be said to explain his action in the sense of saying more fully what action it was: it was doing B as this or for the sake of that. If we include these features in the action, then indeed A's having these reasons is not a distinct existence from and therefore not a cause of the action, and equally there is no explanation of the occurrence of the action, though the action itself is explained or explicated in the sense that it is unfolded, set out more fully. On the other hand, it seems impossible to deny that there is such a thing as a pre-formed

* See n. 20 to Chapter VIII below, p. 114.—Edd.

intention, and hence a state of an agent's having such an intention before he performs the related action which, being temporally separate from the action, must be a distinct occurrence. If so, it is hard to deny that a similar state might occur contemporaneously with the action, and yet be still an occurrence distinct from that action, or, if the action itself is so defined as to include this state, distinct from certain parts of the action. And then not only could the having of a pre-formed intention be a (partial) cause of the whole action, but also the contemporaneous having of the intention could be a (partial) controlling cause of those other parts of the action. In this way the having of intentions could, for all that the logical connection argument can show, be causes of actions or of parts of actions, and so could figure in causal explanations of their occurrence, even if there is *also* the kind of explanation for which von Wright argues which explains, non-causally, not the occurrence of the action but the action itself just by describing it more fully. But what we must not do is confuse these two, and suppose that we have found a non-causal kind of explanation of the occurrence of an action.

This conclusion is not undermined by the consideration that an existentially separate—for example pre-formed—intention is also rationally connected with the action, that the having of it makes it so far reasonable for the agent to do what he does. It is a contingent fact that people do act on the whole fairly reasonably, even though this fact has been taken up into our concepts of wanting, deliberating, choosing and so on. Nor can we build anything on the admitted awkwardness of such a remark as 'He was caused to do *B* by his having earlier formed an intention to do *B*'—a formula which is inappropriate just because it suggests a cause bearing upon the agent from outside. Nor can it be argued that the relation in question cannot be causal on the grounds that there seems to be no way of reducing it to a mechanical process, or that there is no good evidence that what is going on here is deterministic.

All this can be transferred to the realm of ideological explanation; the having of an ideology, like the having of an intention, combines elements of desire or valuing and belief, and it similarly makes a corresponding action so far reasonable. Also, the ideology, like the intention, can figure in two different sorts of explanation. It can be taken in something like von Wright's way as not existentially distinct from the action, but as helping to make it the sort of action that it is. For example, the passing of a bill, and so the making of a law, by a parliament in what Marxists would call a bourgeois democracy is an occurrence for the adequate description of which we need to mention the roles that the various agents see themselves as playing, the purposes of which they are conscious and the powers they take themselves to have. But the ideology can also figure as a partial cause in a causal explanation. If we ask why it came about that there is now this new law, it may well be correct to refer to the ideology shared by most members of the parliament and by many of their constituents as a partial cause of this event.

We can now see that the dilemma that I posed earlier, that an explanation from inside an ideology would be biased and distorted, and that one from outside would ignore something essential to the social phenomena, is almost wholly spurious: neither horn is either hard or sharp. An adequate description of a social phenomenon must indeed include an account of what the agents take themselves to be doing. In one sense they cannot be wrong about this. But it is also possible that their behaviour has some partial causes of which they are unaware, that it will have effects that are not included in their purposes, and indeed that it may have an unknown function in the sense that these unknown partial causes include the fact that such actions tend to produce these effects which were no part of the agents' purposes. Thus there is a sense in which the agents can be wrong about what they are doing. But a full description of what is going on must and can take account of both aspects, both of how their actions appear to the agents and of what is not apparent to them: it can recognize distortions as part of what is there without itself becoming distorted. Accounts of a social phenomenon from inside and from outside the relevant ideology, far from being both inadmissible for different reasons, are both admissible and both contribute to understanding, though in different ways.

This internal/external contrast does not quite coincide with the non-causal/causal one that I used above. It is true that the external account will be in several important and possibly complex respects a causal one. I have suggested that the action (A) will have some unpurposed effects (E) and some unknown-to-the-agents causes (C), and further that C may include the fact that actions such as A have regularly had effects such as E: such actions may have been fostered by their tendency to produce certain results: in this sense they may have a function unknown to the agents. It is equally true that an internal account may be non-causal, it may simply describe actions in which beliefs, purposes, etc., are constituents and so display whatever rationality they have. But there is no reason why an internal account should not also be a causal one, why it should not treat beliefs and purposes, and also quite different sorts of things, as causes of actions or of other effects that are existentially distinct from those causal factors. I mentioned at the beginning of this paper an explanation of inflation given by bourgeois economists: this would clearly be a causal explanation. Being internal to an ideology, such a causal explanation will no doubt be inadequate in some ways, it will leave out relationships which from outside the ideology can be seen to be important. But it is not necessary that the causal statements made within an ideology should be false: many or all of them may correctly or fairly correctly identify some partial causes, subject only to the limitation that the items identified as causes may themselves be seen, from within the ideology, in a somewhat distorted way.

I come back now to my first group of questions, whether all thinking about society is ideological, whether there is therefore a general sociology of knowledge, and whether ideologies have to be false or distorted—or, if they are made so by definition, whether this feature necessarily accompanies the other features that constitute an ideology.

Now it is obvious that for an ideology to perform the sort of function that it is supposed to perform, it must include value-components. Also, it is very natural that what we may be able in principle to distinguish as factual and evaluative components should be almost inextricably combined in the content of the ideology. To put it very crudely, a system of concepts, beliefs and values will be more stable and more effective in controlling and justifying conduct if the evaluative aspect is wrapped up in the concepts and beliefs, if those who have the ideology see things-as-they-are as exerting certain pressures on them. Slanting the news reports is a more potent form of propaganda than printing a rousing editorial alongside a neutral and objective report. For similar reasons, we are less likely to find value merely added to descriptive elements like a surface colouring, than incorporated in descriptions by the addition of fictitious elements and the omission of much that is real, the magnifying of some real elements and minimizing of others, and so on. Ideologies being what else they are, it is to be expected that even in their descriptive aspect they should contain a good deal of error and distortion; and yet it is also necessary for their operation that they should have verisimilitude, so that they cannot afford to be completely false.

I said at the start that I was not primarily concerned with the question how widely applicable the notion of ideology is. This is an empirical question, and can be properly settled only by detailed studies. Still, it may be legitimate to remark that on general grounds one would expect thinking about society to be largely ideological. The basic everyday concepts are those used by men who are practically involved in social action, and who will naturally have a need to justify their actions, to explain them as rational to themselves and others, to see them as having places in a value-pervaded scheme of things. And even if social theorists are not themselves, even in a minor way, men of action, they will unavoidably start from and be influenced by the thinking of those who are. No doubt one should take account here of the Marxist view that the thinking of those who are on the side of ultimately inevitable progress, whether we call it an ideology or not, is likely to be truer and less distorted than that of those whose social role is conservative or reactionary. But all I can say here is that I see neither any *a priori* plausibility in this thesis nor any *a posteriori* confirmation of it.

But although we have some grounds for expecting all thinking about society to be to some degree ideological, we have none for embracing a general doctrine of the sociology of knowledge, for saying that all truth about society is socially relative, that no proposition about society is simply true, but that even the most favoured items are true only from this or that point of view, or only within this or that ideology. It is easy to show that this extreme doctrine is self-frustrating, that taken seriously it would prevent even itself from being enunciated. But equally there is no need to adopt it, since the general grounds that we had for thinking that all ideologies involve some distortion are also grounds for expecting them to contain a fair amount of simple truth as well.

My main message, therefore, is one of tolerance. I have found no philosophical reason for scepticism either about the very concept of ideology or about any of the several kinds of explanation into which it may enter. In conclusion, I want to sum up these possibilities in broad outline and see how they fit together.

An ideology (*I*) makes reasonable certain kinds of action (*A*). Consequently, the possession of that ideology by the members of the society in question is a partial, favouring, cause of actions of these kinds. But also actions of these kinds (*A*) are, in the actual environment (*E*), helpful for the continuance and flourishing (*F*) of a society of that sort. And these two facts together explain causally, in the usual evolutionary way, the growth and persistence of that ideology. *I*'s being a favouring cause of *A*, together with *A*'s being in *E* a favouring cause of *F*, together constitute a favouring cause of *I* itself. (The apparent circularity in this outline account disappears as soon as we introduce the time dimension.) We find, then, that though not everything that can be called ideological explanation is causal, it is within a complex of causal relationships that we can understand both the occurrence of ideologies and their various contributions to explanation. Also, we might develop the pattern just sketched by bringing what Marx called forces of production in under *E* and what he called relations of production as an extension of *A*. We can then see that *wherever this pattern is applicable*, it will be plausible to regard the forces of production in *E* as the independent variable, and the relations of production in *A* as the factor more immediately controlled by it, *I* being more remotely controlled. This yields another sense in which, without making ideology epiphenomenal, we can still say that it is social existence that determines consciousness, rather than the reverse.

VIII

PROBLEMS OF INTENTIONALITY

Some 'problems of intentionality' can be solved by distinguishing this psychological feature ('tee-ality') from the logical feature intensionality ('ess-ality'). We can explain why ess-ality, which arises from an interest in properties and propositions, often accompanies tee-ality, but also why either can occur without the other. These clarifications, however, uncover a deeper problem. Intentional objects are contents of experience masquerading as separable objects. But how can there be one (psychological) state of affairs which is adequately described only through a (partial) description of a different, merely possible, state of affairs?

It seems to me that some of the problems that have been raised about intentionality, and some of the disputes about it in which philosophers have engaged, can be resolved fairly easily; but it has other aspects which I find puzzling, though I may or may not be able to persuade others to share my embarrassment.

But first, if we are to achieve any clarity we must distinguish intentionality from intensionality (tee-ality, perhaps, from ess-ality) and also several senses of 'intentional' from one another. The essential work has been done, and set on a firm historical foundation, by Kneale.[1] An *intentio* in, for example, Aquinas is something whose being consists in its being thought, rather like a Berkeleian idea. Following this, Brentano speaks of intentional inexistence meaning existence as an object of thought. But to intend is also, etymologically, to aim or shoot at something,[2] and Husserl for one calls a state of mind or a mental event intentional meaning that it is directed on an object. (Kneale suggests that Husserl's develop-

Reprinted from *Phenomenology and Philosophical Understanding*, edited by Edo Pivčević (Cambridge University Press, 1977). Mackie's references (in notes 5, 13, and 17) to 'Carr, this volume' relate to David Carr's 'Intentionality' which immediately precedes his own essay in the collection.

[1] W. Kneale, 'Intentionality and Intensionality', *Aristotelian Society Supplementary Volume XLII* (1968), pp. 73-90.

[2] G.E.M. Anscombe, 'The Intentionality of Sensation: A Grammatical Feature', in *Analytical Philosophy*, Second Series, edited by R.J. Butler (Oxford, 1965), pp. 158-80.

ment is due to a misunderstanding of Brentano: certainly—as we shall see—he takes 'direction upon an object' in a sense stronger than Brentano's.) Intensionality, on the other hand, is a logical, or perhaps grammatical, feature or cluster of related features, contrasting with extensionality. A context is intensional if coextensive predicates cannot in general be substituted for one another in it *salva veritate*—for example, since I may know that X is ϕ without knowing that X is ψ, even if everything that is ϕ is in fact ψ and vice versa, 'I know that X is ...' is an intensional context. Again, a context is intensional if co-referring substantival terms cannot be so substituted: 'The vicar is *ex officio* chairman of the school board' may be true but 'The headmistress's lover is *ex officio* chairman of the school board' false even if the vicar is the headmistress's lover: so '... is *ex officio* the Y' is also intensional. Again, a context is intensional if truth-functionally equivalent clauses—clauses which as statements on their own would have the same truth-value— cannot be so substituted: since even if 'q' and 'r' are both true, 'p because q' may be true while 'p because r' is false, 'p because ...' is an intensional context. Again, a statement or a sentence in use is intensional if it does not imply the existence (or the non-existence) of items apparently referred to by substantival terms, or if it gives such items a kind of indeterminacy—as 'I want a cup of tea' does not imply that there are any cups of tea, or that there is a particular cup of tea that I want, or even that there is some specific kind of tea, Indian, China, or Ceylon, say, that I want: lots of questions which can be asked and answered about any actual cup of tea do not arise with regard to the cup of tea which is the object of my want, and to ask them would be to display a failure to understand the meaning-structure of this sentence. Similarly a sentence in use is intensional if it does not imply the truth (or the falsity) of embedded clauses as 'A believes that p' does not imply either the truth or the falsity of 'p'.[3] Chisholm has suggested two further criteria of the same general sort, but since he proposed them especially in order to mark out intentionality as an exclusively

[3] R.M. Chisholm, *Perceiving* (Ithaca; N.Y., 1957), Chapter 11, and 'Intensionality' in *Encyclopedia of Philosophy*, edited by Paul Edwards (New York and London, 1967), Vol. 4, p. 203; A.N. Prior, 'Intentionality and Intensionality', *Aristotelian Society Supplementary Volume XLII* (1968), pp. 91-106; L. Jonathan Cohen, 'Criteria of Intensionality', same volume, pp. 123-42; G.E.M. Anscombe, *op. cit.* (reference in note 2 above).

psychological feature, and since Cohen has shown that they fail to do so, they seem to be of little importance.[4]

But tee-ality and ess-ality come together in, for example, some uses of such verbs as 'look for', 'worship', 'see', and of course 'intend'. An atheist can describe a theist as worshipping God, and Diogenes did not compromise his cynicism when he said that he was looking for an honest man. An action may be intended under one description but not under another which also truly applies to it. And many people have seen ghosts, though there are none. In such cases it is plausible to speak of an object of thought or of a directing of the mind on some object, perhaps linked with some overt behaviour. Something in them, therefore, is intentional; but the sentences we naturally use to describe them are intensional by one or other of the logical criteria.

It is such facts as these that have encouraged Chisholm, following Brentano's suggestion that intentional inexistence is the mark of the mental or of the psychic, to try to formulate logical criteria for the intentional use of language such that psychic phenomena, and these only, require intentional sentences to describe them adequately; he is trying to find some variety of ess-ality which is coextensive with tee-ality and hence with mentality also. But this project seems misguided. I would not, indeed, accept Husserl's view that sensations and certain types of feelings are psychic but non-intentional.[5] They need not involve anything that we can call in a strong sense the directing of the mind on an object. There may be no mental act which deals in any further way with the content of the experience, so that Husserl is rightly reluctant to call these items intentional in his sense. Yet a sensation of pain or of pricking, or a feeling of lassitude, has something that we can call its content but that is not existentially separable from the experience; it exists in and by being the content of the experience and so is an intentional object in Brentano's sense. On the other hand, it does not seem that the description of these experiences calls for intensional sentences. Whereas ghosts can be seen without existing, pain and lassitude exist if they are felt, and unlike wanted cups of tea or imagined castles in Spain, they have no indeterminacy about them: there are no further descriptions of them that we might first think

    [4] Chisholm, 'Intentionality'; and Cohen *op. cit.* (references in note 3 above).
    [5] Carr, this volume, pp. 17–36; E. Husserl, *Logical Investigations*, translated by J.N. Findlay (New York, 1970), pp. 552–3, 569 ff.

of enquiring for, and then realize that they did not allow. But this is surely because the language that we use to describe such sensations and feelings belongs to them alone, whereas the language that we use to describe wants, imaginings, and so on is borrowed from that whose primary use is to describe concrete objects and states of affairs. The description of a desire for a cup of tea is parasitic upon the description of cups of tea, but the indeterminacy in the former results from a mismatch between the two: real cups of tea have far more features than are mirrored in desires for cups of tea. There is no room for any such mismatch in the description of the sensations and feelings mentioned. Here already, therefore, we find tee-ality without ess-ality. But equally we can find ess-ality without tee-ality. It does not seem that intensionality, or any variety of it, will prove to be a sufficient criterion of the mental or psychic. The literature is full of examples of intensional but non-psychological statements. 'Lizards are like dragons' does not entail that there are, or that there are not, any dragons. 'Any offspring of a white rat and a white mouse must be a barren albino' is similarly non-committal about barren albinos. 'Possibly what caused the power-cut was that a swan flew into the wires' does not imply either the truth or the falsity of the embedded clause about a swan. Even if the predicates '... has atomic number 10' and '... has atomic weight 20' are coextensive, the statement that some property of neon is due to its atomic weight does not entail that the property is due to its atomic number. 'It is contingent that grass is green' does not have the same truth-value as 'It is contingent that if grass is green then grass is green', the first being true and the second false, though the two that-clauses have the same truth-value, being equally true. 'This blackcurrant bush needs an extra supply of nitrogen' does not entail that there *is* an extra supply of nitrogen or that there is any particular form which the needed supply takes or is to take. And in general Cohen's examination of Chisholm's successive proposals justifies his conclusion: 'Only by question-begging definitions of intensionality and/or psychologicalness shall we ever demonstrate, it seems, that the logical property of intensionality affords a sufficient and/or necessary condition of a proposition's constituting a psychological description.'[6] It is better to say, with Prior (and in agreement also with Kneale) that 'intensionality' is a rather general

---

[6] Cohen, *op. cit.* (reference in note 3 above); J.O. Urmson, 'Criteria of Intensionality', same volume, pp. 107-22.

phenomenon of which 'intentionality' provides some of the most interesting examples.[7]

If we consider what in general would give rise to ess-ality, it is in no way surprising that there should be non-psychological as well as psychological examples of it. Intensional constructions contrast with extensional ones; extensional ones are those in which we are concerned only with picking out certain things or sets of things or perhaps certain truth-values; but wherever an expression is used not just to pick out things, to identify extensions, but to say something about one or more properties or propositions, so that the connotation or sense of the expression plays some special role, the construction to which it belongs will be intensional. There are some properties that something would need to have if it were to count as a dragon; as well as these, there are further properties which are frequently ascribed to dragons in stories or given to them in pictures. To say 'Lizards are like dragons' is to say that lizards have some of these properties, especially some of the more striking or distinctive ones. The word 'dragons' is here used to indicate a somewhat vague cluster of properties, not to pick out a set of things, and it is irrelevant whether this cluster is instantiated or not. Yet on the surface the sentence is constructed on the same model as 'Zebras are like horses', which is most naturally construed as presupposing the existence of both kinds of animal and stating a relation of resemblance between them. Similarly the sentence about lizards speaks as if there were dragons: there is a conflict between its surface form and its underlying structure, the truth-conditions to which someone who uses it is ultimately committed. Causal statements like those about a barren albino, neon's atomic weight, and the blackcurrant bush's need for nitrogen are again intensional because they assert relations between properties. Both parents' being albino would result in any offspring's being albino; the parents' being of different species would result in any offspring's being barren. It is the absence or shortage of nitrogen in any assimilable form that has caused this bush's poor condition, and it is the supply of anything of that *sort* that would bring about an improvement. The necessity of 'If grass is green then grass is green' and the contingency of 'Grass is green' belong to these respective propositions, they are features that result from their internal propositional

---

[7] Prior, *op. cit.* (reference in note 3 above), p. 91.

structure, and there is no reason why either should survive the substitution of another proposition of the same truth-value.

In saying this we are not, of course, committed to reifying intensions—properties or propositions. To talk about the property of ϕ-ing is just to talk in some, possibly complicated, way about actual or possible cases where something ϕs or does not ϕ; talking about properties is merely (in some circumstances) more expeditious and facilitates generalization. And the same goes for talking about propositions.[8] For example, to say that it is one rather than the other of two coextensive properties that enters into some causal relation is just to say that it is A's being ϕ, not A's being ψ, that caused B's being χ, and the central part of what this says is that if, in the circumstances, A had not been ϕ, B would not have been χ, but that even if A, in those circumstances, had not been ψ, B might still have been χ; there is perhaps also a suggestion that A's being ϕ led on in some continuous way to B's being χ, whereas A's being ψ did not.[9] Similarly to say that a certain proposition, for example that grass is green, is contingent is just to say that grass might not have been green; however this is to be further analysed, it is quite clear that to say this is to say something different from what one gets by substituting any other equally true proposition, for example that gold is malleable, for the proposition that grass is green, and so saying that gold might not have been malleable. Yet to realize this difference it is not necessary to recognize propositions as entities.

(Reference to properties or propositions is not, indeed, the only source of intensionality or referential opacity. In 'Giorgione was so called etc.' references to the man Giorgione and to the name 'Giorgione' are run together, and that is why '... was so called etc.' is a non-extensional context. Similarly 'The vicar is *ex officio* etc.' condenses references to the vicar and to the office of vicar. But reference to properties and propositions is of far more interest and importance.)

Once we have this general understanding of what gives rise to ess-ality, it is easy to see why so many psychological statements are

[8] Cf. A.N. Prior, *Objects of Thought* (Oxford, 1971), Chapters 1, 3, and 4; W. Kneale, 'Propositions and Truth in Natural Languages', *Mind*, Vol. 81 (1972), pp. 225–43.

[9] I discuss the analysis of causal statements in detail in *The Cement of the Universe* (Oxford, 1974).

intensional. Statements about kinds of overt action that are guided
by thought are rather like causal statements. To look for an honest
man is at least to do things that seem likely to put one in touch
with something that is both human and honest, if such there be in
the neighbourhood, and to do them because they seem likely to
have this result. (It is probably more than this—it may indeed
include, say, wondering whether and if so where there is an honest
man, but the more will be covered by one or other of the following
kinds of example.) If I see a ghost, then I have a visual experience
(associated perhaps with a belief) which is most adequately described by describing the content of each, that is, by indicating the
set of properties that I take (in part at least wrongly), or am inclined to take, to be coinstantiated at a certain place and time.
Thinking often (Kneale suggests 'always') involves the entertaining
of propositions; consequently sentences used to describe thinking
commonly express propositions about propositions.[10] Referentially
opaque belief-statements fit into the same pattern. If Tom believes
that Cicero denounced Catiline, the content of his belief is appro-
priately expressed by some such sentence as 'There was someone
who was called "Cicero", and who was famous for this and that,
and who denounced someone called "Catiline".'[11] We need to
mention some such proposition in order to give the content of
Tom's belief, and if we change the proposition, say by using expressions with different senses, or by using condensed formulations
which surreptitiously introduce names other than 'Cicero' or
'Catiline', we shall of course misrepresent the belief. Referentially
transparent belief-statements are in fact more puzzling than opaque
ones, though their logical structure is only different, not more obscure. Formally, a referentially-transparent belief-statement is one
in which the name or definite description of the thing or person
that the belief is about is given larger scope: it may say, in effect,
'As for Cicero and Catiline, Tom believes that the former denounced the latter.'[12] The identifications of the two characters
stand outside the scope of the belief-operator, and consequently
any co-referring expressions will achieve the same identifications

---

[10] Kneale, 'Intentionality and Intensionality', p. 86 (reference in note 1 above).

[11] Prior, 'Intentionality and Intensionality', p. 99 (reference in note 3 above).

[12] Cf. R. Sharvy, 'Truth-Functionality and Referential Opacity', *Philosophical Studies*, Vol. 21 (1970), pp. 5-9; A. Smullyan, 'Modality and Description', *Journal of Symbolic Logic*, Vol. 13 (1948), pp. 31-7.

and yield equally true statements. But if I say this, I am saying that Tom has somehow succeeded in directing his thought towards the very same individual men that I am talking about, and this may well seem to be a more remarkable achievement, and one for which more of a further explanation is required, than merely to have, among the contents of his thoughts, certain clusters of properties which are ascribed, with the help of existential quantifiers, to external reality.

But why, then, do some psychological verbs such as 'know' and 'see' (in its most natural sense, as distinct from that in which people have seen ghosts) fail to obey the logical criteria of ess-ality? I think that Carr, following Cornman, is right to explain this by distinguishing, within the meaning of such verbs, achievement-claims from descriptions of 'genuine mental activity' or 'experience'.[13] If I say, in the most usual sense, that Tom is seeing the Eiffel Tower, I am saying that Tom is having an appropriate visual experience, and is himself taking it as the seeing of something real and external (and this much, in itself, does not require the real existence of the Eiffel Tower within Tom's range of vision, or indeed anywhere); but I am also saying that the Eiffel Tower is there, that Tom has got it more or less right, and that this appropriate visual experience of Tom's is causally dependent in some suitable way on the tower's being there. The visual experience, then, involves intentional inexistence, and any adequate description in terms of a tower, of anything similar, would be intensional for that reason. Again, Tom's taking it as the seeing of an externally real object, the fact that his seeing points towards a supposedly actual tower, although there might not have been one, calls for an intensional description. But my claim that the tower is there and has helped to produce his more or less correct visual experience will refer extensionally to the actual tower.

'Know' works similarly. Knowledge generally involves belief—though there are marginal cases where we would ascribe knowledge, in the absence of belief, on the strength of an ability or disposition to give correct answers, and so on[14]—and such belief on its own will be described by the use of intensional sentences, whereas the success entailed by 'know' will be described by ones

---

[13] Carr, this volume pp. 17-36.

[14] Cf. D.M. Armstrong, *Belief, Truth and Knowledge* (Cambridge, 1973), Chapter 10.

which are in some respects extensional: for example, 'Tom knows that the Eiffel Tower is made of steel' entails the truth of the embedded that-clause.

It seems to me that the points made so far are straightforward and should be relatively uncontroversial: but from here on the subject becomes more difficult. I have accepted Brentano's terminology of intentional objects and inexistence; but just what does this represent, and how is it related to the other kinds of intentionality that are indicated by the metaphors of pointing and aiming? It is useless to think of the intentional object as an internal picture, a real object which actually exists somewhere inside one's head and which is inspected there. For this would force us to make another move of the same kind, to introduce a further intentional object as the content of the experience which is the inspecting of this one.

Again, it will not do to say that where there is an intentional object there is an experience E which is its own object, or even part of its own object, though Brentano seems to have taken inexistence to imply this. The supposition that E is (part of) the object of E leads at once, as I have argued elsewhere, to a vicious infinite regress.[15] One bit of experiencing could not be part of what it was itself an experiencing of, though it could presumably be the object of some other piece of experiencing. We cannot explain inexistence by the use of a relational model, even by making the relation reflexive.

Similarly it will not do to postulate propositions as entities, of which that-clauses are the names, to be real objects of belief and other propositional attitudes. Apart from the stock objections to uneconomical postulation, this move only creates further difficulties. It is quite obscure how believing, fearing, hoping and so on could be analysed as real relations to such entities. It is equally obscure how such proposition-entities, when true, would be related to the concrete states of affairs that made them true. Consequently if belief, for example, were so analysed, it is obscure how Tom's believing-relation to the proposition that-it-will-rain-tomorrow would have anything to do with the actual falling of rain on the next day.

In contrast with all these unhelpful moves, we must insist that

---

[15] In my 'Are There Any Incorrigible Empirical Statements?', *Australasian Journal of Philosophy*, Vol. 41 (1963), pp. 12–28. [Now reprinted as Chapter II above.— Edd.]

the only entity involved is, for example, Tom's having an experience of a certain sort. Talk about its intentional object can be no
more than a way of characterizing it, of saying what sort of an
experience it is by indicating its content. But what gives rise to the
difficulties and to the mistakes we are constantly tempted to make
in this area is that this content, though it is really only a feature of
the experience, though it really only makes it the particular sort of
experience it is, presents itself as if it were a more or less distinct
object to which the subject is related, this whole relational situation
then being the experience. I feel a pain in my leg almost, and yet
not quite, as if it were something in my leg apart from my feeling
of it, and this applies even more to my hearing a sound or my
seeing a patch of colour.

This truth, that a content which masquerades as a separable
object really only makes an experience the sort of experience it is,
holds for beliefs, fears, and so on as well as for sensations. In
consequence, it is more illuminating to punctuate a belief sentence
in the way Prior recommends, '*A* believes-that *p*', than in the more
usual way, '*A* believes that-*p*'.[16] Grammatically we can, of course,
admit that prefixing the word 'that' to any sentence represented by
'*p*' yields a noun-equivalent: this is a device of nominalization. But
this bit of grammar is misleading or at least useless with regard to
ontology: there is no entity for this noun-equivalent to name.
Prior's punctuation, on the other hand, brings out that we are
ourselves using the sentence '*p*' to characterize, by presenting its
content, *A*'s belief-condition which is reported by the larger sentence in which '*p*' is embedded.

It is therefore tempting to accept Husserl's thesis, quoted and
endorsed by Carr,[17] that the intentional object is merely the intended object, and hence that it is none other than the real object:
'the intentional object of a presentation is the same as its actual
object, and on occasion its external object ... I mean the transcendent object named in each case'.[18] This would mean, presumably,
that the intentional object of Tom's belief that it will rain tomorrow
is just rain actually falling tomorrow, which, if it rains, will be a
fully objective, external, state of affairs. But this is no more than a
half-truth. It is true that what Tom believes (or hopes, fears, and
so on: we might say 'intends' in a sense that covers all these) is just

[16] Prior, *Objects of Thought*, pp. 19-21.   [17] Carr, this volume pp. 17-36.
[18] Husserl, *op. cit.*, pp. 595-6 (reference in note 5 above).

that rain falls tomorrow; it is with this possible state of affairs itself that he is concerned, and not with any image or counterpart of it or substitute for it. Yet this object as intended lacks many of the features that the actual external object, if it occurs, will have. This was, of course, our starting point. As intended, it is somewhat indeterminate: rain some time tomorrow, but not for any precise period and not in any exact quantity. And it is no less an intended object if the actual rain should not occur at all. In presenting Tom's state of belief (hope, fear, and so on) we have to speak about the object-as-intended, as distinct from the object as it (perhaps) will be. And the object-as-intended has just those features that distinguish a proposition from a concrete occurrence or state of affairs and tempt us into what we have already noted as the error of postulating proposition-entities. Admittedly Husserl also notes these distinctions. But they entail that it is false to say that the intended object is identical with the real object, except as a way of emphasizing that Tom's belief (and so on) is about actual rain tomorrow, and nothing short of this.

At last we are beginning to get into focus the real puzzle about intentionality. Is it not strange that there should be one state of affairs (Tom's state of believing, hoping, fearing, or whatever it may be) that requires for its adequate description the partial, incomplete, selective, indeterminate description of a quite different and so far merely possible state of affairs? Some remarks of Wittgenstein's about expecting an explosion may help to bring this out,[19] 'Here my thought is: If someone could see the expectation itself—he would have to see *what* is being expected. (But in such a way that it doesn't further require a method of projection, a method of comparison, in order to pass from what he sees to the fact that is expected.)' This presents the problem, but Wittgenstein's surrounding remarks do nothing to resolve it. He says 'The statement "I am expecting a bang at any moment" is an *expression* of expectation' and 'if you see the expression of expectation you see "what is expected"', and he offers the dictum 'Like everything metaphysical the harmony between thought and reality is to be found in the grammar of the language'. This looks profound, but it is shallow. What the grammar of the language, even with Prior's construal, shows is simply that a clause governed, for example, by

---

[19] L. Wittgenstein, *Zettel* (Oxford, 1967), 53-6; cf. *Philosophical Investigations*, 2nd edn. (Oxford, 1958), 444-5.

'believes that' is used, with just the meaning it would have as a sentence on its own, to describe a state of believing (and so on): but this constitutes the problem and does not solve it. After we have understood the logical structure, we still want to know what psychological (or other) reality underlies it and is represented by it.

We might think that since ess-ality is found in other, non-psychological and non-puzzling, cases, notably causal ones, we could make tee-ality less puzzling by assimilating it to such causal relationships. Perhaps what makes a certain state of strain the expectation of an explosion is just the fact that hearing an explosion would relieve it, while nothing else would. Or, if this alone is not enough, perhaps it is this combined with the fact that this tense state has causal antecedents which are themselves somehow connected with an explosion. Perhaps it has been induced by hearing talk about a possible explosion, or by observations of things that are known or believed to be causes of explosions, and so on. If an explosion comes in only at one or more places in a network of causal relationships surrounding the tense state, then there will indeed be true statements about that state in which expressions that seem to refer to an explosion occur intensionally; but this will be no more puzzling than similar intensional occurrences in our causal statements about the blackcurrant bush, the albino rats and mice, and so on.

But let us see just why this would not be puzzling; I suggest that what makes it non-puzzling also makes it inadequate as an account of intentionality. We can distinguish intrinsic from relational descriptions. When a naïve realist says that a rose is red, he takes himself to be describing it intrinsically: the being red, he thinks, is right there in the rose. But when a sophisticated realist says that a rose is red, meaning only that it looks red to normal observers in normal conditions, he is offering a relational description of the rose. Again if I say that a hole is round, I have described it intrinsically, as it is in itself. But if I say that it is such that a square peg would not fit it, though a round peg would, I have described the hole relationally: an adequate intrinsic description of the hole could have been given without mentioning the pegs. Similarly if I say that a state of strain is such that only the hearing of a loud bang will relieve it, I have described it relationally, and so also if I say that it was produced by the observation of something that was thought likely to lead to an explosion. But we can apply the notion of intrinsic description to mental states, though not so simply as to roses and round holes. If I say that this state is one of expecting an explosion, I seem to be describing it intrinsically. That is how it is in itself, how it would be no matter what the rest of the world was like. And yet I cannot adequately describe how it is in itself without mentioning a possible explosion. This is what is puzzling: that the reference to another, merely possible, and in this case future, event should be required for an intrinsic description of the tense state. The assimilation of this sort of case to merely causal examples of ess-ality does away with their difficulty but at the cost of denying something that seems to be significantly characteristic of them.

This problem occurs equally with believing, hoping, fearing, supposing, wondering whether, and so on. It may seem, indeed, to be less acute with believing, just because some cases of believing lend themselves to a dispositional analysis. But it is hard to deny that there are also cases of occurrent belief, as well as of the other propositional attitudes.

There is a well known argument that someone's intending to do *X* is so logically connected with his doing *X* that the former cannot cause the latter. This is a fallacy: the kind of logical connection involved here, the need to describe the intending in terms of the action intended, is no obstacle to their being distinct existences in the sense in which a cause and an effect must be.[20] But the widespread reluctance to admit this, and the prevalence of attempts to make all intending adverbial, all just a matter of doing X intentionally, may reflect some awareness of our difficulty about there being two distinct states of affairs such that an adequate intrinsic description of the one is parasitic upon a (partial) description of the other.

Berkeley said firmly that an idea can be like nothing but an idea.[21] It would have been better if he had merely raised the problem, *How* can an idea be so like something else as to call for a description that is parasitic on the description of that something

---

[20] Cf. A.I. Melden, *Free Action* (London, 1961), p. 53; G.H. von Wright, *Explanation and Understanding* (London, 1971), pp. 94-5 and 115-16; F.M. Stoutland, *The Logical Connection Argument*, American Philosophical Quarterly Monograph *No.* 4 (1970), pp. 117-30; I have discussed this issue in *The Cement of the Universe*, Chapter 11.

[21] G. Berkeley, *Principles*, Section 8.

else? It is, of course, this problem that suggests a theory of images or mental pictures, for a picture can be like what it is a picture of, and we can describe a picture by describing the scene it portrays. Yet, as we have seen, this is a trap, a dead end. Anything that was literally a picture would raise the same problem all over again. The notion of a picture seems helpful if we think of the picture not just as another physical object that in some respects resembles the scene, but as a picture *of* that scene, as pointing beyond itself to an independent (possible) reality. But this feature belongs not to the picture as a physical object, but to the picture as interpreted by us. It is our thinking that points to this reality, not the picture on its own. Pictures taken thus provide us only with another mental example of intentionality, not with a non-mental analogue of it.

It might be objected that my puzzle is a spurious one which disappears as soon as it is clearly formulated. If Jane, say, describes Tom as believing that it rained yesterday, her description of Tom's belief-state is parasitic upon her way of describing the concrete state of affairs, 'It rained yesterday'. But if she can describe this state of affairs, why should Tom not be able to do so too? And why should not Jane's describing of how Tom might describe it be related to her own describing of the same state of affairs?

But this objection misses the point. I am not saying that indirect speech is puzzling whereas direct speech is not, or that there is anything surprising about the relation between them. The real problem is about a capacity which even direct speech expresses. Since Jane can say, and mean, 'It rained yesterday' there is already in her a mental state which points beyond itself to yesterday's rain.

Someone might resort to a transcendental argument here. Anyone who raises the sort of difficulty that I am raising must himself be exercising the capacity that he professes to find strange. This is true, but what does it show? This sort of argument might be effective against someone who went beyond puzzlement to scepticism, who professed to doubt or deny that we have the capacity in question. But it does nothing to resolve the difficulty for someone who does not for a moment doubt that we have this capacity, but who finds it hard to understand *how* we have it.

One way of highlighting the problem is to consider whether, and how, a physicalist theory could cope with intentionality. It would have to give some kind of reductive analysis, aiming eventually, perhaps, at micro-reduction. If the assimilation to causal cases of ess-ality, discussed above, were satisfactory, then there would be no serious obstacle to a materialist account; but if, as I have suggested, such an assimilation is unsatisfactory, it is hard to see how the physicalist could even begin. Irreducible intentionality would be fatal to physicalism. To this extent Brentano was right after all in calling intentionality a mark of the mental. But it would be a rather hollow victory for the anti-physicalist if he could defeat his opponent only at the cost of admitting something of which he was equally incapable of giving any satisfactory explanation.

But it is in this unsatisfactory state that I must leave the question. I have tried to show that some problems about intentionality and its relation to intensionality can be cleared up, but that their removal uncovers a deeper problem. I have not solved this problem, but have merely argued that some initially attractive ways of resolving or avoiding it will not do.

IX

POPPER'S THIRD WORLD— METAPHYSICAL PLURALISM AND EVOLUTION

1 INTRODUCTORY REMARKS

IT was after I had proposed the title 'Popper's Third World', and indeed after I had written most of my first draft of this paper, that David Boyer drew my attention to the article with the same title by Brian Carr in *The Philosophical Quarterly* for July 1977. I think this is a good article and most of what it says seems to be right, but it does not overlap much with what I want to say. I have put in the sub-title 'Metaphysical Pluralism and Evolution' to distinguish my paper from Carr's.

Also, I had better say right at the start that I have mixed feelings about Sir Karl Popper. On the one hand I agree with many of his main views—for example, his realism, his endorsement of something like a correspondence theory of truth, his stress on problems and on the procedures of formulating and testing hypotheses, his fallibilism, his rejection of the search for certainty about starting points or about methods or about conclusions, his insistence on the similarity of rational procedures in the physical and in the social sciences and in other human activities as well, and his defence of the open society. On the other hand I am repelled by his gratuitous sneers at most other philosophers, his constant employment of straw men and Aunt Sallys, his persistent name-dropping, his over-use of superlative terms—so many things are 'incredible,'

Previously unpublished: written 1977. Mackie intended to revise this article before publishing it in his *Selected Papers*, but this revision was never carried out. A few marginal notes indicate that he intended to make minor alterations in Section 3 of this article, to take account of Popper's statement that tools, institutions, works of art, and human products generally, may be included in world 3; hence that there may be said to be at least three sorts of item in world 3, rather than two sorts as stated on p. 120 below. (The reference is to Popper, 'Intellectual Autobiography', in *The Philosophy of Karl Popper*, edited by P.A. Schilpp (La Salle, Illinois, 1974), Vol. I, pp. 144-9). We have not been able to discover what other alterations, if any, Mackie intended to make.

'bold,' 'daring,' or 'beautiful'—his endless repetition of the same points, even the same phrases; and I often deplore his reluctance to do detailed work. 'For heaven's sake, cut the cackle,' one is impelled to say when reading Popper's writings, and there is a great deal of cackle to be cut. Still, when one discards the over-dramatization, there sometimes remain in his work ideas that deserve attention, indeed that deserve closer examination and more clarification than he gives them. I believe that his theory of the third world is one of these.[1]

2   BRIEF EXPOSITION

The phrase 'third world' seems to be due to Frege, and Popper introduces the notion by comparison with some views of Frege, but also with some of Plato and Bolzano[2]. He contrasts the third world, or world 3, with world 1, which is the realm of purely physical things, and world 2, the realm of minds, conscious experiences, and mental states. He rightly refuses to take the word 'world' in these phrases too seriously. Strictly speaking there is only one world, but still, he claims, there are these three kinds of things, or at least three kinds of states and relationships. On the mind–body problem he supports a dualism at least of the double-aspect sort (there are mental states as well as physical states, though not mental and material substances), but he would turn this into a pluralism by adding a third world to the other two. The items that make up the third world are 'possible objects of thought ... theories in themselves, and their logical relations ... arguments in themselves ... problem situations in themselves'.[3] The word 'thoughts' is ambiguous: as bits of thinking, psychological occurrences, thoughts belong to world 2, but as thoughts in Frege's sense, objective contents of thought, they belong to world 3. Such theories, arguments, problems, and so on can be located in books, computers, and the

---

[1] The theory is presented particularly in two chapters in his *Objective Knowledge—An Evolutionary Approach*, namely Chapter 3, 'Epistemology Without a Knowing Subject', and Chapter 4, 'On the Theory of the Objective Mind'. Subsequent references to this book will be to '*OK*', with page numbers.

[2] In 'The Thought: a Logical Inquiry', after distinguishing an inner world of 'ideas' from the outer world, Frege says: '... thoughts are neither things of the outer world nor idea. A third realm must be recognized.' Popper refers to Frege in *OK*, 106-9, 127, 153, 156, to Plato in *OK*, 106, 122-6, 153-8, 300, and to Bolzano in *OK*, 106, 126-7, 153.

[3] *OK*, 154, 231n.

like as well as in minds, and in any case it is the arguments (etc.) themselves that matter, not anyone's subjective thought processes, so we can speak of knowledge in the objective sense as knowledge without a knower, without a knowing subject.[4] Only a formulated theory can be thus objective: 'it is this formulation or objectivity that makes criticism possible'. Popper says that the realization of this point led to his theory of a third world.[5]

With regard to this third world, Popper states at least five theses:

(i) World 3 is a human product, not, like Plato's Forms or Ideas, divine and unchanging. It contains problems, questions, and false theories, not eternal truths or ultimate explanations.[6]

(ii) Although it is a human product, world 3 is not to be reduced to world 2. It is in some important sense (or senses) autonomous, independent.

(iii) World 3 is to be understood in its own terms, rather than in terms of world 2. Understanding world 3 will throw a lot of light on world 2. Most of our subjective thoughts involve world 3 items. Our self-consciousness itself depends largely on world 3 theories about our bodies, about time, about memory, and so on.[7] We can understand better why human beings think and behave as they do by analysing logically the problem situations they confront and by seeing the logical relations between various conjectures and critical arguments. But the converse is not the case. The subjective aspect of thought will not throw light on the growth of scientific knowledge, for example. Psychologism is not a fruitful method either in epistemology or in the human sciences or the humanities.[8]

(iv) Worlds 2 and 3 interact: men's minds produce theories and arguments, but equally objective knowledge, theories and problems in themselves and so on, affects men's thinking. But Hegel was wrong to make this a one-way process, with Objective Spirit and Absolute Spirit simply controlling men's minds, making them their instruments.[9]

(v) Though worlds 1 and 2 also interact, world 1 and world 3 do not interact directly, but only through world 2.[10]

I want to examine all of these theses.

[4] *OK*, 109.   [5] *OK*, 31.   [6] *OK*, 122-3.   [7] *OK*, 74.
[8] *OK*, 114, 162.   [9] *OK*, 125-6.   [10] *OK*, 155.

3 PROBLEMS AND CLARIFICATIONS

My first question is, 'Exactly what are the contents of world 3?' Implicit in what Popper says are two divergent accounts. Sometimes he refers to possible objects of thought. There will be what have often been called propositions, or statements in the sense of what is stated, arithmetical equations, for example, arguments, again in the sense of what is argued, theoretical systems, and so on. These are all what we may call logical entities. They are also abstract entities, and in a reasonably clear sense timeless. We can speak about a certain proposition just because various concrete sentences in use can be seen to say the same thing, and if someone says one thing at one time and something else at another time, it is not that the proposition has changed; he is just asserting a different proposition. But more often Popper stocks his third world with what are plainly historical entities, such as the present state of discussion in physics.* He is greatly concerned with the growth of knowledge; so objective, third world, knowledge is something that grows. World 3 at any time will therefore contain whatever ideas, theories, values, problems, and so on are current at that time, and since, of course, these items also persist through time an important part of its contents will be traditions—traditions of thought or belief, of critical methods, of morality, and so on. These items will have a dimension of relative strength in a sense in which abstract logical items cannot. One theory may be dominant at a certain time, while a rival theory, even if it is held or canvassed by some thinkers at the same time, is less popular, less influential, though the second may be logically the stronger of the two.

It would be pedantic to object to Popper's putting items of these two sorts† into the same third world, especially as he admits that his enumeration is not final, that we might distinguish more than three worlds.[11] There are obvious connections between the two sorts of item. But at least it should be realized that these are two very different sorts, and that we cannot in general take what we rightly say about one sort and simply transfer it so as to apply it to the other sort of item. In particular 'interaction' must be taken

---

* A marginal note at this point refers to Popper, 'Intellectual Autobiography', pp. 148-9.—Edd.

† See note on p. 117 above.—Edd.

[11] *OK*, 107.

differently with regard to the two sorts of item, which I shall call, to distinguish them, 'logical' and 'historical' respectively. It is the historical items that are plainly human products. It is more questionable whether propositions, theory-contents, and such logical items are man-made. But perhaps we can allow this way of speaking, saying that a proposition or question or theory in the logical sense is produced when it is first propounded or formulated. Also, conversely, it is the historical items that are causally efficacious, that act upon the thoughts of individual human beings and so bring about changes in physical things. For example, it is the contemporary dominance of a certain view of persons that largely determines my individual self-consciousness. Again, it was the state of physical theory around 1940 that suggested to several people the possibility of making nuclear weapons, so that this project was actually implemented and realized. Of course, this historical state of physical theory had this effect only because it had as its content certain logical items, but it was not their logical features as such that were effective, but rather the fact that these propositions were fairly firmly accepted. Popper is inaccurate, therefore, when he speaks of the '*universe of abstract meanings*' having an influence on human behaviour.[12] What has such an influence is the concrete historical instantiations of these abstract meanings.

My second question is, 'In what sense, or senses, is world 3 autonomous or independent?' In the first place, do world 3 items *exist* independently of physical things and minds? Some might want to take a 'Platonic' view of the existence of at least some logical items, in particular of some or all mathematical entities; but Popper himself explicitly rejects this.[13] He must do so if he holds that the logical as well as the historical items are a human product. Such entities could hardly be produced but then left standing around by human minds, as a spider may leave behind a web or a bird a nest that it has constructed. So I shall leave such Platonism aside. If this problem is shelved, we shall say that the existence of the logical third world items is parasitic partly upon that of the historical ones, and partly on that of world 2 items. Propositions, theory-contents, and the like exist either as the contents of thought-traditions (or of books and computer memory stores as interpretable by such traditions) or as the contents of minds, as actual (not merely possible) objects of thought. But precisely because any particular

[12] *OK*, 230. [13] *OK*, 118.

world 3 item is likely to have multiple location, to occur among the contents of the thoughts of more than one person, or to be the content of a tradition that is widespread both in space and through time, or to be recorded in many books and many libraries, its existence will usually be independent of any particular mind, equally of any particular book, and even of any small space-time-slice of a tradition. The existence of any historical world 3 item, in turn, is parasitic upon that of minds, though of course, just because traditions are widespread, it is independent of the existence of any particular mind. We might be tempted to say that since a theory can be recorded in books and computers, its existence is then independent of all minds, even though it was originally produced by minds, just as there might be coral reefs or birds' nests or bridges even if coral polyps and birds and engineers became extinct. Popper's use of these analogies sometimes suggests this, but it would be a mistake, and he also says things that should guard against it. It is only the possibility of being understood that makes a lot of black marks on paper into a book, a third world item; otherwise it would be just a physical object, resident wholly in world 1.[14] And the possibility of its being understood requires minds—not necessarily human minds—and traditions of language use and meaning. So historical world 3 items are dependent for their existence on world 2 ones, and therefore the same holds, indirectly, for logical world 3 items as well. Popper seems reluctant to say this, but his denial that world 3 exists only as contents of world 2 items can amount merely to this: historical world 3 items are not *contents* at all; they are existentially dependent in a different way on world 2 items in general, though not on this or that particular mind, and the logical world 3 items are also existentially dependent, as contents, on minds in general or on historical world 3 items that are in turn existentially dependent on minds in general, though not on this or that particular mind. Popper's insistence on autonomy simply fails to get this straight.

However, both logical and historical world 3 items may be autonomous in other ways. Whether or not we agree with Popper that mathematical entities, even the series of natural numbers, are man-made, it is, as he says, beyond dispute that truths and problems arise with regard to them which are in no way planned or anticipated. We may lay down the rules which generate the number

[14] *OK*, 116.

series, but these rules have unintended and non-obvious consequences. We do not further lay down that there should be just four
prime numbers between ten and twenty, or that the sequence of
prime numbers should be infinite. These are firm but unexpected
consequences of the initial rules. So, clearly, is either the truth or
the falsity of Goldbach's conjecture—or, perhaps, on an intuitionist
view, its indeterminacy. And all sorts of logical relations will be
autonomous in this kind of way.

It is not only such logical relations that will be independent of
any intention or plan, and often beyond the range of anyone's
foresight. The same will be true, for other reasons, of the causal
relations of historical third world items. Bodies of knowledge and
belief, of error and myth, other traditions, and cultural items of all
kinds, such as languages and systems of law and economic and
political structures, grow, persist, change, and decay in ways which
are largely the outcome of human thoughts and intentional actions,
but because they are resultants of many different, separate, uncon-
certed, choices, often of competing or conflicting purposes, these
developments are not themselves planned or in general foreseen by
anyone. Yet it may be possible to understand them, either by seeing
how they are the resultants of masses of separate choices, or more
directly in terms appropriate to the third world items, logical or
historical, themselves. For example, where there is a general climate
of scientific criticism, we can understand how a once-popular
theory comes to be abandoned just by noting how difficulties arise
in it or evidence piles up against it. The logical relations involved
will explain its decline in favour not, indeed, in themselves but in
relation to the critical climate. And, as Popper stresses, to understand why a scientist propounds a particular theory it will usually
be more useful to analyse his intellectual background and problem
situation than to study any essentially subjective aspects of his
thought processes.[15]

My third question, which constitutes a possible objection, runs
as follows. If the historical third world items are dependent for
their existence on minds, how could they be causally independent?
And if they are causally dependent on minds, will not the only
adequate understanding of them be that which traces and follows
this dependence? However, this does not follow. A historical world
3 item will indeed occur if and only if some conjunction of mental

[15] *OK*, 109, 170-7.

states and perhaps also non-mental, physical, states occurs. It will still have whatever logical features and relations it has in the third world, and it will be reducible to world 2 and world 1 items only if they also are allowed to have logical features. Subject to the same qualification, changes and causal processes involving world 3 items will also be in principle reducible to changes and processes involving only items in worlds 1 and 2. For example, the development of a tradition will consist in some large conjunction of causally connected changes in a great many minds, causally linked also with the production and exchange of certain physical records, documents, and suchlike materials. So it is true, in a way, that everything that happens in the historical part of world 3 could in principle be adequately described and causally understood in terms that involve only worlds 1 and 2. But only in principle. Not merely is there no reason to suppose that such descriptions and such understanding will be more accessible to us than descriptions and explanations in world 3 terms: in general there is every reason to suppose the opposite. We may well know that a certain tradition has grown and changed, and understand in general terms why it has changed, without having access to the individual details of this process. If one scientist propounds a new theory, ten others gradually come to accept it provisionally, but a twelfth scientist then criticizes it cogently, and the other ten, and even the original propounder, then abandon it, no doubt there is a complex sequence and interplay of mental processes in all twelve thinkers and this interplay will also involve some purely physical processes—sound waves that convey speech, pieces of paper, perhaps printing presses and trains or trucks or aeroplanes to carry the written or printed materials about—but it is neither necessary nor in practice possible for us to trace the causal processes at these levels and in this sort of scattered detail. What is accessible to us is an explanation which would be merely an expansion of the account I first gave, filling in the content of the new theory, the intellectual context—Popper's problem situation—which made it worth propounding, the tests or evidence which made it acceptable, and the arguments and/or further tests which refuted it. Such details as these, which belong in either the logical or the historical part of the third world, combined with the information that the twelve scientists are all intelligent and reasonable men and are caught up in the tradition of critical enquiry, will be enough to explain what happens. This will be a quite genuine explanation, tracing quite genuine causal connections, despite the fact that the processes involved are in principle reducible to processes at another level. And, as I said, it is the explanation at this level, in third world terms, not the reductive explanation which is open only in principle, that is likely to be accessible to us. There is a general principle of which this is one instance: we can accept a metaphysical reduction—for example, some variety of metaphysical individualism—without being thereby committed to the corresponding methodological reduction—for example, the corresponding methodological individualism, which may well be practically impossible. And conversely we can reject a methodological reduction and insist upon the opposing methodological autonomy of enquiry at some higher level without being thereby committed to denying the corresponding metaphysical reduction, that is, without having to defend what may well be an implausible metaphysical or existential autonomy. But none of this is made clear by Popper's account.

My fourth question concerns the alleged interaction between the worlds: is it correct to speak of interaction between worlds 1 and 2, and also between worlds 2 and 3? I have argued in another place that once we have a correct analysis of causal asymmetry we see that a pair of causally inseparable items cannot compete with one another for a causal role.[16] Thus some mental state, and its neurophysiological basis, may consist of distinct sets of properties, but if they are causally inseparable in a strong sense it will be true to say of each of them that it causes whatever the other causes. So even if there is, in principle, a complete and adequate account at the neurophysiological level of, say, a piece of intelligent and intentional behaviour, this will not show that the mental features, the intelligence and the intentions, are causally idle or irrelevant. There can be, therefore, quite genuine causal relations in either direction between mental states and bodily states: sensory inputs can give rise to conscious experiences, and choices and decisions can give rise to bodily movements. This is, of course, what we all ordinarily assume. But the point is that this ordinary assumption can be retained even along with the denial of property-identity between brain and mind and along with the supposition that there is in principle a complete and adequate causal account of sense-percep-

---

[16] Mind Brain, and Causation', in *Midwest Studies in Philosophy*, Vol. IV (1979). [Now reprinted as Chapter X below.—Edd.]

tion and voluntary action at the neurophysiological level. It is not, indeed, that a mental state interacts with the physical state which is its own neurophysiological basis; rather it interacts with whatever that basis interacts with; it and its basis share a causal role. But the outcome is that world 2 items can be said, properly and literally, to affect and be affected by world 1 items.

The same holds, by analogy, for the interaction between world 2 and the historical part of world 3. For any historical world 3 item, there will be some combination of world 2 and world 1 items on which the world 3 item wholly depends for its existence. Since here too there may not be property-identity, we should not say that the world 3 item is identical with this combination. Nevertheless, it will be causally inseparable from it in a strong sense: given only the basic laws of working of the actual world it will be impossible to have that combination of world 1 and world 2 items without the world 3 feature, or to have this world 3 feature without some such combination of first and second world items. So, again, whatever causal relations this combination enters into with other items in worlds 1 and 2, the world 3 item equally enters into these. It will interact not with its own mental and physical basis, but with whatever that basis interacts with.

This analysis has the consequence that, contrary to what Popper says, there is no barrier in principle to direct interaction between world 3 and world 1. Popper's belief that world 2 must enter as an intermediary seems to be due to a conflation of two points which his account fails to clarify.

First, every historical world 3 item depends partly on some world 2 items, and it is only when these are involved that the world 3 item, as such, can act or be acted upon. If a pure world 1 part of the basis of a world 3 item has some effect elsewhere in world 1— say, if a book's pages reflect light differentially because of the black print on the white paper—this would not be an effect of the world 3 item. Similarly, if a pure world 1 part of the basis of a world 3 item is directly affected by something else in world 1—say, if a recording thermometer operates automatically, collecting data to check some meteorological theory—it will not be the world 3 item that is affected unless some world 2 items, mental states, are also involved. But still it is not strictly that world 3 acts on world 2, and then world 2 on world 1, or vice versa. And, despite Popper's hostility to linguistic philosophy, this point turns out, on examination, to be little more than a verbal one: it is simply that it does not count as the world 3 item acting or being acted upon unless world 2 items are involved.

Secondly, if we think of logical world 3 items—propositions, argument-contents, and so on—it is obvious that, not being historical entities, they cannot, strictly speaking, act or be acted upon at all. It is only their concrete realizations that can interact with anything, and these must include world 2 components. But again it is not really that world 3 acts on world 2, and then world 2 on world 1, or vice versa.

It is these two points that between them constitute the truth which Popper expresses loosely by saying that world 3 cannot interact with world 1 directly, but only through world 2.

In answering these four questions I have not fully endorsed Popper's five theses, though I have shown that there are truths to which they roughly correspond. But to get these matters straight, and not just roughly right, it is essential to draw distinctions which Popper fails to draw, in particular that between what I have called the logical and the historical components of world 3. Once these are distinguished, other matters fall neatly into place. But when we do get things straight, there is little left that could be called a pluralist metaphysics. On examination, Popper's metaphysical fanfare dies away. What remains is his stress on understanding the logic of problem situations and on the importance of public, inter-personal, and multi-personal traditions of knowledge and critical enquiry.[17]

4   CULTURAL EVOLUTION

Although *Objective Knowledge* has the sub-title 'An Evolutionary Approach', and although Popper stresses the analogy between the evolution of organic species through natural selection and the growth of scientific knowledge through the critical selection of hypotheses and conjectures,[18] I do not think that he makes enough of the analogy between biological evolution and the development of the third world.

To show this I shall borrow from a recent brilliant and fascinating book, *The Selfish Gene* by Richard Dawkins.[19] As the title

---

[17] This agrees with Brian Carr's main contention.
[18] *OK*, 112, 144-5, 156, 260-1.   [19] Oxford, 1976.

indicates, Dawkins puts the gene at the centre of his neo-Darwinian account of evolution. Biological history is seen as a struggle for survival not between animal and plant individuals, nor between species, but between genes. Individuals are only loose temporary federations of genes: you and I are gene-machines, whose biological function is to carry genes around and enable them to replicate themselves. And not only individuals but also groups, populations, and species are, as genetic units, too temporary to qualify for natural selection. Only genes are the true units of natural selection.

Of course, when Dawkins speaks of the gene as the subject of selection, he means not an individual or token, nor even a gene-type, but rather a gene-clone, the family of gene-tokens descended by replication from any one gene-token. It is this clone or family that survives and multiplies, or dies out, in competition with other gene-clones.

Though the gene is the hero of Dawkins's book, it is not necessarily of unique importance. What matters about it is a certain cluster of logical features. Genes are replicators. Each gene-token is capable, in favourable conditions, of producing multiple copies of itself. But it is also capable of occasionally producing imperfect copies—mutations—which can then replicate themselves just as the original gene did. Anything that has these logical features is a suitable subject for evolution by natural selection. And as Dawkins points out, what we might call cultural items are also replicators— a song, a language fragment, a religious doctrine, a legal rule, a tradition of child-rearing, a concept, and, of course, a scientific theory. The appropriate environment for these cultural items is, of course, a collection of human minds with powers of imitation and memory. To emphasize the analogy with genes, Dawkins coins the name *memes* for such cultural items—a word with echoes of 'mimesis' (imitation) and of 'memory'.

And now comes the important point. Memes can evolve and multiply in much the same way as genes. The explanation of the widespread flourishing of a certain meme, such as the idea of a god or the belief in hell fire, may be simply that it is an efficiently selfish meme. Something about it makes it well able to infect human minds, to take root and spread in and among them, in the same way that something about a virus makes it well able to take root and spread in human or animal bodies. There is no need to explain the success of a meme by reference to any benefit it confers on individuals or groups; it is a replicator in its own right. A cultural trait can evolve, not because it is advantageous to society, but simply because it is advantageous to itself.

Dawkins's memes would include the historical components of Popper's third world, but would comprise other things as well. For example, Popper regards the third world as a by-product of language,[20] so that language cannot itself belong to the third world; but language itself consists of memes. Also, there are memes which do not depend on language—tunes, fashions, traditions of craftsmanship—and others, including many technical skills, which depend only slightly upon language. But it is surely better to see concepts, theories, and the like as merely some memes among others, subject to the same general principles of evolution. It is also significant that just as some genes supply part of the environment in which other genes are selected, so some memes supply part of the environment in which other memes may flourish or die.

One merit of the notion of memes, and the analogy between these and genes, is that it brings out more clearly a respect in which historical world 3 items are autonomous. In the appropriate conditions each meme tends to replicate itself, with occasional variations, and to compete with other memes for the resources on which they live—essentially, the components of world 2, or the time and mental energy of human beings. The history of the third world can be better understood from this point of view.

Another merit of a wider, more inclusive, view of memes is this. We can see that Popper, by being too selective, takes an over-optimistic view of evolutionary pressures in the third world. He speaks of 'a competitive struggle which eliminates those hypotheses which are unfit', and says that 'while animal knowledge and pre-scientific knowledge grow mainly through the elimination of those holding the unfit hypotheses, scientific criticism often makes our theories perish in our stead, eliminating our mistaken beliefs before such beliefs lead to our own elimination'.[21] I agree that this may happen. But false beliefs are not necessarily lethal, or even harmful, to their possessors, and in the competition of hypotheses factors other than rational falsification may affect their fitness to survive. The human acceptability or non-acceptability of a view may in practice be more important than its logical confirmation or refutation. Once again, a clear distinction between logical and historical

<hr>

[20] *OK*, 137.   [21] *OK*, 261.

third world items makes it easier to appreciate this point. What is true, however, is that there is a kind of critical tradition of scientific procedure, a critical climate of opinion, within which the rational merits of hypotheses will be more than usually relevant to their survival; this tradition, this climate, itself consists of memes, and it would be worth while to consider how and in what further conditions they are able to flourish. An evolutionary approach to knowledge should be put in the setting of an evolutionary understanding of a much wider range of cultural items, among them the very conditions in which knowledge, rather than error, is likely to evolve.

X

MIND, BRAIN, AND CAUSATION

ALTHOUGH minds are not distinct things from brains, mental properties are distinct from physical properties, and mental facts are different from neurophysiological facts. But what, then, is the causal role of mental facts and properties? When desire and belief (or knowledge) together lead to a decision and an action that involves bodily movement, do the relevant mental facts and properties help causally to bring about that movement and that action? Or do the physical (including neurophysiological) facts and properties constitute a sufficient cause of that movement and that action, so that the related mental elements are causally idle and redundant? Is epiphenomenalism right in treating the mental elements as only effects of physical factors, and not also causes? At first sight, neither answer seems acceptable. The epiphenomenalist view that the mental aspect of our desires, beliefs, and decisions is causally idle is strongly at variance with our ordinary understanding of these matters. It is also hard to reconcile with an evolutionary theory: if consciousness evolved through natural selection, it must have contributed causally to the survival of the species in which it was developing. On the other hand it seems plausible to suppose that it is one neurophysiological occurrence that causes another, so that what brings about the bodily movements that constitute the action (or else are part of it, and in conjunction with external circumstances causally determine the other parts of it) is not the agent's desires and beliefs as such, but their neurophysiological basis. The continuity of the causal process is on the physical side, and there is no room for mental elements to intervene and make a difference.

These problems arise only if mental elements such as desires, beliefs, and conscious experiences are distinguished from the physical features of brain states and processes. Defenders of the mind-brain identity theory have argued from such difficulties to the denial of the distinction. It would indeed be awkward to recognize mental features but leave them causally idle. We should need one-way causal laws to connect them with their neurophysiological basis, and these laws would be loose ends in the network of scientific laws, 'nomological danglers'. But we cannot deny that there are conscious experiences, and (as I shall show) there is no way in which they can be reduced without remainder to their physical basis.

We are faced, then, with what looks like an inconsistent triad of propositions, each of which is highly plausible on its own. Mental facts and properties are distinct from physical ones. Mental facts and properties are causally operative in human action, not idle or redundant. Yet physical (including neurophysiological) elements constitute sufficient causes of the bodily movements that determine actions.

I want to treat this as an ontological problem, not a linguistic one. It is sometimes argued that language could change so that talk about brain processes and the like would replace talk about experiences. Well, suppose that it could, and did: this would not settle our problem. Part of this problem is whether this reformed language would be adequate, whether it would cover the world, not merely in the sense of reporting and predicting all concrete occurrences under some description, but also in the sense of not leaving undescribed some perfectly real and (to us at least) interesting features. It is argued more plausibly on the other side that whatever discoveries science comes up with, and whatever arguments physicalist philosophers deploy, we shall always go on speaking in terms of experiences and intentional thought, and that talk about actions belongs firmly within this branch of ordinary language. But, even if this is so, it does not settle the issue in the opposite sense: the question remains whether this persistent way of speaking expresses a truth or a systematic error. To take an analogous case, it might well be that we shall always go on speaking of coloured objects in a way that implicitly treats colours-as-seen as objective. But the doctrine of secondary qualities may none the less be correct; this way of speaking may embody an error. The practical indispensability of the language of consciousness might indeed result from and be indirect evidence for the presence of irreducible mental properties, but it does not settle the issue directly or in itself. Our problem is about what properties actually are there, and their causal relations; it is not about our present language and conceptual scheme, nor is it about how these could or could not be altered.

I should briefly sum up the case for the distinctness of mental properties. There are several sorts of feature that are, *prima facie* at least, distinctively mental. First, there are the 'raw feels' or phenomenal qualities: almost all of us know what it is to feel pain, to see something red, to hear a high note, to feel cold, and so on. Secondly, we have perceptions that are as of independently existing things in an objective spatio-temporal order. Thirdly, we have propositional attitudes, beliefs, desires, and so on, that concern various things other than those mental states themselves in such a way that they cannot be adequately described except by including a description of whatever it is they are about. The desire that it should be fine tomorrow is just that: no way of describing it will do justice to it unless it somehow captures and encapsulates the possible state of affairs, its being fine tomorrow. Features of both the second and the third sort have been put under the heading of intentionality, and we need not discuss whether they are really different from one another, or whether the second is analysable in terms of the third. The important point is that no features of these three sorts seem to be exhaustively analysable into or reducible to any system of features of sorts other than these three, that is, uncompromisingly physical features.

This becomes plain if we examine what are offered as analogous cases of reductive identification: the table is nothing but a cloud of particles, lightning is nothing but an electrical discharge, heat is nothing but the kinetic energy of molecules, and the gene is nothing but the DNA (or RNA) molecule. Granted that where the table is there is no persisting continuous solid, though to sight and touch there appears to be one. We can explain away the continuous solidity as an appearance: that is just how what is there looks and feels to us. We replace some of the supposed qualities of the table with parts of the content of our conscious experiences. Similarly, where we see the lightning there is nothing but an electrical discharge and photons being sent out from it; but we see it as a bright flash. Again the brightness is shifted from the external object to become part of the content of consciousness. And the same with heat as we feel it. But it is obvious that this method of explaining things away will not do for experiences themselves and their contents. Its looking thus and so to us is one of the features that is embarrassing for the physicalist, and the explanation that it only looks to us as if it looks thus and so is not only absurd but useless:

Logic and Knowledge

it would leave us with an unexplained item of the same sort on our hands. The gene is in a different position. It is initially introduced only as a hypothetical entity, as that which plays a certain causal role, interacting in regular ways with other genes, in determining the inheritance of characteristics. To start with, it is simply that, whatever it may be, that does such and such. It is therefore freely up for identification with whatever may later be discovered to do this job. There is no appearance here to be explained away. If mental features were analogous to genes, if they were introduced simply as otherwise unknown causes of behaviour, as the grounds, whatever they may be, of dispositions, there would be no obstacle to reductive identification. If my desire to do X were merely something or other in me which brings it about that in favourable circumstances I (tend to) do X, then indeed it could be exhaustively identified with some neurophysiological condition that has only impeccably physical properties. Similarly, if, as in Smart's notorious example, my having a certain after-image were known to me simply as something going on in me which is like what goes on in me when my eyes are open (etc.) and there is a yellowish-orange patch on the wall, then my having of this experience could be exhaustively identified with a brain process. Identity theorists have therefore been tempted to give accounts of these sorts. But implausibly. I know what an orange after-image looks like, and I know at least the central cases of my desiring to do X as involving fully conscious thought about doing X. The phenomenal and intentional features cannot plausibly be denied, and once they are recognized even as merely apparent they cannot be explained away. The only available method of explaining apparent features away fails here through circularity.

Our problem is that once we have accepted an irreducible distinction between mental and physical facts and properties, and have allowed that physical facts and properties constitute sufficient causes of actions, we seem to be forced to admit that mental facts and properties are epiphenomenal, causally idle; yet this conclusion is itself implausible. This problem, however, involves two important items of causal theory. First, it arises, on our assumptions, only if we take facts and properties as causes. If a cause were always a concrete thing or a concrete event, we could say that what was causally responsible for an action was a neurophysiological structure or event: this structure or event could have mental features as well as purely physical ones, but, given this approach, there would be no sense in asking which features were operative and which were idle: what was causally operative was the concrete whole. But though this sort of report is allowable, it is not the only sort that is allowable, and it cannot cover on its own everything that is important about causation. We can and frequently do distinguish, within concrete things and events, those features that are relevant to a certain outcome. Although it was the one concrete event, Tommy's eating of a number of apples, that caused both his immediate stomach ache and his later poisoning, it was the fact that the apples were unripe that caused the stomach ache and the fact that they had been sprayed with paraquat that caused the poisoning. We have to recognize fact- and property-causes as well as concrete event- and thing-causes. So once the mental features have been distinguished even as features of a physical thing, we can ask intelligibly whether they are causally relevant to actions or not. Secondly, our problem involves the direction of causation. It is only on the assumption that any particular causal relationship is asymmetrical that we can formulate epiphenomenalism and suggest that there is only a one-way causal path from the neurophysiological to the mental, and hence that even if certain mental facts are necessary and sufficient (in the circumstances) as temporal antecedents of actions, they are none the less causally idle and redundant. Also, it is natural to suppose that each mental item occurs at the same time, or has the same temporal duration, as its neurophysiological basis, so that if there is causal asymmetry here it must consist of something other than succession in time. It may be, then, that the key to our problem lies in the understanding of causal asymmetry. I have tried more than once to analyse it, but with less than complete success;[1] I shall try again, from a different starting point.

Here, as elsewhere, there are three sorts of questions, conceptual, epistemological, and ontological, that are liable to be mixed up with one another. We can ask what concept we have of causal asymmetry; again, what knowledge we have of it and how we acquire that knowledge; and thirdly, what constitutes causal asymmetry in the objects, what directedness there is in the objective relation between a cause and its effect. The answers to questions of these three sorts may be related to one another, but they could diverge radically. Let us start with conceptual analysis, and then,

[1] Especially in Chapter 7 of *The Cement of the Universe* (Oxford, 1974).

if we can elucidate the concept of causal direction, consider what knowledge we have that applies this concept and what observations could have generated it, and whether we can claim objective validity for it or for anything related to it.

We often think of the direction of causation as a direction of conditionality: the effect is conditional upon, depends upon, the cause in some sense in which the cause is not conditional upon the effect. Now some conditional relationships are non-symmetrical: if A is a necessary condition of B, B need not be a necessary condition of A, and equally if A is a sufficient condition of B, B need not be a sufficient condition of A. (Though on some analyses if A is necessary for B, B is sufficient for A, and vice versa, so that if A is necessary and sufficient for B, B must also be necessary and sufficient for A.) But these non-symmetries are not what we want. A cause, or a causally relevant factor, may be sufficient (in the circumstances) for its effect; again, it may be necessary; the causal asymmetry is different from and cuts across the contrast between necessity and sufficiency. Causal priority can combine equally well with necessity or with sufficiency. In fact, on the most natural interpretation something must have causal priority to count as a necessary condition, or as a sufficient one, or both. On this interpretation it will not follow that if A is a necessary condition of B, B is a sufficient condition of A, and so on. If A and B are single (token) events, such converse relationships cannot hold, and even if they are event types there is no reason to expect them to hold.

It seems, then, that we cannot derive a direction of conditionality from necessity and sufficiency, whether or not we add 'in the circumstances'. We have either to add the conditional and causal priority as a further factor, or to follow the natural interpretation which takes it to be included, but as something not yet analysed or explained, in the relation of necessity, or sufficiency, or their conjunction. I have previously, on this account, despaired of finding an analysable direction of conditionality. But an article by David Sanford has persuaded me that it is possible, though the analysis I shall offer is rather different from his.[2]

Let us work with examples of what are, so far as we can tell at the start, simultaneous causes and effects. One such example is von Wright's of a box with two buttons on top, so connected inside

[2] David H. Sanford, 'The Direction of Causation and the Direction of Conditionship', *Journal of Philosophy*, Vol. 73 (1976).

that if you press either button both go down together; let us call the buttons A and B. In the circumstances A's going down is necessary and sufficient for the simultaneous going down of B, and vice versa: but on some one occasion when I press A, A's going down is causally prior to B's. We can believe this even if we think there is strict simultaneity—B starts to go down at exactly the same instant as A. Our concept of causal priority is not that of being earlier in time. I have argued elsewhere that in such cases as this we rely on the continuity of causation: since it is A that my finger presses, I am confident that A's movement is causally prior to B's because I believe that the movement of my finger is causally prior to both, and A's movement comes between that of my finger and that of B in a physically continuous causal line. But this is pretty clearly not what we mean when we say that A's movement is on this occasion causally prior to B's, and it is unhelpful because it merely refers us to the still-to-be-analysed causal priority of my finger movement, or perhaps of my decision to press A. What we mean is rather this. Although in these circumstances the movement of either button is necessary and sufficient for that of the other, it is not so in other possible circumstances. We could open the box and cut or disconnect whatever it is that links A with B, and then the movement of neither button would be necessary or sufficient for that of the other. If the connection between them had been broken, A would still have gone down when I pressed A, but (other things being equal) B would not. It is, I suggest, in this sense that in the actual case, where the connection is not broken, B's movement is conditional upon A's: it wouldn't be occurring but for the connection with A. The conditionally dependent (and therefore, in our concept, causally posterior) item is the one which would or might have been absent if the connection between them had not been there, but things had been otherwise as far as possible the same.

This is offered as a conceptual analysis, but it also indicates how observations and especially experiments could suggest and confirm such directed conditionality. By making various changes and then pressing either button again I could check what it was that linked them, and I could note which moved and which failed to move when I pressed each with the connection broken. Of course, our general experience tells us to expect that it will be the one we press that moves in these circumstances, but that is only because our experience includes plenty of roughly analogous experiments. *A priori* it is conceivable that, when I press A with the connection broken, only B should go down. If it did, I should conclude that when they were connected and I pressed A and both went down, it was B's movement that was conditionally and causally prior to A's. So the detection of conditional and causal priority is independent of the physical continuity of the causal line, and it is a synthetic truth that we can in general rely on such continuity as an indicator of causal priority, a truth for which we need, and have, empirical evidence.

Another example (used by Sanford) takes as the two causally related items the rotation of the drive shaft (propeller shaft) and the rotation of the rear wheels of a car. When the engine is moving the car along a level road, the rotation of the wheels depends on that of the drive shaft. On our conceptual analysis, this means that if the connection between the two rotations had not been there—say, if the differential had failed or had been missing—but things had otherwise been as far as possible the same, the drive shaft would have been rotating but not the wheels. In fact it is a bit more complicated: the drive shaft would have been rotating faster. That is, there are both conditional and causal priorities running in both directions. The drive shaft's rotation is maintaining that of the wheels, while that of the wheels is holding back that of the shaft. That the wheels are rotating at all is conditional upon the rotation of the shaft, but that the shaft is rotating no faster than it is is conditional upon the frictionally limited rotation of the wheels. And, of course, all this is reversed when the car is being pushed.

Generalizing, then, if on a particular occasion A's doing X is causally related to B's doing Y, and if they had not been so related but things had otherwise been as far as possible as they were, A would still have been doing X but B would (or might) not have been doing Y, then A's doing X is conditionally and causally prior to B's doing Y. And this holds whether A's doing X is necessary for B's doing Y, or sufficient, or both.

We can thus formulate directed conditionality in terms of appropriate counterfactual conditionals, of which the key one is 'If the connection had not been there ...' These, like other counterfactuals, can be supported, though not conclusively established, by observation of closely analogous but slightly changed situations.

An assumption about the uniformity of the course of nature in the relevant respects allows us to take what happens there and apply it, counterfactually conditionally, to the present case. And this direction of conditionality seems to be the core of our concept of the direction of causation. The experiments and observed regularities that support these counterfactuals are the source of our knowledge of causal asymmetry.

I have treated the button and car examples as ones in which cause and effect are contemporaneous. In reality, there will be a small time lag (for example, between the instant at which the rotation of the shaft reaches a certain speed and that at which the rotation of the wheels reaches the corresponding speed) owing to the elasticity of the connecting materials. But the temporal order thus set up between cause and effect is something quite different both from the direction of conditionality as it figures in our concept of causal order and from the observed contrasts and regularities that give rise to and justify that concept. We could make these observations and assert the conditional dependence in complete ignorance of the time lags. Their coincidence is a synthetic and empirical truth, like the agreement, noted above, between physical continuity and causal priority.

This account can be extended to examples where there is not even an appearance of simultaneity, where the effect plainly follows the cause in time. What here corresponds to breaking the connection will be making a small change in the circumstances such that the causal relation no longer holds. For example, the near end of a fuse is lit, the flame burns along it and a heap of gunpowder which the far end of the fuse is touching explodes. We repeat the experiment with the end of the fuse not touching the gunpowder and there is no explosion. So we say, about the original case, that if the far end of the fuse had not been touching the gunpowder, the near end would still have burned but there would have been no explosion. This is the analysis of the claim that the burning of the near end of the fuse is the cause and the explosion the effect.

It might be objected that we are begging the question by taking as the most nearly analogous case without the connection one in which the near end is lit: why not take one where, though the fuse is not lit and its far end is not touching the gunpowder, there still is an explosion? Would not this suggest that if the connection had been absent, the explosion would have occurred in the original case but not the burning of the near end of the fuse, thus reversing, on our analysis, the direction of conditionality? Yes, this would follow if we found a lot of cases, all otherwise very similar, divided into a class where there was contact between fuse and gunpowder, an explosion, and an earlier fuse-burning, and a class in which there was no contact, an explosion, and no earlier fuse-burning. This would constitute *prima facie* evidence for time-reversed conditional dependence of the earlier burning on the later explosion. But, of course, we do not get this pattern of evidence. Consider a case in which the explosion occurs but there is no contact with the fuse. In cases most like this, except that there is contact, there is no strong tendency for there to have been an earlier burning of the near end of the fuse. We do not need to make a question-begging estimate of similarity to conclude that the counterfactual supported by the actual pattern of resemblances and differences is 'If the connection had not been there, the near end of the fuse would have burned but there would have been no explosion', not 'If the connection had not been there, there would have been an explosion but the near end of the fuse would not have burned'. The observed evidence, in the light of our analysis, supports a synthetic, empirical, judgement that the conditional and causal order here coincides with the temporal order.

What I have sketched here is a conceptual analysis of causal asymmetry based on the direction of conditionality, and a related epistemic analysis. Since I deny that counterfactual conditionals with unfulfilled antecedents (other than those whose antecedents entail their consequents) can be simply and straightforwardly true, I cannot offer it also as a factual analysis, as an answer to the ontological question about causal asymmetry. But such asymmetry in the objects will consist at least in those contrasting regularities, those patterns of resemblances and differences, the detection of which gives rise to and supports those counterfactual judgements. It is a further question whether this account can be developed so as to accommodate my earlier suggestion that the direction of causation is linked with the contrast between fixity and non-fixity, and that an effect is fixed only by way of its cause. Leaving this aside, the account so far given may be enough to throw some light on the causal relations between mental and physical features and on the suggestion that mental features may be causally redundant.

If we apply our conceptual analysis here, the suggestion that the mental features are epiphenomenal amounts to this: if the connection between the neurophysiological basis and the mental features had been missing, but things had been otherwise as unchanged as possible, that basis would have been as it is but the mental features would not have been there. Similarly, the suggestion that these features are causally idle or redundant amounts to this: if the connection between the neurophysiological basis and the mental features had been missing, but things had been otherwise as unchanged as possible, then although the mental features would have been lacking, the actions to which we ordinarily take those mental features to be causally contributing would still have occurred. (Of course, if we take these mental features to be constitutive elements in those actions, to be contributing to them logically, we cannot say that *those actions* would still have occurred: the suggestion must then be that something just like those actions except for the absence of these mental features would still have occurred; it does not matter whether we should call this an action or not.) It is a confirmation of our analysis that this is just what we would ordinarily take these suggestions to imply.

But, then, what if the connection between the neurophysiological basis and the mental features could not have been missing? On this supposition, neither of the above-stated possibilities could arise. If the connection between two items could not have been lacking, then on our analysis there can be no direction of conditionality between them, and neither can be causally prior to the other. (Also, as I suggested earlier, the mental features and their basis may be strictly contemporaneous, so that neither is temporally prior to the other.) Nor will it make sense to say that the mental features are idle: the actions could not have occurred without them. Two items neither of which could have occurred without the other do not compete for a causal role: even if one is a sufficient as well as a necessary cause of some outcome, the other will be a necessary and sufficient cause of it too.

However, this suggestion that the connection *could not* have been lacking, that neither item *could* have occurred without the other, needs to be made more precise. Let us distinguish the derived biological laws that govern the behaviour of various living things, but which themselves depend partly on structures developed by evolution, from basic physico-chemical laws that constitute the framework within which evolution takes place.[3] The suggestion that matters for our purposes is that our 'neither item could have occurred without the other' should be a consequence of those basic laws, not conditional upon any particular evolved structure. For this suggestion would at once solve one part of our original problem. 'If consciousness evolved through natural selection, it must have contributed causally to the survival of the species in which it was developing.' If mental features had been causally idle, how could they have been naturally selected? The reply is that if these features were linked to their neurophysiological basis by laws of the framework within which evolution occurred, and this basis gave rise to actions that were useful for survival, these features would automatically be selected along with their basis: evolution simply could not have developed the basis without the consciousness.

But this seems to solve only one part of the problem, leaving another part unsolved. Would what I have offered validate our ordinary conviction that mental features play a real part in bringing actions about? Or is it somehow cheating? Have I really left the mental features idle and redundant after all, and merely blocked the simplest way of formulating that redundancy? Would the present suggestion make consciousness merely an unavoidable accompaniment of something causally operative and useful, but not causally operative and useful itself?

However, it is not easy to pin down any sense in which the mental features would, on this account, be idle. Perhaps it is, as I have said, that the continuity of causation would lie on the physical side. Some continuous processes would connect the neurophysiological basis, rather than the mental features, with the movements that determine or constitute an action. Before that, other continuous processes would connect whatever the causally relevant antecedents were with this basis rather than with the mental features. Putting these two together, we have a picture in which continuous causal lines go through the basis but by-pass consciousness. But this picture does not really justify the inference that consciousness is idle or redundant if, given only the fundamental laws of the

[3] The former would have been different if evolution had happened to get off to a different start, or if conditions had been different along the road, and if there are highly evolved life forms in other planets somewhere, the derived biological laws that govern their behaviour may well be different from those that hold on earth. But the basic laws, whatever they are, will be the same everywhere, and would still have been the same here even if evolution had taken some quite different turn.

natural world, that particular basis could not have occurred without it.

Moreover, there are other connections that link antecedents and consequents more particularly with the mental side. Suppose that I visually perceive, fairly accurately, some three-dimensional scene. This achievement will be partly the result of very complicated learned methods of processing sensory input, but these methods are by now built into me and work automatically. No doubt the neurophysiological states and occurrences that are the basis of my now seeing things roughly as they are must somehow represent the way these things are: the scene must be somehow neurally encoded. But the content of my visual experience represents the things as they are far more directly: how the things look *resembles* how they are much more than does their neural encoding. And this resemblance is invariant through widely different sensory inputs: I keep on seeing the scene as it is from different positions and under different lighting conditions. The inbuilt methods of processing sensory input have been selected and reinforced primarily by their success in achieving this. Much the same holds also on the output side: in innumerable ordinary successful performances there is, in an obvious sense, a resemblance between what I intend to do and what I actually achieve, and this resemblance is invariant through changes in the conditions and the details of such performances. Economical and explanatorily simple accounts of both perception and intentional action turn upon these resemblances, and could not be replaced by purely physical accounts without loss of this simplicity. This is one reason among others why talk about experiences and intentions is most unlikely ever to be replaced by any physicalist substitutes. The possible substitutes would be not only unfamiliar to us but also more complex and so less explanatory. Donald Davidson is, I think, wrong in saying that there cannot be psychophysical laws, but what is true is that there will be only complex, not simple, psycho-physical laws, and therefore that the physical accounts to which psychical accounts will be correlated by those laws will be far less simple and straightforward. This applies not only to accounts of single processes of perception and action, but also to any evolutionary account of how our powers of perception and action have come into existence. The utility or survival value of seeing things roughly as they are and of being able to bring about states of affairs that we desire is more obvious, and more open to general description, than the value of their purely physical bases. The most economical general causal accounts will often be ones that use not-simply-replaceable mentalistic terms. This can be set against the admitted fact that the related causal continuities in each individual sequence of events will lie on the physical side.

However, the main point is that the members of a pair of causally inseparable items cannot compete with one another for a causal role. Whatever one item causes, its inseparable companion causes too, despite the fact that the items in question may enter into different relations of continuity and resemblance. While in general we can, and in formulating explanatory causal statements we do, discriminate between the features or aspects of a concrete event, picking out some rather than others as causally relevant to some outcome, we cannot do this with the members of a causally inseparable cluster of features. To this extent and in this special sort of case we cannot improve upon a concrete event as a cause.

I have not, of course, shown that mental features and their neurophysiological bases are in fact causally inseparable in the required strong sense.[4] I merely offer it as a suggestion that is made plausible just by the fact that it could solve the otherwise very puzzling problem set out at the beginning of this paper. I offer it particularly to those who feel the force of the arguments for the mind–brain identity theory, but who are (rightly) sceptical of the assertion that mental features are identical with physical ones, who find a property-identity thesis (as opposed to a thing-identity or concrete event-identity thesis) untenable or even incomprehensible. Perhaps what is or should really be meant is not strictly the identity of mental and neurophysiological features, but rather their causal inseparability in a strong sense, related to the fundamental laws of working of the natural world.

----

[4] It is, indeed, likely that the relation is a bit more complicated, that while there could not be just this basis without this mental feature, it is only that there could not be this mental feature without *some* member of a disjunction of alternative physical bases. But this complication is irrelevant to the present problem.

NEWCOMB'S PARADOX AND
THE DIRECTION OF CAUSATION

NEWCOMB's paradox was first presented by Robert Nozick[1] and has been discussed by a considerable number of writers. You are playing a game with a Being who seems to have extraordinary predictive powers. Before you are two boxes, in one of which you can see $1,000. The other is closed and you cannot see what it contains, but you know that the Being has put a million dollars into it if he has predicted that you will take it only, but nothing if he has predicted that you will take both boxes; you may take either both boxes or the closed one only. The Being has correctly predicted the choices of all who have so far played with him. What should you do?

Let us call the Being the seer, and his opponent the player. I should also like to reduce the amount that may, or may not, be in the closed box to $10,000. Nearly everyone could make good use of $1,000 and better use of $10,000 or $11,000, but it is hard to say whether a million dollars would be a blessing or a curse. Besides, I want the $1,000 in the open box to be a significant addition, even if one can get the larger sum in the closed box, and I also want to consider the possibility of playing the game repeatedly, and even if one were happy about the first million, the possibility of repeated millions is just too much to contemplate.

The obvious argument for taking the closed box only is that there is good inductive evidence for the proposition that everyone who takes only it gets $10,000, whereas everyone who takes both boxes gets only $1,000. The equally obvious argument in favour of taking both boxes is that since there is, visibly, $1,000 in the open box, there must be $1,000 more in the two boxes together than in the closed box alone, whether the latter contains $10,000 or nothing. The strategy of taking both boxes 'dominates' that of

Reprinted from *Canadian Journal of Philosophy*, Vol. 7, No. 2 (June 1977).

[1] R. Nozick, 'Newcomb's Problem and Two Principles of Choice', in *Essays in Honor of Carl G. Hempel*, edited by N. Rescher (Dordrecht, 1969).

Diagrams

I   Cases where it is reasonable to take only the closed box

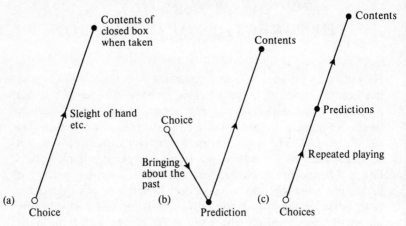

II   Case where it is reasonable
to develop the character of
a closed-box-only-taker

III   Case where it is reasonable
to develop the character of
a both-box-taker

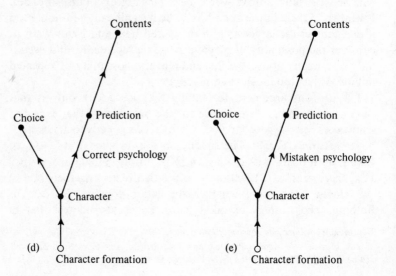

IV Cases where *if* one were free it *would be* reasonable to take both boxes

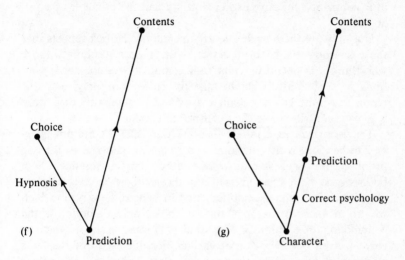

(f) (g)

V Cases where it is reasonable, and one is free, to take both boxes

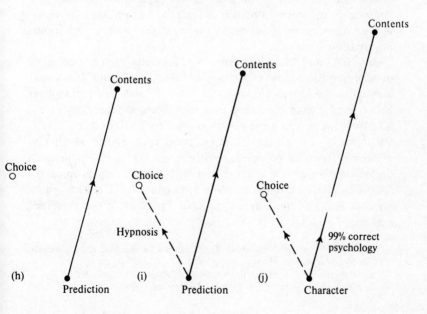

(h) (i) (j)

taking only the closed box. Nozick and many others have seen the paradox as setting up a conflict in decision theory between the two principles on which these arguments respectively rely, the principle of maximizing subjective expected utility and the principle of dominance.

Not only are there these two arguments, but Nozick reports that those to whom the problem is put divide almost evenly into those who think it is obviously right to take both boxes and those who think it is obviously right to take the closed box only; and this report is confirmed by a similar division of opinion among those who have contributed to the published discussion.

This is, of course, a purely theoretical puzzle. We are not likely ever to be faced with situations even roughly analogous to the one proposed. But I believe that we can state a complete solution which both is of some interest in itself and throws light on certain metaphysical notions and assumptions that lie behind the ways in which we are inclined to reason about it. The complete solution is the conjunction of a number of partial solutions, each of which is correct given one or other of various possible views of the facts involved in the problem situation. In effect, I shall be spelling out in more detail the remark with which James Cargile[2] concludes his discussion: '... there is no warrant for serious use of the term "paradox" in conjunction with the puzzle, and no basis for determining one course of action as the right one without additional information'.

Bar-Hillel and Margalit[3] point out, correctly, that the principle of adopting the dominant strategy is not always sound. It is sound only when the alternative states, in each of which one action gives better results than the other, are themselves independent of the actions between which the player has to choose. They gave in 1972 the following still topical example. Israel must decide whether to withdraw from its occupied territories or not, and Egypt must decide whether or not to go to war with Israel. They propose the following matrix, the figures being a measure of the relative goodness for Israel of the different possible outcomes of the combined actions.

    [2] J. Cargile, 'Newcomb's Paradox', *British Journal for the Philosophy of Science*, Vol. 26, No. 3 (September 1975).
    [3] M. Bar-Hillel and A. Margalit, 'Newcomb's Paradox Revisited', *British Journal for the Philosophy of Science*, Vol. 23, No. 4 (November 1972).

		Egypt	
		war	peace
	withdraw	0	2
Israel	remain	1	3

If Egypt goes to war, Israel will do better by having remained in the occupied territories than by having withdrawn, and the same is true if Egypt keeps the peace. But if withdrawal is very likely to ensure peace, while remaining is very likely to provoke war, it may be a better policy for Israel to withdraw than to remain, thus securing the pay-off scored as 2 rather than that scored as 1. The dominant strategy is not here the best. But though they are right about this, Bar-Hillel and Margalit formulate the required qualification incorrectly. They say that what is wrong here is that the states of the world (Egypt's going to war or keeping the peace) are not probabilistically independent of Israel's actions, and that the principle of dominance holds only where there is such probabilistic independence. But what is important in the example is surely not probabilistic but causal dependence. The strategy of withdrawal is (on the assumptions stated) preferable because withdrawal is very likely to *bring about* a lasting peace, whereas remaining in the occupied territories is very likely to *bring about* a renewal of the war. It is essential that the direction of causation here is from Israel's action as cause to Egypt's action as effect. A probabilistic connection founded on some different causal pattern would not necessarily carry this implication. For example, if Egypt's giving evidence of an intention to renew the war would encourage Israel to remain, whereas Egypt's showing an eagerness for peace would encourage Israel to withdraw, the resulting probabilities would not give Israel any *reason* for departing from the dominant strategy, though on this hypothesis Egypt's actions might *influence* Israel in this direction. Nozick states the point correctly: 'if the actions or decisions to do the actions do not affect, help bring about, influence, etc., *which* state obtains, then whatever the conditional probabilities (so long as they do not indicate an influence), one should perform the dominant action'.

On the most natural interpretation, the situation in the Newcomb paradox does not incorporate the right direction of causation to undermine the principle of dominance. The seer has already made his move before the player chooses. What the player does cannot affect what is in the closed box. It is this, and not the principle of dominance alone, that seems to make it reasonable to take both boxes. However, if the player thought that the seer was relying not on foresight but, say, on sleight of hand or telekinesis— that he was regularly putting $10,000 into the closed box but surreptitiously removing it each time a player went for the open box— or that the $10,000 disappeared into a false bottom that was electronically operated by the removal of the open box, then of course it would be reasonable for him to take the closed box only. For now he would assume that taking the open box would *cause* the absence of the $10,000 from the closed one, and the Newcomb situation would be strictly analogous to the Israel-Egypt one, where remaining would be likely to *bring about* war. This possibility is represented in Diagram (a).

The same choice could, alternatively, be defended with the help of the far more extravagant assumption that there occurs the extreme form of backward causation, the bringing about of the past. By now taking the closed box only the player brings it about that the seer some time ago foresaw that the player would take this box only, and so brings it about that the seer has already put $10,000 into it. (See Diagram (b).)

If we reject backward causation and exclude sleight of hand and suchlike trickery, how are we to understand the ascription of extraordinary predictive powers to the seer, and how are we to explain his observed successes? One possibility is that the seer is really a hypnotist. He chooses, quite arbitrarily, sometimes to put $10,000 into the closed box and sometimes to put nothing. When he has put in $10,000, he hypnotically controls the player so that he takes the closed box only; when he has put in nothing he controls him so that he takes both boxes. But the player, like other victims of hypnotic suggestion, thinks he is choosing freely. If this is what is going on, the question 'What is it reasonable for the player to do?' is idle. If the player were free, then taking both boxes *would be* the better of the two courses that would then be open to him, whatever the seer had put into the closed box. But this counterfactual cannot serve the player as a guide to action. He will do whatever the hypnotist-seer has directed him to do. Admittedly, he will finish better off if the seer happens to have directed him to choose the closed box only. So if we slightly alter our supposition and let the player know that he is under hypnotic control, but still assume that he cannot break free from it, and knows this, he may reasonably *hope* that he has been directed to take the closed box only, and be pleased if he finds out that this is in fact so. But this does not make it reasonable for him to *choose* this strategy: on the present hypothesis, no such choice is open to him. (See Diagram (f).)

In fact, if we modify this hypothesis further, and allow that the seer's hypnotic control, though almost totally effective, just may be overcome if the player makes a supreme effort, it will be reasonable for the player to endeavour to break free if he feels himself being hypnotically forced towards taking the closed box only; for then there will be $10,000 safe in the closed box, and another $1,000 in the open box available for the taking, if only he can bring himself to take both. On the other hand, if he feels himself being hypnotically pushed into taking both boxes, he cannot do better than to go along with this and settle for the $1,000. This situation is represented in Diagram (i). Here we have the ironical but not really paradoxical result that it is reasonable at one and the same time to hope that one is being hypnotically directed towards taking the closed box only but to make every effort to free oneself from this direction and take the open box as well.

Another possibility is that the seer is really an extremely good psychologist, who can tell by observing his opponents how each of them will reason—whether he is the sort of person who will be impressed by the inductively established probability of greater gains for those who take the closed box only, or the sort of person who will rely on the principle of dominance, arguing that his choice cannot affect what is already in the closed box. On this hypothesis the player is free in a sense which compatibilists might find sufficient: he makes his own choice, subject to no external constraint, but how he will make it flows with strict regularity from a character which he already has and which can in principle be detected, so that his choice is, for someone with enough knowledge, securely predictable. (See Diagram (g).)

It seems to me that on this hypothesis, no less than on that of hypnosis, the question 'What is it reasonable for the player to do?' is idle. We can say which of the two courses of action that, so far as external constraints are concerned, are open to him would be the better. But no such statement can, on this hypothesis, function as a recommendation: it cannot supply a consideration that might affect the player's choice. Each player will rigidly follow his own characteristic style of reasoning and so do whatever the psychologist-seer has predicted, which may or may not be in accordance with our pseudo-recommendation. If our statement could still operate as a reason leading the player to act otherwise than he would have acted without it, the seer's prediction would, contrary to the present hypothesis, be insecure. We can state the counterfactual conditional recommendation that if the player were still free to choose, in a sense stronger than that mentioned above, then taking both boxes *would be* the reasonable thing to do. But if we go further and say that on this view of how the seer operates taking both boxes *is* the reasonable thing to do, we are displaying a curious sort of arbitrariness or inconsistency. As the contrast with the Israel–Egypt example showed, the case for taking both boxes rests essentially on the assumption that the seer has made his move, irrevocably, already, and there is no trickery about the closed box—no false bottom, for instance. The state that the closed box will be in when it is taken is fixed, independently of what the player decides. But if we genuinely recommend taking both boxes as the reasonable choice for the player to make, we are treating that choice as still open, at least to the extent that this recommendation could help to decide it. Yet on the present hypothesis the player's choice is just as fixed, recommendation or no recommendation, as the future state of the closed box. The latter is fixed by way of the persistence of material things and the absence of any interfering causes, while the former is fixed by the player's already established character. It would be arbitrary to rely on the causally determined fixity of the one and yet to ignore or propose to override the equally causally determined fixity of the other.

Compatibilists and soft determinists are likely to interpret the question 'What is it reasonable to do on this occasion?' as equivalent to 'What sort of action is in general most advantageous in situations of the sort to which this one is known to belong?' or to substitute the latter question for the former. In many kinds of situation the answers to these two questions will indeed coincide; but it is a peculiarity of that set up by Newcomb's paradox that it splits them apart. Admittedly we could say, in answer to the second question, that the best pattern of behaviour of all would be one which fooled the psychologist-seer, which gave him the impression that the player was a closed-box-only-taker while he was in reality a both-boxes man. But on the present hypothesis this is ruled out: the seer is too good a psychologist to be fooled. If so, the best possible pattern of behaviour is that of the closed-box-only-taker, whereas the answer to our first question is, as we have seen, that it would be better to take both boxes if the choice were still open, but that, since it is not open, no serious recommendation can be made.

In this discrepancy between the answers to the two questions, Newcomb's paradox is not, indeed, quite unique. It is characteristic of the many situations of the Prisoners' Dilemma type that it may be more advantageous for both (or all) of two (or more) people if they have certain fixed habits or principles of action other than that of each choosing what is the (dominantly) preferable course of action for him. But what is peculiar to the Newcomb situation is there is such a divergence, even for a single individual, between what *would be* the better choice (*if* one had a free choice) on each occasion and what is the better regular habit or principle of action.

This fact has a further consequence. We are still assuming that any particular player's choices, occasion by occasion, are settled by and predictable in the light of his already established character. But we can add the supposition that at some early stage in each player's life it is genuinely open to him to develop in himself one sort of character or another. We can then ask, about the choice that is open at this early stage, what is the best sort of character for someone to develop, on the admittedly implausible expectation that he will spend some important part of his later life playing this game against psychologist-seers of the proposed sort. The best character of all to develop, if it were possible, is one which would fool these psychologist-seers—the player should appear to be a closed-box-only-taker, and should perhaps start by intending to take the closed box only, but then change his mind at the last minute and take both boxes; if the game is to be played repeatedly, he must appear at the start of each new game to be a reformed character who, despite his former lapses, will take only the closed box *this* time, and yet he must in the end yield to temptation again and take both boxes after all. (See Diagram (e).) However, this possibility is excluded by our hypothesis that the seer is too good a psychologist to be taken in by such a systematic recidivist. The next best character, and therefore the one that the prospective player should choose to cultivate in his youth, is that exemplified by Bar-Hillel and Margalit, the intellectual make-up that is so impressed by inductively established probabilities, in defiance of the direction of causation, that one will really take only the closed box each time. It is no good having such a character as to make what would be, if one were free, the rational choice occasion by occasion, if one is up against a psychologist-seer who can detect and take advantage of one's rationality. Rationality as a character trait, defined as a strong tendency always to do what, if one were free to choose, would then be the more advantageous thing to do, is not necessarily the most advantageous character trait to have. (See Diagram (d).)

This suggests a further possibility. Suppose, contrary to what we have been assuming for some time now, that the player is in fact free to make either choice on each occasion, unrestricted by any established character, but that the psychologist-seer thinks that the player's actions are determined by his character, and suppose that the player knows that the seer believes this. Suppose, besides, that the game is to be played repeatedly by the same player against the same seer. Then it will be sensible for the player to take only the closed box every time, since on these assumptions this will ensure that the seer regularly puts $10,000 into it. These assumptions—in particular that of repeated playing of the game—reverse the direction of causation and enable the player's choices to determine the seer's moves, just as would happen if the seer were using clairvoyance or sleight of hand. (See Diagram (c).)

There are cases where it is both reasonable for the player to take both boxes and genuinely open to him either to do so or not. These occur when his choice neither is causally determined by a set of factors that does not include our recommendation nor determines what the contents of the closed box will be when it is taken, either through the seer's prediction (by backward causation or repeated playing) or through sleight of hand or similar trickery. In the extreme case the player's choice is causally disconnected from the whole prediction–contents sequence, as in Diagram (h). But this hypothesis deprives us of all possible systematic explanations of the seer's predictive successes. If we adopt it, we must say that it is a sheer coincidence that all the seer's predictions to date have been correct, and that we have therefore no reason to expect that he will have any more than a chance proportion of successes in the future. However, we can include under this heading the supposition that the seer has successfully used sleight of hand, etc., with all previous players, but that the present player is taking adequate precautions against this. In either case we can adopt a hypothesis represented by Diagram (h) only by dismissing the claim that the seer has predictive powers in relation the present game.

There is, however, a related, less extreme case, where the players have established characters which strongly influence their choices, but do not rigidly determine them: a player *can* break free from his own established character by a heroic effort of will, but this hardly ever happens. This hypothesis, combined with the supposition that the seer is a very good psychologist, entails that he will predict the players' choices correctly nearly all the time, and only a little extra luck is needed to account for his faultless record to date. This is represented in Diagram (j). Here, as in the analogous case of not totally effective hypnosis represented in (i), it is sensible for the player to take both boxes if he can bring himself to do so: he may well hope that his established character will tend very strongly to make him take the closed box only, but if it does he should make a supreme effort to break free from it and take both; but if his established character tends to push him into taking both boxes, he cannot do better than to go along with it.

We have, then, not a unitary solution of the paradox but a multiplicity of partial solutions, differentiated by the various possible explanations of the seer's predictive success, including the marginal explanation of (h) that it is sheer coincidence.

Running over this array of partial solutions, we note that wherever the seer's predictions are completely reliable but the player's choice is really open—not already fixed irrespective of any recommendation—it is reasonable for the player to take the closed box only ((a), (b), or (c)) or, as in (d), to develop the character of a closed-box-only-taker. This survey seems, therefore, to support Bar-Hillel and Margalit and those who agree with them. Yet every one of these cases for which the closed-box-only recommendation holds diverges in one way or another from what it is natural to take as the intended specifications. They involve some species of trickery, or the bringing about of the past, or repeated playing, or a choice not about what to take on a particular occasion but about what sort of character to cultivate in advance. These situations are all off-colour in some respect. But so, it must in fairness be pointed out, are all the situations which make reasonable the contrary choice. They are cases where the player does not really have an open choice ((f) and (g)), or where the seer does not really have predictive powers, and his past successes must be set aside as co-incidence ((e) and (h)), or at least where his predictions are not a hundred per cent reliable and his faultless past record owes something to luck ((i) and (j)).

The survey as a whole, therefore, shows that every possible case is somehow off-colour. There is no conceivable kind of situation that satisfies at once the whole of what it is natural to take as the intended specification of the paradox. We simply cannot reconcile the requirements that the player should have, in a single game, a genuinely open choice, that there should be no trickery or back-ward causation, and that the seer's complete predictive success should be inductively extrapolable. While the bare bones of the formulation of the paradox are conceivably satisfiable, what they are intended to suggest is not. The paradoxical situation, in its intended interpretation, is not merely of a kind that we are most unlikely to encounter; it is of a kind that simply cannot occur.

But what should the player do if he is confronted with the situation described but given no further information? Presumably he should try to estimate the likelihood, relative to the information available, that the situation is of kind (a) or (b) or (h) or (i) or (j)—these being the only ones in which the player has a real choice and just one game to play. Let us call these probabilities P_a, P_b, etc. If the situation is of kind (a) or (b), taking only the closed box gives the player $9,000 more than taking both boxes; if it is of kind (h) or (i) or (j), it gives him $1,000 less than the contrary choice. Assuming that their utility to the player is proportional to the sums of money—which one could certainly not assume if the key sum were a million dollars, but which is not too absurd if it is only $10,000—the expected relative utility of taking the closed box only is

$$((P_a + P_b) \times 9000) - ((P_h + P_i + P_j) \times 1000)$$

If this difference is positive, he should take the closed box only, if negative, both boxes. This reasoning is, of course, in line with orthodox decision theory, but the probabilities of which we have to take account are the likelihoods of the situation being of this or that causally characterized sort. It is worth noting that P_b is surely negligibly small and that the player can reduce P_a by taking appropriate precautions.

These considerations seem to me to wrap up the paradox and to confirm Cargile's conclusion quoted above. But some morals can, I believe, be drawn from the discussion. First, to deal satisfactorily with this problem we must take explicit account of the different possible lines and directions of causation—whether rigid or not. These are the features that are displayed in the diagrams and that distinguish the cases which call for different treatment and sometimes for different solutions. And it is just these features that are left out by a pure Humean analysis of causation in terms of regular succession and merely temporal order.

Secondly, a number of our cases suggest that there is some connection between the direction of causation and the contrast between what is, at any given time, fixed and what is then still open, undetermined. On most of the diagrams some item is represented by a small white circle, which signifies that this item is open up to the time when it occurs. Where we have such an item, no firm directed lines of causation lead to it, though broken, that is non-rigid, ones may, and firm lines may lead away from it. I am not claiming that these examples prove that, wherever there is directed causation, it occurs in some line that starts from an item which is open until it occurs. I have argued for this thesis in my *Cement of the Universe*;[4] all I am saying now is that there seems to be some connection between causal asymmetry and the contrast between openness and fixity.

But, thirdly, to leave room for genuine recommendations, choices need not be open in the sense of being causally undetermined. All that is needed to differentiate (i) from (f) and (j) from (g) is that there should be some chance of our recommendation itself helping to decide what the player does. A subtle compatibilism or soft determinism which requires for freedom that an agent should be thus open, at least to some extent, to rational persuasion, not firmly tied to a certain course of action by hypnosis or established character irrespectively of any reasons for doing otherwise that may be put before him, could still find room for our cases (i) and (j), and might well confine not only the term 'free' but also some of its moral associates to actions where the agent was thus rationally persuadable.

4 Chapter 7, 'The Direction of Causation'.

ADDENDUM

The editors of the *Journal* have drawn my attention to the article by Allan Gibbard and William L. Harper, 'Counterfactuals and Two Kinds of Expected Utility', in *Northwestern Studies in Management*, Discussion Paper No. 194 [1975]. This article draws a clear distinction between two possible definitions of the expected utility of an act, one of which—u (A)—measures the utility that the performing of the act A is likely to produce, while the other—v (A)—measures the welcomeness of the news that one will perform the act. These authors rightly consider v-maximization an irrational principle of action. It relies on probabilistic (as opposed to specifically causal) relations, such as I have dismissed when discussing Bar-Hillel and Margalit. But they point out that standard works on decision theory often use this misleading definition of expected utility as v (A). In ordinary cases this will yield the same value as the correct definition, but it is a merit of the Newcomb situation (and of some related examples which these authors construct) that it destroys this coincidence, and should then force us to state decision theory in terms of the correct measure of expected utility, u (A).

These authors have not noted, however, that there are odd causal hypotheses (my cases (a) and (b)) which make it rational to take the closed box only, not to maximize v (A), the welcomeness of the news that one will so act, but to maximize u (A), the genuine expected utility of one's action.

XII

A DEFENCE OF INDUCTION

I INTRODUCTORY SURVEY

To many people, justifying induction seems rather like squaring the circle. It has so often been shown to be impossible that anyone who attempts it risks the suspicion of being mildly insane. Yet it seems evident that we do reason inductively, we accept and believe, perhaps with some reservations and caution, the conclusions of that reasoning, and we rely on them in practice. It would be nice if we could show that it is in some sense rational or reasonable to do so, that this is not merely an instinct that we cannot help following or a convention that we just happen to have adopted.

Sir Karl Popper's many forceful objections to what he calls inductivism do not dissolve this problem. We can concede that science is not much concerned with simple inductive generalization or extrapolation from the observed to the unobserved; that science does not in general proceed by mere fact-collecting—that we have to ask questions, frame hypotheses, put nature to the test; that there are no methods guaranteed to advance science significantly; and that good scientists do not, at the price of lack of content, prefer hypotheses that are highly probable, or merely try to confirm their hypotheses or to save them in the face of contrary evidence, but rather follow procedures that expose their hypotheses to a high risk of falsification. Again, we can concede that we should not aim at certainty, or even, perhaps, at established truth; and perhaps that we cannot find starting points or data which are themselves certain partly because they are theory-free. But none of these concessions affects the fact that we accept both common-sense and scientific generalizations about the causal behaviour of material things and rely upon them in practice. We do not accept them merely as worthy subjects for further testing: we act on the assumption that well tested generalizations are either true or near enough to being true to have true entailments for applications fairly similar

Reprinted from *Perception and Identity: Essays Presented to A.J. Ayer with his Replies to them*, edited by G.F. Macdonald (The Macmillan Press, 1979).

to those for which they have been tested. It is the rationality of such beliefs, taken tentatively, and of the connected practical policies that is to be defended. We are not seeking a proof that bread will always nourish us. Of course we may become allergic to it, or if it is made from ergot-infected grain it may poison us; what we want is merely to justify a presumption that bread will not gratuitously start to poison us, without some cause that could in principle be discovered.

But the problem is wider than that of such causal generalization or of the equivalent ascription of dispositional properties to things. Any grounds that Hume or anyone else has for denying the rationality of belief in empirical generalizations, particularly causal laws and quasi-causal statistical laws, apply equally to the belief that material objects will persist more or less as they are if not interfered with. The belief equally involves extrapolation beyond what either has been observed or can be validly deduced from observations. The inductive question is not merely whether bread will continue to nourish us, but also whether pieces of bread will continue, even for the next minute, to be bread. Or, if we take our ordinary terms for material objects to entail such persistence for a time if not interfered with, the question will be whether we are ever justified in applying these terms. Is this really bread, or merely something superficially like bread but too ephemeral to deserve that description? Also, the belief in an objective world goes along with the belief in such persistences and regularities of behaviour: if the latter belief is not rationally justifiable, neither is the former. Selective scepticism about induction, conjoined with unquestioning acceptance of the objective and continuous and extrapolable existence of material things, would be arbitrary. But of course this only widens the problem; it does not resolve it.

We should distinguish between all such extrapolations from observed to unobserved things or time-slices of things or processes or sequences of events—in particular from the past to the future— and inferences from what is more directly observed to a deeper explanation. The latter are of far more interest to science, the former being normally taken for granted. Of course, the two cannot in practice be separated. Even with the former there is the question of what to generalize or project, what to take as a causal or quasi-causal law; while deeper explanations are ordinarily extrapolated without hesitation. Also, both raise the inductive problem. We may reasonably be more tentative about explanatory theories than about causal generalizations connecting readily observed features, more willing to admit that they are likely in the end to be abandoned and replaced by better ones; but such theories are at least provisionally accepted and relied upon in practice, and there is a real question whether, and if so why, this is rational. Also, I believe that ultimately similar answers can be given to both halves of the inductive problem. Nevertheless, the two halves can be distinguished: it would be one thing to justify the generalizing, the especially temporal extrapolation, another to justify the preference for this or that deeper explanation. Nor would the latter carry the former with it, or make the former unnecessary. However good and reliable an explanation we had of why something had worked as it had to date, there would still be a question whether and why we could expect it to go on so working and could believe that that explanation would still hold. In what follows I shall concentrate on the first half of the problem, that of justifying generalization or extrapolation.

This is of course Hume's problem. But Sir Alfred Ayer, at several places in *Probability and Evidence*, reports and endorses Hume's argument that our belief in law-like connections between events can never be rationally justified, that we can never have good reason to accept an empirical generalization, and he criticizes attempts, such as that of Harrod, to answer Hume, to solve the problem of induction by justifying at least some projective procedures. However, he refuses to see this as a reason for scepticism.[1] And elsewhere, in what is admittedly an *argumentum ad hominem* against Popper, he argues that there would be little point in testing hypotheses if they gained no credit from passing the test.[2] Like many others, Ayer is reluctant to give up the belief that inductive reasoning is reasonable, and yet he neither can find, nor will allow, any escape from Hume's proof that it is not. I shall try to show, however, that Hume's argument and some related ones are not as conclusive as they seem, so that a rational defence of inductive

[1] A.J.Ayer, *Probability and Evidence* (London, 1972), esp. pp. 3-6, 63, 88, and 91-110.

[2] In *The Philosophy of Karl Popper*, edited by P.A. Schilpp (La Salle, Illinois, 1974), p. 686.

reasoning is not ruled out *a priori*; and then I shall offer the outline of such a defence.

2   CRITICISM OF SCEPTICAL ARGUMENTS

Hume argues that, if it were reason that guided our causal thinking, when we go from observed past sequences to unobserved future ones, it would be relying on the principle that 'the course of nature continues always uniformly the same'. If this principle itself is to be proved, it must be either by 'demonstrative arguments' or by 'probable reasonings'. But the former is impossible and the latter would be circular, because probability always rests on causal relations, and therefore on the very presumption of uniformity which we are trying to establish.[3] These alternatives, 'demonstration' and 'probability', mean for Hume not valid deduction and non-deductive support, but, rather, valid deduction from *a priori*, analytic truths and valid deduction from synthetic, empirical truths. Only on the assumption that the second alternative requires deductive validity is Hume justified in saying that the uniformity principle itself is needed here. For, suppose that we allow that there is such a thing as relational epistemic probability—that is, the logical-relation kind of probability proposed by Keynes and Carnap, or what is often misleadingly called subjective probability. Then, for all that Hume has said it might be that an observed constant conjunction of *A*s with *B*s somehow *probabilified* that this new *A* would be conjoined with a *B*, or that in some such way evidence non-deductively supported an inductive conclusion that went beyond it. Given this approach, there would be no need to rely on the principle of uniformity, and hence no vicious circularity. Hume's dilemma as he intended it does not exclude this possibility; it does not even consider it. Hume appears to consider and reject this possibility only if his 'probability' is misinterpreted as referring to a conceivable probabilification and his 'demonstration' correspondingly extended to cover all deductive arguments. But with this misinterpretation Hume's claim that 'probability' would have to appeal, circularly, to the uniformity principle would be false.

In reporting Hume's argument, Ayer considers the possibility

---

[3] D. Hume, *A Treatise of Human Nature*, Book I, Part III, Section vi. My interpretation follows that of D.C. Stove in *Probability and Hume's Inductive Scepticism* (Oxford, 1973), which criticizes scepticism about induction on much the same grounds as I rely on in this part of the paper.

that 'we can at least show [the principle of uniformity] to be probable'. But he says that any judgement of probability must have some foundation, which 'can lie only in our past experience. The only ground we can have for saying that it is even probable that the course of nature continues uniformly the same is that we have hitherto found this to be the case. But then we are arguing in a circle....' He adds that

the same objection would apply to any attempt to by-pass the general principle of uniformity of nature and argue that inferences from one matter of fact to another, although admittedly not demonstrative, can nevertheless be shown to be probable. Again, the judgement of probability must have some foundation. But this foundation can lie only in our past experience.[4]

and then the circularity breaks out again.

The first part of this *resembles* Hume's argument; the second part (as he has conceded privately) is Ayer's own extension, not a paraphrase of anything in Hume. But both parts are plainly intended by Ayer to exclude any showing of induction to be 'probable' in some modern sense, not in the queer sense that Hume, as he tells us, took over from Locke and found 'ridiculous' even when he wrote Section xi of Book I, Part III, of the *Treatise of Human Nature*. But, if it is intended to exclude epistemic probabilification, the essential premiss, that probability must have a foundation which can lie only in our past experience, does not hold. A frequency or a propensity, say, would need to be empirically established, but not a logical relation of non-deductive support. Ayer's argument requires that anything like a logical relation of probabilification, any principles of non-deductive support that were acceptable *a priori*, should be excluded from the start.

Ayer could reply that he has a separate argument against the logical relation theory of probability. Indeed, in *Probability and Evidence* he refers to this argument, first published fifteen years earlier, and says that he has not yet seen any effective rejoinder to it. However, I think that effective rejoinders have since been published.[5] The argument is essentially that the logical relation theory

[4] *Probability and Evidence*, p. 5.

[5] *Op. cit.*, p. 57, referring to A.J. Ayer, 'The Concept of Probability as a Logical Relation', in *Observation and Interpretation*, edited by Stephan Körner (New York, 1957); repr. in A.J. Ayer, *The Concept of a Person and Other Essays* (London, 1963). For rejoinders, see R.G. Swinburne, *An Introduction to Confirmation Theory* (London, 1973), pp. 27–8; and J.L. Mackie, *Truth, Probability, and Paradox* (Oxford, 1973), pp. 196–202.

cannot explain why we should prefer one to another of the different degrees of probabilification that would, on this theory, relate different pieces of evidence to the same conclusion, all holding as logical truths. The rejoinder turns upon the distinction between a simple epistemic probability and a relational one. We prefer one logical relation to another only in that it is the probabilification by all the relevant evidence that someone has that determines the simple epistemic probability for him, the degree of belief that it is rational for him to give to the conclusion. Ayer also asks why it is sensible, sometimes, to look for more evidence rather than to be content with the 'logical' degree of support by the evidence you already have. The answer is that in general if you do so you are more likely to be right in accepting or rejecting the conclusion, where this 'likely' represents another epistemic probability. This argument of Ayer's, like a related one of Popper's,[6] shows only that the logical relation theory does not cover the ground: we have to recognize probabilities, even epistemic ones, which are not purely relational, and of course we also have to recognize various non-epistemic items, such as frequencies and perhaps propensities, that can also be called probabilities. But none of this has any tendency to prove that there cannot be such logical or quasi-logical relations, which might be acceptable *a priori*, of non-deductive support. Yet it is such a proof that would be needed to fill the holes in the argument that Ayer has constructed by reinterpreting and extending Hume's dilemma.

Yet another argument can be developed from Hume's by reinterpretation. If we use 'induction' in a very broad sense, to cover non-deductive reasoning as a whole, and ask whether it can be rationally defended, it seems clear that induction cannot be justified deductively; it cannot without circularity be justified inductively; therefore it cannot be justified at all.

The cogency of any dilemma depends on the exhaustiveness of the alternatives. Here the alternative methods of justification are made exhaustive simply by defining 'inductively' so that it covers all rational procedures other than deduction. But then all that the argument shows is that this body of non-deductive procedures cannot be justified as a whole. Any justification must start somewhere, with something other than deduction. There is no way of rationally overcoming the scepticism or curing the doubts of someone who is

[6] Karl Popper, *The Logic of Scientific Discovery* (London, 1972), pp. 407–9.

systematically suspicious of all reasoning that is not deductively valid.

But this conclusion leaves open the possibility of justifying some procedures that are inductive in this very broad sense in terms of others. In particular, we may take 'induction' in a narrower but still fairly broad sense as including the two things that we distinguished earlier: generalization or extrapolation, and inference to a deeper explanation. And then there are other kinds of reasoning which are neither deductive nor inductive in this sense. For example, there is that which yields judgements of epistemic probability about games of chance. I have a bag which I know to contain nine black balls and one white one, all equal in size, weight, and so on. The balls have been stirred around, and I now put my hand into the bag and take hold of one ball. I have no way of telling what colour it is, and no reason to expect one rather than another of the ten balls to have come to hand. In this mixed state of knowledge and ignorance I say that the ball I have is probably black: my information and lack of information together probabilify the judgement 'This ball is black', and, if something of importance turned upon my stating the colour correctly, the practically reasonable thing to say would be that it was black. And, if there had been ninety-nine, rather than nine, black balls to one white one, both the theoretical and the practical conclusion would have been more strongly supported. This kind of reasoning seems cogent. (Most people admit that, in the ninety-nine-to-one case, if their lives depended on a correct answer, they would say that the ball was black.) Yet it is not deductive. Nor is it inductive in the sense just defined. It makes no extrapolation from observed to unobserved cases, and no inference to a deeper explanation. You need never have played a game of this sort before and you need no theory about it. There is no appeal to Hume's uniformity principle or to any specifically causal judgements. (No doubt in setting up the example I have assumed that the balls have not changed colour, that the black ones have not all shrunk, and so on, since they were examined; but this extrapolation forms no part of the reasoning the example is intended to illustrate: from the premiss that there are now so many similar black and white balls in the bag and I have hold of one of them, along with the lack of any further relevant information, to a conclusion about the colour of this ball.) Now, it is at least conceivable that we should be able to justify what was defined above as inductive reasoning by showing it to be supported by some kind of application of the probabilistic reasoning illustrated here.

We have to take account, then, of three proposed dilemmas which seem to show that induction cannot be rationally defended. The first is Hume's own. Induction rests on the uniformity principle; this cannot be established by deduction from *a priori* truths; to deduce it from empirical truths we should need the principle itself as a premiss; so this principle, and hence the inductions which rest on it, cannot be (deductively) justified at all. The second is Ayer's. Induction cannot be conclusively justified; to show it to be probable, we should need a judgement of probability resting on past experience, and therefore an induction from that past experience to the present application, and this would be circular; therefore induction cannot be rationally supported at all. The third equates induction with non-deductive reasoning as a whole. Induction so defined cannot be deductively justified; it cannot without vicious circularity be inductively justified; therefore it cannot be rationally supported at all. But there is a suggestion that escapes all three dilemmas: the suggestion that induction in a sense which covers generalization or extrapolation (especially temporal) and inference to deeper explanations may be rationally justified by showing that in each such inference the conclusion is probabilified by the premisses or evidence in accordance with the apparently cogent sort of reasoning illustrated by the example of balls in a bag. This suggestion escapes Hume's dilemma because it does not claim that the conclusion is reached by a sound deductive argument. It escapes Ayer's, because Ayer's begs the question against any such probabilification by assuming that any judgement of probability must rest on past experience. And it escapes the third because what this rules out is a justification, from no starting point, of non-deductive reasoning as a whole; it does not exclude the possibility of defending one variety of non-deductive reasoning by the application of principles on which we rely in non-deductive reasoning of another sort.

However, this proposal still seems to be threatened by Goodman's 'new riddle of induction'.[7] The suggested probabilification is of a logical or quasi-logical sort. It is not an empirical probability,

---

[7] Nelson Goodman, *Fact, Fiction and Forecast* (Cambridge, Mass., 1955), Chapters 3 and 4.

such as a frequency or a propensity, but is supposed to rest on purely formal relations between the premises and the conclusion to which they are alleged to give non-deductive support. In order to be acceptable *a priori*, it must have such a formal basis. But Goodman's use of such predicates as 'grue' shows that the temporal extrapolations we make cannot even be described in any purely syntactical way, since rival, unwanted, extrapolations are syntactically on exactly the same footing. It seems to tell not merely against the traditional aim of justifying induction, but even against the more modest aim of describing systematically what we count as confirmation or as respectable inductive reasoning. 'Formal', however, may be more exacting than 'syntactical'. We can stick to the common-sense view that things which are green (especially if they are of the same shade of green) at different times resemble one another in a way that things called grue by Goodman's definition at different times may not. And then it is plausible to suppose that any formal principles of probabilification there may be will take account of the presence or absence of real resemblances rather than the merely syntactical forms which 'grue' can satisfy as well as 'green'. The new riddle, therefore, does not undermine our proposal.*

3 OUTLINE OF A POSITIVE JUSTIFICATION

So far I have been defending the mere possibility of a justification of induction, replying to various arguments which seem to rule this out completely. To go further and actually sketch such a justification we must formulate some principles of probabilification. In the balls-in-a-bag example, we were relying on some version of the principle of indifference or insufficient reason—say, that an incomplete body of information (a mixture of knowledge and ignorance) equally probabilifies each of a set of exclusive possibilities to which that incomplete information is similarly related. This principle has, of course, often been criticized. Yet (as I have argued elsewhere) it is implicit in every transition from a frequency or a propensity, no less than from a classical set of alternatives, to a simple epistemic probability about a particular case.[8] Ayer argues, I think correctly,

---

*Here (in his own copy of *Perception and Identity*) Mackie has added the note: 'N.B. Goodman's pseudo-problem results from over-attention to language.'—Edd.

[8] Mackie, *Truth, Probability, and Paradox*, pp. 161-2 and 197-204.

that Harrod in effect uses this principle, though he explicitly rejects it; and so does Ayer himself.[9] Much of the criticism it has incurred applies not to the principle itself as determining epistemic probabilities, but to plainly fallacious attempts to use it to determine frequencies or propensities. Another criticism is that it yields contradictory results where there is more than one plausible way of dividing a range of possibilities into exclusive alternatives. For example, when we ask what is the probability that a chord of a circle will be shorter than the side of the inscribed equilateral triangle, we can get the rival answers $\frac{1}{2}$, $\frac{1}{3}$ and $\frac{3}{4}$ by classifying possible chords in different ways; we seem unable to reach a determinate conclusion unless we think of the chords as being generated by some particular randomizing mechanism which would have equal propensities to generate chords along some one scale.[10] Now, if we could apply the principle of indifference only where there was some such range of propensities, the principle would indeed be useless for our purpose, since it will always be an inductive conclusion that something has such-and-such generative propensities. But this criticism shows only that, where a range of possibilities does not divide unambiguously into similar alternatives, we must have recourse to the propensities of a generative mechanism; where the division is unambiguous, we can apply the principle directly.

However, whereas this principle immediately applies only to problems in direct probability, it is pretty clear that any justification of induction along the lines suggested will involve some inverse probability argument. We want to argue that, because some result which the falsity of a certain hypothesis would render improbable has been observed, it is now likely that that hypothesis is true. But, when we try to formulate the principle involved in such an argument, we naturally have recourse to Bayes's theorem, and this gives us a final probability for the hypothesis only as a product of its initial probability. We have

$$P(h,\ b\ \&\ e) = \frac{P(e,\ b\ \&\ h) \times P(h,b)}{P\ (e,b)}$$

where b is background knowledge, h is the hypothesis in question, and e the observed evidence. Adding e to b raises the probability

    [9] Ayer, *Probability and Evidence*, pp. 107 (Harrod) and 62–3 (Ayer's own use of an argument in which there is an implicit appeal to the principle).

    [10] J.M. Keynes, *A Treatise on Probability* (London, 1921), pp. 47–8.

of *h* in the same proportion as adding *h* to *b* raises the probability of *e*. I have argued elsewhere that this theorem holds for epistemic probabilities, that it tells us what degree of belief it is reasonable to give to *h* when what we know is the conjunction of *b* and *e*, on the assumption that the probabilities on the right-hand side also represent degrees of belief that are reasonable for us.[11] However, this formula leaves us with several problems. How are we to establish initial or antecedent probabilities—that is, probabilifications of *h* and *e* by *b*? If the initial probability of *h* either is or may be very low, even strongly favourable evidence—an *e* the probability of which is very markedly increased by adding *h* to *b*—may leave the final probability of *h* too low for this hypothesis to be reasonably accepted. And, if the initial probability of an unrestricted generalization is always zero, its final probability will also remain zero, no matter how strong the evidence in its favour. We shall have to see to what extent these difficulties can be overcome.

It is a striking fact that we do not generalize with equal confidence all observed conjunctions of features and events. It is primarily causal sequences that we are prepared to generalize, and those analogous ones that we can call causal in an extended sense, such as the persistence, more or less unchanged, of material objects and the growth processes and metabolic processes of animals and plants. Where we do generalize the coexistence of features not related as cause and effect, as in such stock examples as that all birds of the shape, size and so on that make them count as ravens are black, we suppose that there are underlying causal relations—that the raven shape and the black colour stem alike first from a certain genetic make-up, and more remotely from connected processes of natural selection, that blackness was somehow advantageous for birds with the life-style for which the raven features fitted them. A Humean might say that it is a trivial tautology that it is causal sequences and causally based coexistences that we are prepared to generalize, that it is just the fact that we are prepared to generalize certain sequences that makes them count as causal. But their causal or quasi-causal character is linked with other matters. There are the manipulative experiments that suggest various conditional statements: if I do this, that will happen; if I had not done that, this would not have happened; if I put this cup here, there will be a cup here a moment later; if I smash this cup, there will not be a

[11] Mackie, *Truth, Probability, and Paradox*, pp. 214-23.

cup here a moment later; and so on. Also, a causal process typically consists of a change in one thing following closely upon contact of another thing with it, or of a chain built up from such episodes, while our quasi-causal processes consist of successive states of the same substance, either just like one another or varying only gradually. Even where a cause and its effect are superficially separate and unlike one another, there is commonly some underlying causal mechanism the discovery of which reveals persistences and continuities of features from which the superficial discontinuities result. Causation is a matter of one time-slice of a thing or process producing the next—or, rather, the latter is the result of 'producing' the former in something like the sense in which a line is 'produced' in geometry: clusters of features project themselves into the future. In Hume's terms, the assumption on which our inductive extrapolations and generalizations proceed is not merely that unobserved instances resemble observed ones, but that the *course* of nature— that is, the time-flow of events—continues uniformly the same. Or, if we speak of instances, we must ask, 'Instances of what?', and the answer will be 'Instances of laws of working' as I have tried to distinguish these elsewhere, or of what Mill tried to pick out by contrasting uniformities of succession with uniformities of coexistence.[12]

This suggests that Hume and Mill were not so wrong after all, that in the order of justification the primary induction is that which supports some principle of the uniformity of nature with respect to its ways of operating through time, and that particular generalizations and extrapolations are supported by the conjunction of this principle with specific experiments and observations. But the content of this principle can be more fully brought out. It says, first, that individual things and goings-on tend to persist as they have been; secondly, that a confluence of two (or more) goings-on tends to produce goings-on which partly continue each of the original ones; and, thirdly, that most detectable events flow in this sort of way from detectable neighbouring antecedents and likewise lead to detectable neighbouring sequels to which they are related by at least approximate generalizations. This third part includes something like the traditional formulation 'Every event has a cause', but it adds to it something like 'Every event has an effect'. It

---

[12] See J.L. Mackie, *The Cement of the Universe* (Oxford, 1974), pp. 208-28; J.S. Mill, *A System of Logic*, Book III, Chapter V, Section ix and Chapter XXII.

strengthens these by requiring that the antecedents and sequels should be neighbouring and detectable, but it also restricts the subject to detectable events and weakens the claims from 'Every' to 'Most'.

I have shown elsewhere how Mill's eliminative methods of induction can be tightened up and made more accurate by exhibiting each of their variants as combining a standard pattern of observations with an assumption which says that a certain kind of occurrence is related to some necessary and sufficient condition drawn from or built up out of a restricted range of possibly relevant factors.[13] We can apply this result here with modifications. The restricted range of factors, in any particular case, will be supplied by the qualifications 'neighbouring' and 'detectable' The principle that most detectable events fit into a certain pattern will make it epistemically probable that events of a certain specific sort do so, if we have no special reason to suppose that they do not: this is just a rough direct probability argument. The fact that our principle speaks only of at least approximate generalizations adds a further respect in which the argument along the lines of an eliminative method has to be reduced from a deductively valid one to a probabilistic one. On the other hand, our principle is so framed as to allow the identification of (partial) effects as well as that of (partial) causes: we can simply invert the observation pattern for the method of difference, for example, as between antecedents and sequels, and by an exactly similar argument reach an (incomplete) generalization about the effects to which a certain phenomenon leads. Also, the first and second parts of our principle will aid the process of elimination, telling by direct probability arguments against the causal character of sequences where no such continuities can be found. Altogether, then, it is plain that if we had such a principle we could, by conjoining it with suitable observations, probabilify just those sorts of causal and quasi-causal generalizations that we ordinarily accept and rely upon in practice—elliptical generalizations, with implied clauses about other things being equal, taken to hold only in certain rather vaguely specified fields or background conditions, and so on. But they would be generalizations, going beyond the observations on which they were based, and they would be epistemically probable—that is, supported in some degree by the mixture of knowledge and ignorance that we have, in accordance

[13] Mackie, *The Cement of the Universe*, pp. 297-321.

with the principles of epistemic probability illustrated by our balls-in-a-bag example. This support would make it reasonable for us to accept them provisionally and to rely on them, with something less than complete confidence, in practice.

The crucial question, then, is whether we can defend, by an inverse probability argument, the primary induction that supports the proposed principle of uniformity. Surely we can. We might consider first the simple pair of alternative metaphysical hypotheses, that there is a world which conforms throughout to our principle, and that the world as a whole is purely random, a fortuitous concourse not indeed of anything as solid and persistent and moderately well behaved as Epicurean atoms, but (to borrow a phrase from Ayer) of 'variations of scenery in a four-dimensional spatio-temporal continuum'.[14] Now, we have countless observations that conform to and illustrate our principle, the general pattern of which, therefore, is expectable on our first alternative hypothesis but improbable in the extreme on the second. If we had just these alternatives to choose between, it would be reasonable to prefer the former in the light of our observations, unless it was antecedently almost infinitely less probable than the second. As far as I can see, the only line of thought that would suggest that the hypothesis of uniformity is almost infinitely less probable than that of randomness is one which rests on what is in this context the question-begging assumption that things are really totally random, and that order could be achieved only by a fantastically improbable piece of luck. Since this assumption is question-begging, I see no good reason for assigning so low an initial probability to the uniformity hypothesis that the observations which tell so massively in its favour are unable to make it more acceptable than its rival.

However, it may be objected that to offer only these alternatives so oversimplifies the issue as to introduce fallacy. It is true that we could split our principle into its three parts, and consider various more modest hypotheses saying that the world conforms to some of these parts but not to them all. But it is obvious that for each part of our principle there is any amount of observed evidence which illustrates it, and which would be left unexplained by, and extremely improbable in relation to, any hypothesis which omitted that part. So there is no need to work tediously through such complications as these.

[14] Ayer, *Probability and Evidence*, pp. 10–11.

A complication which deserves to be taken more seriously is one introducing, as rivals to our alternatives of uniformity throughout the world and pure randomness, hypotheses of extensive but still limited order—that uniformity holds only over some range that is limited spatially or temporally or both, and then terminates or gradually fades out. But we can cope with these. First let us consider the indefinitely large set of hypotheses all of which assign the same spatio-temporal extent to uniformity, but locate it differently—for example, that uniformity holds for this, that and the other stretch of time, where each stretch lasts a million years. It seems a legitimate application of the principle of indifference to assign equal antecedent epistemic probabilities to the various hypotheses of this set. Some of them, however, will have been ruled out by the already-observed spread of uniformity. Suppose that this covers, say, 100,000 years. Then, of the hypotheses not so ruled out, if the extent which is common to the hypotheses of the set (here a million years) is considerably greater than the observed spread of uniformity, relatively few will say that uniformity will terminate either at once or very soon—few of the surviving hypotheses of this set will locate the cut-off of uniformity either at or near the edge of its observed spread. So, taking the not-yet-ruled-out hypotheses of the set as equally probable, we can conclude that, even if uniformity lasts only for this limited extent, it is not likely to end very soon. But, secondly, let us consider the set of sets of such hypotheses, comparing all million-year hypotheses with all 110,000-year ones, and so on. Clearly, the shorter the extent characteristic of each set of hypotheses, the smaller the proportion of the hypotheses of that set that will cover the observed spread of uniformity: this proportion falls dramatically when the characteristic extent is little greater than the observed spread. Consequently, by an inverse probability argument the observation of, say, a 100,000-year spread of uniformity raises the probability that *some* million-year hypothesis holds much more than it raises the probability that some 110,000-year one holds, and so on. The observation of a certain spread of uniformity raises the probability that the extent of uniformity is considerably greater than that spread much more than it raises the probability that that extent is equal to or only a little greater than that spread. Now, we cannot, perhaps, use the principle of indifference to assign equal antecedent epistemic probabilities to the various hypotheses as to the extent of uniformity—100,000 years, 110,000, a million, and so on—but we can appeal to a similar but weaker principle of tolerance to justify our not giving a zero antecedent probability to all hypotheses assigning more than a certain extent to uniformity.[15] So long as the greater-extent hypotheses are not ruled out by such an unfair initial assignment, they can come out more probable in the end, their probability being raised more by the observation of some considerable spread of uniformity. Assuming that the observed spread is 100,000 years, it is more likely that uniformity holds for some extent of more than 110,000 than that it holds for some extent less than this. And, as we have seen, once we have confirmed such a greater-extent hypothesis, we can go on by a direct probability argument to infer that uniformity is not likely to end very soon. We can still reach such a modest but mildly reassuring conclusion even if we bring into consideration hypotheses of extensive but limited order.

It may be objected that this argument must be fallacious, because it would prove too much. For it seems to show the following: even if there were a purely random distribution of uniformity, so that there was an even chance of its occurring or not occurring in any small region, and such persistences of uniformity as did occur were the product of pure chance, it would still be more probable than not that uniformity would continue significantly beyond the region over which it has been observed. But of course this cannot be right: the conclusion would contradict the assumption. However, the argument is not committed to generating this absurdity. The assumption of a purely random distribution would entail that greater-extent hypotheses were initially much less probable than smaller-extent ones: this assumption is equivalent to an assignment of initial probabilities so extreme, so adverse to greater-extent hypotheses, that the raising of probabilities by the inverse argument could not outweigh it. This is similar to the proposal which Carnap considers, but rejects, to give equal initial probabilities to all state descriptions. If we start with such an assumption, then indeed no amount of inductive evidence will enable us to advance. We shall in effect have ruled out from the start any possibility of inductive support. But it is enough to see that this is an extreme assumption; it is arbitrary to lay it down dogmatically *a priori* that the distribution of uniformity must be purely random. If, instead, we allow

[15] Cf. Mackie, *Truth, Probability, and Paradox*, pp. 229-30.

from the start that there is some better-than-zero probability of some not purely random pattern—as opposed to purely local appearances of order which really result from chance—then the inverse argument can work in the modest but reassuring way outlined above.

We can go thus far even if we treat the problem as one of generalization or extrapolation alone, of determining the likely extent of a certain kind of uniformity among what are in themselves no more than variations of scenery in a four-dimensional continuum. But we can also take our principle as indicating a deeper explanation: that the hypothesis that what is really there is not adequately captured by this talk of four-dimensional scenery, and that our ordinary way of thinking in terms of persisting things, and of what there is now producing what there will be, which makes the time dimension significantly different from any purely spatial one, approximates to some metaphysical truth.[16] On the four-dimensional scenery view, such uniformity as we have observed was antecedently highly improbable. As I have said elsewhere, it is remarkable that nearly all the four-dimensional worms we have encountered are temporal ones, occupying possibly causal lines, and hardly any are (purely) spatial ones, occupying what could be lines of simultaneity. On the hypothesis that all that is really there is four-dimensional scenery, the observed distribution of four-dimensional worms is a surprising coincidence; but on the rival hypothesis, which is hard to formulate but the point of which is that it finds some metaphysical truth in the thought of things as persisting through time and processes as projecting themselves in time, the general pattern of what we have observed is expectable. So, unless the latter hypothesis is antecedently far more improbable than the former, it will have been made the more probable by what we have observed. I can see no reason for saying that the latter hypothesis is antecedently less probable. An objection that might be raised is a phenomenalistic attack on its meaningfulness or intelligibility as an alternative to the four-dimensional scenery view; but I have argued elsewhere against the theory of meaning on which such an objection would have to rest.[17] The inference to the suggested metaphysical truth as a deeper explanation is, then, a good inverse probability argument, and this metaphysical truth, whatever its

[16] Cf. Mackie, *The Cement of the Universe*, pp. 225-8.
[17] J. L. Mackie, *Problems from Locke* (Oxford, 1975), pp. 56-60.

precise formulation should be, would make it more reasonable to accept the principle of uniformity which we need for the support of specific extrapolations and generalizations. It clearly entails the first and second parts of that principle. It does not entail the third part, and yet it suggests it in a way that I cannot make precise. If what was there at one time simply and exactly persisted into the succeeding time, there would be exact generalizations relating all detectable items to detectable neighbouring antecedents and sequels. I should like to have a weakened variant of this thesis, that if there is some persistence and some projecting of processes it is likely that these will be in accordance with at least approximate generalizations; but I do not see clearly how to establish this. Even without this thesis, however, the inverse probability argument for our suggested metaphysical truth gives some further support to the extrapolation of uniformity, which in any case can be defended in a modest form by an inverse probability argument of its own. And, once we have even a modest form of our uniformity principle, claiming only that such uniformity is likely to hold for some considerable time to come or generally over a spatio-temporal range significantly greater than that in which it has been so far observed to hold, we have the necessary assumption on which observations in the style of the eliminative methods will support similarly modest inductive generalizations.

That is, we can do the trick. The rational defence of inductive extrapolation is not only left open as a mere possibility by the rebuttal of the sceptical arguments which purport to show it to be impossible: we can also see the main lines of an argument by which it can be carried through. The materials used in this argument are all extremely familiar—the support of causal generalizations by eliminative induction; a principle of the uniformity of nature; inverse probability; and the principle of indifference—but I have defended their use against the stock objections. My argument resembles Harrod's in its emphasis on the probability of limited extrapolations, but the method of supporting them is different, making explicit use of the principle of indifference, which Harrod tries to do without—though, as Ayer argues, it is implicit in his procedure after all. My argument resembles Mill's in its two-stage procedure, eliminative methods supporting specific causal generalizations and a separate argument in favour of the causal principle which they have to assume; but, whereas Mill treats this separate argument as a simple induction,[18] I rely here on inverse probability. My central idea is that we must use inverse probability somewhere to give epistemic probabilistic support to an ampliative or extrapolating induction, and that we must rely on the principle of indifference (or some weakened variant of it, such as my principle of tolerance) to supply the antecedent or initial probabilities on the right-hand side of Bayes's theorem, but that these moves can be made more legitimately in the case for an appropriate version of the uniformity principle than in attempts to vindicate specific inductions, starting from cold. In the order of justification, therefore, the primary induction is that which supports a certain general view of the world—either our uniformity principle or the metaphysical conception which would provide a deeper explanation of at least part of the pattern of phenomena which that principle describes.

There is a possible weaker claim than the one I am making. Someone who rejected the inverse probability argument for our uniformity principle could admit that such a principle may well be *true*, while denying that *we* can establish it or even show it to be probabilified by the information we have. If it happens to be true, there is a sense in which the eliminative inferences by which we support specific causal generalizations will in fact be rational, even if we cannot show them to be so. On this view, our correct causal beliefs would constitute knowledge in the sense that it was no accident that these beliefs were true, though they would not constitute what I have called authoritative knowledge.[19] It may be worth noting that there is this second line of defence to which we could, if necessary, fall back; but I would rather try to hold the forward position.

[18] J. S. Mill, *A System of Logic*, Book III, Chapter XXI, Section ii.

[19] For the distinction between authoritative knowledge and knowledge in the sense of non-accidentally true belief, see Mackie, *Problems from Locke*, pp. 217-20. Ayer suggests a similarly weak justification of factual inferences in *Probability and Evidence*, pp. 86-7.

XIII

CAUSATION IN CONCEPT, KNOWLEDGE, AND REALITY

I PRELIMINARY DISTINCTIONS

THERE are three kinds of analysis—conceptual, factual, and epistemic—which should be distinguished but are often confused. 'What is our present established concept of causation, of what causes and effects are, and of the nature of the relation between them?' That is a problem of conceptual analysis. Factual analysis would answer the very different question, 'What is causation in reality, in the objective world: what actually goes on in what we take as typical cases of causation?' Half-way between these two lies epistemic analysis, seeking answers to such questions as this: 'What is causation in reality so far as we know it? What can we observe or discover or establish or reasonably believe about what we take as causes and their effects?'

The answers to these three questions may well fail to coincide. We may have a concept of causation which has no basis in reality, and which goes beyond what we can reasonably claim to know. Equally there may be actual relations between causes and effects of which we know nothing, or of which we know only in a few special cases, while our ordinary knowledge of causal connections is much more restricted.

Another preliminary distinction, cutting across this one, is highlighted by the question, 'Are causes and effects events or facts: to what category do causes and effects belong?' A simple example will illustrate this distinction. I toss a coin and it falls heads: did my tossing of it cause its falling heads? Well, presumably the concrete event which was my tossing of this coin on this occasion caused the later concrete event which was its falling on the table, which included the feature of being a case of falling heads. But the fact that I tossed it did not cause it to fall heads (rather than tails). The cause of the fact that it fell heads would be some more complex fact, that I tossed it with just such-and-such a force, just so far

Previously unpublished; typescript dated January 1977.

above the table, and so on. Or suppose that the tossing of a coin were really an indeterministic process; if so, then nothing at all would have caused the fact that it fell heads; that would have been a product of pure chance. And yet even if the process were indeterministic, the concrete event that was the coin's falling was still caused by the concrete event that was its being tossed.

This example shows that both facts and concrete events can be both causes and effects: this clearly holds in conceptual analysis; and probably in factual and epistemic analysis too. It also shows that for an accurate treatment of particular cases we may need to be clear which category we are speaking about. But for many purposes this does not matter: much that needs to be said applies equally to events and to facts, and it would be needlessly pedantic constantly to specify one category or the other.

We might hope, having drawn these preliminary distinctions, to take up the great debate between rationalist and empiricist views about causation. Empiricists have held that causation is nothing but regularity in the succession of events, while rationalists have claimed that it is something more than this, that it includes some kind of power or necessity, some making of things to happen, which mere talk about regular sequences, or even laws, leaves out. But I shall try to show that this issue is rather misleadingly formulated, particularly because David Hume, the leading figure on the empiricist side—and indeed the greatest single contributor to philosophical thought about causation—went badly astray, not so much in the answer he gave but rather in the very questions he asked.

2   WHERE HUME WENT WRONG

It is ironical that despite the importance of Hume in the philosophy of causation, and of causation in his philosophy, it is not the primary subject of the sections in which he discusses it. His primary subject is inferences about matters of fact, the ways in which we can extend empirical knowledge beyond what we immediately observe; causation comes in because he thinks that causal inferences, especially ones from effect to cause, are our main and perhaps our sole means of so extending our knowledge; that is why he says that causation is 'to us, the cement of the universe'. But Hume's concern with inference is not only his reason for studying causation: it affects—and indeed distorts—his whole treatment of it.

He starts, reasonably enough, by asking what we find if we examine some individual instance of a cause and its effect. Two elements are relatively uncontroversial: succession and contiguity. The effect-event follows the cause-event in time, and in the central cases it follows immediately, with neither a spatial nor a temporal gap. Where there is a spatio-temporal interval between cause and effect, this interval is ordinarily bridged by a series of intermediate steps in each of which an effect follows its cause immediately. Admittedly, neither this contiguity nor even the temporal succession is entirely uncontroversial, in any kind of analysis, conceptual, factual, or epistemic: it is not clear that time-reversed causation is either factually or conceptually impossible, nor is this clear for action at a distance. I am saying only that these points are relatively uncontroversial, and that Hume does not bother much about them. What does matter to him is that even together contiguity and succession are not sufficient to constitute causation: we distinguish causal sequences from merely accidental sequences, *propter hoc* from merely *post hoc*. All of Hume's interest is focused on whatever may be the ground of this distinction.

But it is here that he begins to go astray. He should have enquired, in an open-minded way, what this third element in causation is, what is the difference between causal sequences and mere sequences, considering both our concept and what we can discover in observed causal sequences. But he does not. He simply assumes that the third element in our concept of causation is the idea of a necessary connection. And what does he mean by that? He interprets it as something which, if we knew it, would constitute a firm basis for *a priori* causal inferences, something which we might discover in a cause by itself which would then tell us that just such an effect would follow, or which we might discover in an effect which would then tell us that just such a cause was responsible for it. He assumes that our idea of necessary connection, that is, of what differentiates causal sequences from non-causal sequences, is that of a licence for *a priori* inferences.

Having assumed that this is what we must look for, Hume has no difficulty in pointing out how hard it is to find any such thing. Since cause and effect are distinct events, occurring as they do at different times, though in close succession, there cannot be any analytic, logically necessary, connection between them. So far as logic is concerned, either could exist without the other: no purely intrinsic description of either will entail that the other, under a similarly intrinsic description, must occur. Nor can we find anything, either in a physical causal sequence or in that by which a bodily movement follows a voluntary decision, which would give us *a priori* knowledge of the synthetic truth that one stage would be followed by or would have been preceded by the other. Analytic connections between cause and effect are out of the question, and synthetic *a priori* connections simply cannot be found. All we can find is regular successions, that is, sets of sequences in which similar antecedents are repeatedly followed contiguously by similar successors: whenever an event of kind *C* occurs, one of kind *E* occurs immediately afterwards, and one of kind *E* occurs only when one of kind *C* has preceded it.

It is then easy for Hume to go on to argue that this idea of a necessary connection between cause and effect is a fiction. We cannot discover any licence for *a priori* causal inferences. The truth of the matter is just that when sequences of a certain kind have been observed a number of times an association of ideas is set up, so that on observing the antecedent we expect a successor like those which have commonly followed similar antecedent events. This expectation constitutes an inference which has no rational basis, but is due simply to custom and the imagination: but by projecting this expectation onto the objective sequence of events we create the fiction of a necessary connection between them. Instead of the causal inference being based on a perceived necessity, the supposed necessity is itself based on the inference.

This is an ingenious and plausible explanation. It could perhaps account for our having such an idea of necessity as Hume supposed that we have. Yet it almost completely misses the mark. The idea of necessary connection which it would explain is not in fact the idea that we ordinarily employ to distinguish causal from non-causal sequences. This idea of an *a priori* inference licence, of something that would make causal sequences rationally expectable, in advance of experience, and intelligible when fully known, is indeed a notion that many scientists and philosophers have had. It is particularly favoured by rationalists, yet Locke, who counts as an empiricist, endorsed it no less than Descartes. But it is not part of our ordinary everyday working concept of cause and effect.

What has gone wrong is very curious. In his epistemic analysis, his account of causation in reality so far as we know it, Hume was a regularity theorist, and perhaps in his factual analysis also. But not in his conceptual analysis. Far from saying that our concept of causation is that of regular succession alone, he accepted far too readily and uncritically the rationalist interpretation of this concept, and then displayed admirable but quite needless ingenuity in explaining it away as a fiction. It seems plain that it was his concentration on causal inference, to the relative neglect of causation itself, that led him astray, or at least made him over-ready to accept this erroneous view.

But it is not only this mistaken conceptual analysis that reflects his interest in inference: Hume's regularity theory, his own proposed epistemic and factual analysis, seems also to be adapted to this end. For a statement about a regular succession, a synthetic universal proposition connecting kinds of event, however we may have come to know it or believe it, is just what we should need as the major premiss for an inference from an observation to an unobserved matter of fact.

I have said that Hume went wrong, but I have not yet shown that he did. To establish this, I must start again and do what Hume failed to do, that is, enquire in an open-minded way what makes the difference between a causal and a non-causal sequence. So let us take an example. A man drinks a fair quantity of wine. At the same time he eats a fair quantity of bread. Soon after he shows some of the familiar signs of intoxication. Here we have two sequences, wine-drinking followed by intoxication and bread-eating followed by intoxication. So far as temporal succession and contiguity are concerned, the two sequences are exactly alike. But we would say that the first sequence is causal, the second non-causal. Never mind, for the moment, how we know this or why we believe this, or even whether we are right: let us concentrate first on what we mean when we say that the wine-drinking caused the man's drunkenness, but the bread-eating did not. Plainly, what we mean concerns this particular episode: we do not *mean* that wine-drinking is regularly followed by intoxication whereas bread-eating is not. This may or may not be the case, but it is not what we mean. But equally we do not *mean* that if only we knew enough, about the detailed structure of the wine on the one hand and of the man's body on the other, we could know *a priori* that the putting of one into the other would be followed by just such symptoms. That, too, may or may not be the case, but it is not what our singular causal statement means. Surely what it means is rather something like this: if the man hadn't drunk that quantity of wine, but everything else had been as it was, he wouldn't have become intoxicated. And when we deny that the second sequence was causal we are saying that if the man hadn't eaten the bread, but everything else (including the wine-drinking) had been as it was, he might still have become intoxicated. And, in general, when, speaking about some past sequence, we say that X caused Y we mean not only that X was followed by Y—perhaps contiguously or with a chain of contiguous links—but also that if in the circumstances X had not occurred, Y would not have occurred either; or, briefly, that X was necessary in the circumstances for Y.

This holds whether we think of the cause as this concrete event, the man's drinking of this wine, or as a fact, the fact that he drank at least so much wine. But the point comes out more clearly where we wish to distinguish different facts which are aspects of the same concrete event. I touch a red hot piece of iron and burn my finger. This concrete event, my touching of this piece of iron, caused the burn; that is, if I hadn't touched it I wouldn't have been burned. But, distinguishing various facts, here, we would say that it was not the fact that I touched this piece of iron that caused the burn— that would have been harmless if the iron had been cold. Nor was it the fact that I touched the iron when it was red—it might have been merely painted red. The fact-cause was that I touched the iron when it was above a certain temperature; for it was just that, and none of the concomitant facts, that was necessary in the circumstances for my being burned.

Such counterfactual conditionals as these, then, are the distinctive components of causal statements about the past. But when, speaking of the future, we say that X would cause Y, other conditional statements come into view. If I say that striking a match would cause an explosion, I mean that if, with things as they now are, a match were struck, an explosion would immediately follow, whereas if no match is struck—and things are not otherwise altered—no explosion will follow: the striking of a match is necessary and sufficient in the circumstances for an explosion. These are open conditional statements, and not counterfactual ones, though they may be expressed in either the subjunctive or the indicative. But, like the counterfactuals, they are non-material conditionals: their meaning is not adequately captured by the formal logician's truth function which makes 'If *p* then *q*' equivalent to 'Either not-*p* or *q*' and to 'Not both *p* and not-*q*'.

There are various sorts of causal statements, and an accurate account of them would require additional detail and precision. But these are not needed for my present purpose. What matters is that the third element in the analysis of our established concept of causation—the item that Hume failed to find, or even properly to look for, and for which he wrongly substituted the rationalist notion of an *a priori* inference licence—is something expressed by certain non-material conditional statements.

And yet it is not quite fair to say that Hume failed to find it, though he did fail to look for it. For in the *Enquiry*, though not in the *Treatise*, he mentioned it, inadvertently. Repeating from the *Treatise* his definition of causation as regular sequence he adds 'or in other words *where, if the first object had not been, the second never had existed*'. This is exactly the counterfactual conditional on which I have been insisting. But it is not, as he claims, merely his previous regularity definition in other words, but a quite different analysis and, at least as conceptual analysis, a far more correct one. But Hume never realized its importance.

3   CONDITIONALS AND POSSIBLE WORLDS

Even if this is a correct initial analysis, however, it opens up more problems than it solves. Even if we stick to conceptual analysis, we may well ask what those non-material conditionals themselves mean. And if we try to proceed to epistemic and factual analysis they create further difficulties. How can we observe or verify or even confirm a counterfactual conditional? What reality could such a conditional describe or reflect? It seems that factual and epistemic analysis will come apart from the conceptual analysis of causation and we may have difficulty in finding any relation between them.

An illuminating and widely favoured step is to introduce the notion of possible worlds: we can replace our conditionals by appropriate categorical statements about such systems of possibilities. 'If in the circumstances *X* had not occurred, *Y* would not have occurred' means something like this: 'In the possible world that is, of all those in which *X* does not occur, the closest to the actual world, *Y* does not occur either'. Since this is a counterfactual, it also suggests that that closest world is other than the actual one. The open conditional 'If in the circumstances X were to occur, Y would occur' means something like 'In the possible world that is, of all those in which X occurs, the closest to the actual world, Y occurs also'; but it allows that this closest world may be the actual world itself. To assert non-material conditionals is, from this point of view, to speak about possibilities; but not about anything and everything that is barely logically possible, but only about possibilities that are somehow particularly closely related to the actual course of events.

This is a useful device for studying the meaning and the logic of non-material conditionals, but it is surely a mistake to take possible worlds very seriously or literally. It is only the actual world that really exists, and possible worlds must be explained in terms of it, including, perhaps, our operations in the actual world. Talk about possibilities, I would say, merely reflects the fact that human beings sometimes suppose things to be otherwise than they are, or otherwise than they are yet, or otherwise than they are known to be.

If conditionals, then, are equivalent to statements about certain sorts of possibilities, and possibilities are products of the human faculty of supposing, that is, of a variety of imagination, can they ever be true or false? Curiously enough, they can. For when it happens that the antecedent of a conditional is fulfilled, the possible world about which it speaks turns out to be the actual world. The actual world must then be, of all the possible worlds in which the antecedent is fulfilled, the one closest to the actual world—that is, to itself. Then if the consequent is fulfilled also, what the conditional says has turned out to be the case, so it is literally true; while if the consequent then remains unfulfilled, the conditional is as literally false. On the other hand, if the antecedent is not fulfilled— and a counterfactual presupposes this—then the conditional cannot be, strictly speaking, either true or false, since the possibilities of which it speaks remain mere possibilities, that is, expressions of our supposings; but such a conditional can be reasonable or acceptable, if it conforms to the rules and principles that standardly guide our supposings.

It would be natural, then, to go on to consider what observations and other considerations might justify our use of various non-material conditionals, and what the related realities might be. But before we do this, we must repair an omission. There is something vital that has been left out of our conceptual analysis of causation.

To see what this is, let us consider a case in which some cause has two effects, and is, in the circumstances, both necessary and sufficient for each of them. For example, suppose that there are, on a table, a glass of water full to the brim and a pendulum clock in good order and wound up, but not going. I jerk the table; the clock starts and the water spills over. The movement of the table, we shall say, caused the starting of the clock and also the spilling of the water: that is, if the table hadn't moved, the clock would not have started and the water would not have spilt. But as well as these counterfactuals which agree with our causal judgement, there are others which do not. Can we not say that if the water had not spilt, the table would not have moved: since the movement of the table was sufficient in the circumstances for the spilling, the spilling was necessary in the circumstances for the movement. Yet we do not say that the spilling caused the movement. Again, if the water had not spilt, the clock would not have started, and if the clock had not started, the water would not have spilt; yet neither of these caused the other. Similarly, if we were speaking about such events before they occurred, we might use various open conditionals: not only 'If the table moves, the clock will start' but also 'If the clock starts, the water will be spilt'. But only some of these will correspond to causal assertions.

It seems, then, that our conditional analysis has left something out, and what it has left out is the lines and directions of causation—what we would very naturally represent on a diagram like this

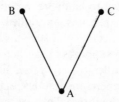

where 'A' represents the movement of the table, 'B' the spilling of the water, and 'C' the starting of the clock. But someone might protest that these features have not been left out, that they are covered by the conditional analysis, if it is handled properly. Some conditionals, it may be said, are much more natural than others: 'If the table moves, the clock will start' is more natural, more acceptable than 'If the clock starts, the water will be spilt', and similarly among the counterfactuals, 'If the table had not moved, the clock would not have started' is more acceptable than 'If the water had not spilt, the clock would not have started'. This point may be at least partially conceded. But what it shows is that there is a specially favoured sub-class of non-material conditionals, in which the antecedent and consequent correspond respectively to a cause and its effect. In terms of the possible worlds account of conditionals, this amounts to a specially favoured way of choosing the closest possible world. Of all the worlds in which the antecedent is fulfilled, the closest to the actual world is taken to be that in which something intervenes from outside the particular system under consideration (here the table and what is on and immediately around it) directly to secure the fulfilment of the antecedent, but otherwise the situation is the same, and things go on in accordance with the same regularities as in the actual world. Thus 'If the table had not moved, the clock would not have started' is acceptable, because in the possible world in which something intervenes to keep the table still, and the set-up and the laws of working are otherwise the same as in the actual world, the clock does not start. But 'If the water had not spilt, the clock would not have started' is not acceptable; for this would describe a possible world in which something intervenes directly to keep the water in the glass, but since the set-up and the laws are otherwise unchanged, the table still moves in this world and the clock still starts.

I concede that this is a specially favoured way of handling conditionals and possibilities, though I would also stress that it is not the only conceivable or even acceptable way. For some purposes we might take the closest world in which the water is not spilt to be the one in which this comes about with the least unusual sort of intervention, and hence by way of the table's not moving, not by something holding the water in, and the events in this possible world would license the conditional claim that if the water had not spilt, the clock would not have started. Since conditionals may be handled in this way, what we need for the conceptual analysis of causation is not just non-material, including counterfactual, conditionals as such, but a particular variety of these, or, what comes to the same thing, these taken along with one particular way of deciding what is to count as the closest possible world.

4   EXPERIMENTS AND LAWS OF WORKING

How can we justify our acceptance of conditionals of this specially favoured sort? On what sorts of observation do we rely? Now in practice our acceptance of such conditionals as those mentioned is linked with a whole complex body of information and belief and theory; but clearly the crucial question is, 'How do we get off the ground?' 'How could we begin to support beliefs of this sort starting from cold, without a body of relevant already established knowledge?' And the answer is, 'By bringing together similar cases in which we ourselves sometimes do and sometimes do not intervene'. At t_1 the table is still, the water remains in the glass and the clock doesn't start; at t_2 I jerk the table, the water spills and the clock starts. So I construct in imagination a possible world in which something intervenes to stop my moving the table at t_2, and I construct it on the model of the actual, observed, world at t_1, so as to say, 'If the table had not moved, the clock would not have started'. Having done this once, at some later time t_3 I have an exactly similar set-up, with everything stationary. I try to describe a possible world in which the table moves at t_4, and which is closer than any other such world to the actual one—it will, of course, turn out to *be* the actual one, if the table is in fact moved at t_4. Basing my description on what happened at t_2, I say that in this possible world the clock starts at t_4, so I endorse the open conditional, 'If the table moves at t_4, the clock will start'. On the other hand, just as I start to move the table at t_4 I clap a cover over the glass of water and it does not spill, but the clock still starts. Constructing a possible world for t_2 with the t_4 events as my model, I reject the conditional 'If the water had not spilt at t_2, the clock would not have started'. And so on.

This example is highly artificial, but it shows the sorts of observation from which basic causal beliefs would in the first instance be derived. But granted that this is how we think when we come to make causal claims, what, if anything, might make it reasonable to think in this way? Since the key procedure is the transfer of features from one (observed) case to another very similar (supposed) one, we are in effect invoking regularities. But not just any regularities; what we are implicitly relying upon is regularities with respect to what Hume called 'the course of nature', the ways in which events within some system run on from something we can see as an intervention into that system. Moreover, we are acting on the assumption that these regularities are discoverable at least in part, so that some similarities that we detect can with some degree of confidence be projected so as to apply to unobserved cases. *The sort of world in which it will be reasonable to think in the ways that generate our causal assertions is one in which events take place in accordance with such laws of working.*

These regularities need not be, and indeed are not, simple. Typically, a certain result comes about only when some number of causally relevant factors are present together: the total cause is a conjunction of many contributory causes. Also, there are counteracting causes: even when we have a set of factors which is normally sufficient to produce some result, the presence of some additional item may prevent that result. Again, there may be what Mill called a plurality of causes: effects of the same sort may be produced in more than one way, so that the subject of a complete regularity statement, if it could ever be formulated, would take the form of a disjunction of conjunctions of terms. Also, the regularities are likely to involve not merely the presence and absence of features but also quantitative relationships between them: the laws will be in part at least ones of functional dependence. And some of them may be probabilistic, not strictly deterministic ones.

The laws by which the world works are thus highly complex; but we hardly ever know all or even most of their complexities. Regularities as we can claim to know them are elliptical: they have gaps where there should be terms. But, surprisingly perhaps, this is not fatal: we can test and confirm and employ for practical purposes laws of working which are very incompletely stated. Such incompletenesses are represented by the well known *ceteris paribus* clause—'other things being equal'—and by the phrase 'in the circumstances' which I used when formulating non-material conditionals as an initial analysis of singular causal statements. In our example we certainly do not know, and do not need to know, the whole disjunction of conjunctions of factors which, in a true and complete regularity statement, would be both necessary and sufficient for such a clock as this to start. What we can reasonably believe after very little experimentation is that there is some set of relevant circumstances, instantiated here, such that this sort of movement of the table is both necessary and sufficient, along with those circumstances, for this result. But this conclusion is reasonable, in the light of our experiments, only on the assumption that there is some such, doubtless very complex, regularity or law of working covering all the cases where such a clock does or does not start.

This is just a very hasty survey of a complicated subject, which I have tried to explore in some detail in my book [*The Cement of the Universe*]. I cannot now go into any such details, rather I want to draw out some morals with respect to the factual and epistemic analysis of causation. It might seem that we have come back to one of Hume's main conclusions by another route. Regularities in the succession of events are what constitute causation in so far as it is a feature of the objective world, and incompletely known regularities constitute all that we can claim to know about this objective feature, though we commonly express this knowledge by framing what are either explicitly or implicitly non-material conditional statements, including counterfactual ones. But this is not the whole of the story. It was an essential part of our conceptual analysis that there are lines and a direction of causation. These features are reflected in the experiments by which we acquire basic causal beliefs, as illustrated in our artificial example of the table, the glass, and the clock. These turned upon what could be seen as interventions, as intrusions into some system, with continuous sequences of events running on from those intrusions. The continuities are essential: how do I know that it is the table that I am moving directly, and hence that it is its movement that is necessary in the circumstances for the starting of the clock, rather than the other way round, except by noting that it is with the table that my hand makes contact? And this kind of thinking will be reasonable only if there are similar continuities and directedness in the objective causal processes themselves.

Of course, much more needs to be said. Exactly what constitutes the directedness or asymmetry of causation, and how this is related to the direction of time, is a very difficult problem, and I am by no means confident that I can solve it: I am, however, reasonably certain that no one else has solved it yet. Nor is it easy to describe adequately the sorts of continuity that are to be found in causal processes. However, it is plain that all three of our analyses of causation, conceptual, epistemic, and factual, diverge in varying degrees from those that Hume gave. Our conceptual analysis is radically different from his, for it centres not on the idea of an *a priori* inference licence but on that of counterfactual and other non-material conditionals, and hence on what are called possible worlds, that is, systematically related possibilities handled in a distinctive way. Our epistemic and factual analyses are closer to Hume's, since they centre, like his, on regularities in the succession of events, laws of working. But our analysis stresses the complex forms of those regularities, to which Hume paid little attention, and also the elliptical or gappy character of the regularities as known by contrast with what we reasonably suppose the objective laws to be like, and also adds what he left out, an asymmetry of cause and effect that is something other than mere temporal succession, and continuities of process that go beyond the spatio-temporal contiguity which he half-heartedly recognized. But though our account diverges thus from Hume's, it does not move at all close to the rival rationalist one. Indeed, as we have seen, Hume's primary mistake was to admit, quite gratuitously, a rationalist notion into his conceptual analysis. My main task has been to repair the damage done to the theory of causation by this false start and by Hume's excessive concern with causal *inference*.

XIV

THREE STEPS
TOWARDS ABSOLUTISM

I INTRODUCTION: ISSUES AND GENERAL ARGUMENTS

QUITE a number of philosophers of science have argued, in recent
years, for at least some kind of absolutism about space or time or
space-time; but most philosophers who do not specialize in this
area seem to take a relativist view, and indeed a fairly extreme
form of relativism, to be simply obvious, or to be established beyond the need for controversy. This paper is addressed primarily
to such general philosophers, and its purpose is at least to disturb
their complacency.

There are many issues, not just one, that come under the heading
of 'absolutism *versus* relativism about space and time', and the first
task is to distinguish them. One question is whether space and time
are entities, existing independently of things and processes, whether
they are proper objects of reference, or whether we should speak
only of spatial and temporal features—qualities and relations—of
things and processes. This is the issue about absolute or relative
existence. But we might decide that space and time are not altogether distinct from one another, that we have rather space-time
which can be sorted out into spatial and temporal dimensions only
relatively to some arbitrarily chosen frame of reference; even so,
there will still be an issue about the absolute or relative existence
of space-time, the question whether it is a proper object of reference, whether it exists independently or only as a collection of
features of things and processes. Distinct from these issues of ex-

Reprinted from *Space, Time, and Causality* (Royal Institute of Philosophy Confer-
ences Volume for 1981), edited by Richard Swinburne, copyright 1983 by D. Reidel
Publishing Company; this volume is a collection of revised versions of papers read
at a conference at the University of Keele in September 1981. Professor Swinburne
writes in a note: 'The paper printed here consists of the paper read to the Keele
conference, with a number of minor corrections which Mr Mackie made before his
death. He was also intending to write an additional note, in part commenting on
some of the objections made in the course of the discussion at the conference, but
the note was never written.'

istence is the issue about position: are there absolute positions in space and dates in time (or, again, points in space-time), or does one thing or event have a position or a date or a space-time location only relatively to some other thing(s) or event(s)? Again, is there an absolute difference between motion and rest, or can one thing move or not move only in relation to another? Similarly, is there an absolute difference between acceleration—change of motion, including rotation—and non-acceleration, or is there change or non-change of motion only relatively to some arbitrarily chosen frame of reference? There are further issues about metrical features. One kind of absolutism will say that things have intrinsic spatial lengths, or that there are intrinsic metrical relations of distance between spatial positions—whether such positions themselves are absolute or merely relative—and similarly that processes have intrinsic temporal lengths or durations, or that there are intrinsic metrical relations of time-interval between occurrences—whether these occurrences in themselves have absolute or merely relative dates, positions in time. The relativism opposed to this kind of absolutism will say that all such metrical features are merely relative, that the most we have is that one thing or process or interval is equal or unequal in spatial or temporal length to another. But this kind of relativism still leaves room for a more limited kind of absolutism, namely the thesis that there are absolute equalities and inequalities of spatial length and distance and of temporal interval and duration. Opposed to this kind of absolutism is the relativism which holds that even these metrical relations are themselves relative to some arbitrarily chosen metrical system or method of measurement, or to some 'observer'—for example, that equalities or inequalities of temporal duration hold only in relation to some chosen clock or set of clocks. And even this does not exhaust the range of questions. For it can be at least plausibly argued that even if the measures of space and time separately, the equalities of length or distance on its own and the equalities of duration on its own, are thus relative to clocks or space-measuring procedures and instruments, yet there are intrinsic equalities and inequalities of time-like length and space-like length along space-time paths, so that, as we may put it, space-time has an intrinsic metric even if space and time separately do not: this would be a further kind of absolutism, while the denial of any such intrinsic space-time metric would be a yet more radical relativism. In fact, when we set them out systematically we find that there are at least fourteen distinct issues, fourteen possible absolutist theses (as shown in Table I), with a relativist thesis as the denial of each of these.

But of course these issues are not wholly independent of one another. Roughly speaking, as we go down the table we come to progressively weaker absolutist theses—and by contrast to stronger and stronger or more and more radical relativist theses. Equally, the conjunction of the separate theses about space and time on any one line will entail the corresponding thesis about space-time on the same line, but neither of those separate theses will be entailed by the corresponding space-time thesis. For example, absolutism about spatial positions and dates requires, but is not required by, absolutism about motion, and absolutism about motion requires but is not required by absolutism about acceleration; if space-time paths have intrinsic lengths, then there will be absolute equalities and inequalities between them, but there might be such absolute equalities and inequalities even if they had no intrinsic lengths. If space and time each exist as independent entities, we should at least expect this fact to carry with it all the other absolutisms—though they *might* perhaps be amorphous entities, with no metrical features or even with no distinguishable parts—but the various absolutisms lower down the table might hold without such absolute existence; and the same applies to absolutism about the existence of space-time and the various absolutisms below this in the right-hand column.

TABLE I
Varieties of absolutism and relativism

There may be absolutisms and contrasting relativisms about:

1.1. the *existence* of space	1.2. of time	1.3. of space-time
2.1. *position* in space	2.2. in time	2.3. in space-time
	3. *motion/rest*	
	4. *acceleration/non-acceleration*	
5.1. *length/distance* in space	5.2. *duration/interval* in time	5.3. *time-like and space-like lengths* of paths in space-time
6.1. *equality/inequality of length/distance* in space	6.2. *equality/inequality of duration/interval* in time	6.3. *equality/inequality* of *time-like and space-like lengths* of paths in space-time

There is a connection of another kind between these issues. In each case the relativist view is commonly supported by the same general line of argument. We cannot observe space or time by itself apart from things or processes, so we have no right to assert its existence as an independent entity. We cannot fix a thing's position except in relation to other things. There would be no detectable difference if everything in the universe were a mile further north than it is, so this form of words fails to specify any real difference. We cannot tell whether one thing is moving or not on its own, but only whether it is moving in relation to other things or to ourselves. There would be no way of detecting whether the whole universe was moving together. And so on. The relativist typically argues that whatever the particular absolutism which he is opposing asserts is unobservable, or at any rate not directly observable, and therefore cannot be real.

But how does the alleged unobservability bear upon the issue in each case? The relativist must be relying not on the unobservability alone but also on some philosophical principle which authorizes him to deny or reject or dismiss whatever cannot be (directly) observed. In fact, several such principles have been put forward.

One of these is Leibniz's principle of sufficient reason: nothing happens without a sufficient reason, and in particular God does nothing without a sufficient reason. But, Leibniz argues, there could be no sufficient reason why everything in the universe should be where it is rather than all together being a mile further north; so there can be no real difference between these alternatives, as absolutism about spatial position holds that there is. If there were absolute positions in time, God would have been faced with the choice whether to create the world at one time or, say, twenty-four hours later, letting it run on in just the same way. But since the difference between these would be utterly undetectable for anyone within the universe, and neither course of events could be better than the other in any way, he could not have had a sufficient reason for preferring one to the other. But if there are no absolute temporal positions, God is spared the embarrassment of such an unresolvable choice. In this way the principle of sufficient reason would support various relativisms. However, there is no sufficient reason why we should accept this principle.

Another suitable principle is the verificationist theory of meaning. If the meaning of every statement is constituted by the method(s) by which it would be verified, a supposed statement which was utterly cut off from the possibility of verification would lack meaning, and so would not really be a statement after all. So if absolute motion, for example, is undetectable, the statement that something is moving absolutely, or that it is absolutely at rest, must after all say nothing.

Even if this principle is accepted, it seems to leave room for a defence of at least some varieties of absolutism. For example, it has been argued, by Newton and by others following him, that although absolute acceleration is not directly observable, it is indirectly observable, and indeed measurable, by way of its dynamic causes and effects. For example, if there were two equal metal spheres joined by a spring, then if we knew the masses of the spheres and the elastic characteristics of the spring we could determine whether, and if so at what angular velocity, this little system was rotating absolutely merely by seeing whether, and if so how much, the spring was extended.

But the verificationist-relativist will reply that if absolute acceleration is never directly observed, we cannot infer it from such effects—or, likewise, from any causes. We cannot establish or even confirm the causal law on which such an inference must rely unless we directly observe, sometimes at least, each of the terms that the law connects. And in default of such an inference, if we claim that, for example, the extension of the spring is a measure of absolute rotation, we must simply be introducing the name 'absolute rotation' as a name for such a directly observed change: 'The system is rotating absolutely with such-and-such an angular velocity' can only mean 'The spring is extended so far'. And in general instead of being able thus to introduce indirectly observed items, we succeed only in introducing what are likely to be misleading names for the features which are directly observed, and which the absolutist was trying to use as evidence for something else.

However, I shall show (in Section 2) that this reply cannot be sustained. The criticism of it there will bring out the weakness of the verificationist theory of meaning; but this theory has in any case some very unpalatable consequences in both scientific and commonsense contexts, and it can, I believe, be decisively refuted.[1]

Another principle on which the appeal to unobservability may

[1] See, for example, my 'Truth and Knowability', *Analysis*, Vol. 40, No. 2 (March 1980).

rely is that of economy of postulation, Ockham's razor. An entity, or a quality, or a relation, that is never directly observed is one that we are not forced to admit, and therefore one that we could do without. However, there is more than one kind of economy, and I shall show (in Section 3) that it may be more economical in an important sense to postulate at least some of the items favoured by absolutism than to do without them as the relativist would prefer.

A fourth principle is the operationalist one, that science should use only operationally defined terms. But this would at most exclude absolutist terms and theses from science: it would not settle any philosophical issues about the existence or non-existence of absolute space or time or space-time, or about the absolute or relative status of the various other features. In any case operationalism derives whatever plausibility it has as a programme for science either from a verificationist theory of meaning or from some principle of the economy of postulation. If these fail, it has no independent appeal.

I maintain, therefore, that there is no cogent general argument for the different varieties of spatio-temporal relativisms, based on the impossibility of observing directly each of the controversial absolute entities or features. Rather, the specific issues have to be examined one by one, to see whether, in each case, the absolutist has good grounds for postulating the item(s) in question. *That is, absolutisms cannot be systematically ruled out: nevertheless each particular absolutism will need to have a case developed for it before it can be ruled in.*

Obviously, I cannot hope to deal with all these issues in one paper; instead, in the three following sections, I shall discuss a few of them, but I hope, in doing this, to illustrate some general principles which should guide us in this area as a whole.

2   ABSOLUTE ACCELERATION

I shall treat the problem of absolute acceleration fairly summarily, because it has been thoroughly discussed by (for example) Newton, Mach, Reichenbach, and Swinburne, and most of what needs to be said about it emerges directly from their discussions.[2]

[2] I. Newton, *Principia*, Scholium following Definition viii; E. Mach, *The Science of Mechanics* (La Salle, Illinois, 1960), Chapter 2; H. Reichenbach, *The Philosophy of Space and Time* (New York, 1957), Chapter III, §34; R. Swinburne, *Space and Time* (London, 1981), Chapter 3.

As everyone knows, Newton argued that since, if we rotate a bucket of water, we find that the surface becomes concave—and the more concave the more rapidly it rotates—we have here an indication of absolute acceleration: the 'centrifugal force' which seems to push the water outwards so that it builds up at the sides of the bucket is really a symptom of the fact that the water is constantly being forced to accelerate towards the centre of the bucket. Similarly, with the two spheres joined by a spring, the tension of the spring is needed to exert on each sphere the force which makes it accelerate towards the centre as the system rotates. The result of the bucket experiment can be checked by anyone in his back garden; observations that are practically equivalent to the two-sphere experiment can be made on planetary and satellite systems and double stars. So far, these results favour Newton: there is independent evidence for the presence of forces which are just the ones that we should expect to find if there were absolute rotations and therefore absolute accelerations involved in them. Moreover, these rotations are not in general rotations relative to some nearby body. The bucket's rotation is indeed relative to the earth, but there is nothing corresponding to this in the other cases. But, as Mach points out, the rotations that are doing the work need not be interpreted as absolute rotations. For they are, obviously, rotations relative to 'the great masses of the universe', the fixed stars and beyond them the galaxies. However, Mach erred in arguing *a priori* that it must be this relative rotation that is doing the work. As Reichenbach points out, it is an empirical question whether this is so. Suppose that we find centrifugal phenomena on an earth E_1 which is rotating relatively to a surrounding shell of fixed stars F_1; then if there were, far away, another earth E_2 stationary relative to F_1, but with a shell of stars surrounding it, F_2, which is stationary relative to E_1, then E_1 and E_2 will each have the same rotation relative to its own surrounding shell. But it is an empirical question whether the same centrifugal phenomena are in fact found on both. If they are, this will confirm Mach's hypothesis: since the effects are correlated with the relative rotations between each earth and its own star shell, it is these relative rotations that are doing the work. But if the centrifugal phenomena are found in E_1 but not in E_2, Mach's hypothesis is disconfirmed. We may be tempted to say that in this case Newton's interpretation, that it is an absolute rotation of E_1 that is producing these effects, is confirmed; but

Reichenbach argues that this would be too hasty a conclusion. *Some* absolute rotation, he concedes, is responsible; but it might be either an absolute rotation of E_1 or an absolute rotation of its surrounding shell F_1. And Reichenbach thinks that we shall be unable to decide which it is. But, as Swinburne says, this is not so: some further additions to the possible observations could decide this. If we have other earths, E_3 and E_4 and so on, with various different rotations relatively to E_1 but within the same star shell F_1, we shall be able to decide, by seeing what centrifugal effects, if any, they exhibit, whether these effects are correlated with what would have to be the different absolute rotations of each earth or with the rotation of the common surrounding star shell F_1. The whole discussion is a straightforward application of the methods of eliminative induction that are known as Mill's Methods. With a sufficient range of partly similar and partly different situations, we could show that various proposed factors in turn are not causally responsible for the 'centrifugal effects'; and the elimination of enough rival hypotheses could in the end powerfully confirm Newton's view that these effects are being produced by an absolute rotation of the body in which these effects appear, and hence by an absolute acceleration of its parts. Of course, the empirical outcome of such a range of observations could go the other way, and confirm, say, Mach's relativist interpretation. All I am insisting on at present is that it is an empirical question; I am protesting against the tendency of many relativists to suppose that the relativist account is the only possible one, that it can be established on some general philosophical grounds without waiting for the empirical evidence.

But now we have a puzzle on our hands. How does this manage to survive as an empirical question? How does it escape the general argument sketched in Section 1 against the possibility of introducing items which are never directly observed, for which we have at best indirect evidence? Specifically, how can we first give meaning to a statement of the form 'X has such-and-such an absolute rotation' and secondly confirm it? If the very notion of rotation is first introduced in connection with the observed rotation of one thing in relation to another, how can we even frame, without internal contradiction, the concept of a rotation that is not relative to anything?

Well, we can first introduce, quite arbitrarily, the notion of a purely abstract standard or frame of reference. There is a frame of reference, for example, with respect to which this book is rotating clockwise as seen from above about an axis perpendicular to its cover through its centre of gravity at sixty revolutions a minute; and there is another frame of reference with respect to which the same book is rotating about the same axis in the opposite direction at twice that angular velocity. Abstract frames of reference are cheap: you can have as many of them as you like at no cost at all; and as such they have no physical significance. But suppose that there is some one abstract frame of reference such that certain dynamic causes and effects are systematically associated with rotations (which vary in magnitude, in their axes of rotation, and in direction) relative to it. Suppose, that is, that there is one 'preferred' frame of reference rotations relative to which do, as it turns out, have physical significance. Next, we may have either of two alternatives. Perhaps there is no physical object at all, and no set of objects, which are associated with this preferred frame (by being, say, at rest in it, or having their motions with respect to it somehow complementary). Or perhaps, as in the Reichenbach–Swinburne worlds, there *is* a set of objects thus associated with the preferred frame, but other observations or experiments show, by Millian methods of eliminative induction, that these objects are *not* causally involved in the cause–effect relationships which pick this out as the one preferred frame. Then we must conclude that what is doing the work is rotations relative simply to this preferred abstract frame of reference itself. Briefly, experiments and observations can show that there are causally significant rotations, but that, as causally significant, they are rotations relative to no *thing* at all. That, I suggest, is what we mean by 'absolute rotation', and the possible observations I have sketched show how we might confirm its reality. It is, of course, a trivial and merely technical task to extend this account from rotations to accelerations of all sorts.

This account shows how, on thoroughly empiricist principles, meaning can be given to such a term as 'absolute rotation'. This is what Locke or Hume, for example, would call a complex idea, and empiricists generally have seen no difficulty in constructing new complex ideas, provided that the materials out of which they are constructed are found within the content of our experience. It is only a 'simple idea' that has to be copied from a preceding 'impression'. Essentially the same principle is expressed in Russell's dictum, "Every proposition which we can understand must be com-posed wholly of constituents with which we are acquainted".[3] This general empiricism is much more plausible than the verificationist thesis that each form of sentence or statement as a whole must be given meaning by a method by which it could be verified, or, equivalently, that each meaningful term, however complex, must be correlated with some direct observation. That more extreme form of empiricism would preclude the constructing of complex ideas or meanings out of simpler empirical components, and there is no good reason for accepting any such restriction. In the parti-cular case we have been studying, there is a set of possible observa-tions which, interpreted by the ordinary (roughly Millian) canons of causal investigation, would show that it is *rotations* that are at work, and further possible observations which would show that what is causally relevant is rotations relative to no *thing*. These are the constituents out of which the required complex concept of absolute rotation (or, more generally, of absolute acceleration) are put together. (In effect, I am here rejecting what Swinburne, in his reply to Sklar elsewhere in this volume, calls 'verificationism pro-per', but, like Swinburne, I am accepting what he calls 'word-veri-ficationism', and using it to show how the term 'absolute accelera-tion' has meaning†.)·

By analogy with absolute acceleration we can readily explain how meaning can be given to the term 'absolute motion', and how it is at least conceivable that observations and experiments should confirm its reality. If there were some one preferred frame of refer-ence such that even uniform motions (rather than rest) relative to it systematically required causes and had effects, without any *things* associated with that frame being causally relevant to these pro-cesses, then we could call motion or rest relative to that one pre-ferred frame absolute motion or rest. To say in general that there is absolute motion would therefore be to say that there is some one such preferred frame; and this might conceivably be confirmed by the discovery of such systematically causally relevant motions with-out any *things* that could account for their relevance. However,

---

† Mackie's reference is to R. Swinburne, 'Verificationism and Theories of Space-Time' and L. Sklar, 'Prospects for a Causal Theory of Space-Time', both printed in *Space, Time and Causality* in the section entitled 'Time and Causal Connectibility', pp. 45–76.—Edd.

[3] B. Russell, *The Problems of Philosophy* (London, 1912), Chapter 5.

while both 'absolute acceleration' and 'absolute motion' are meaningful, there is dynamic evidence that supports the view that the
former term has application, but there is no such dynamic evidence
to show that there is absolute motion. A different kind of argument
for absolute motion will be put forward in Section 4 below.

3   ABSOLUTE DURATION

Another topic with which I want to deal fairly summarily is that
of absolute duration.This has not been discussed so widely as that
of absolute acceleration, but I have myself written and read
(though not published) papers about it on a number of occasions,
and while the conclusion I shall reach in this section is not uncontroversial, it may be not too difficult for unprejudiced people to
accept.

Let us consider initially how in a single frame of reference—to
which our situation on earth and in the neighbouring solar system
is a close enough approximation—we decide whether two time intervals A-B and C-D, marked out by four near-instantaneous
events A, B, C, and D, are equal or not. We use, of course, various
sorts of 'clocks', where the term 'clock' can include not only man-
ufactured devices of many kinds but also the rotations and revolutions of planets and satellites, the decay of radioactive materials,
and so on. All such clocks are probably inaccurate to some extent,
because of causally relevant variations in the circumstances in
which they go through their characteristic performances; but we
can identify the causes of inconstancy by seeing how similar clocks
running side by side may diverge from one another, and once we
have found these causes we can either correct the deviant clocks or
allow for their inconstancies. For example, we find that of two
otherwise similar pendulums swinging side by side, the longer
swings more slowly. We can use this knowledge, along with the
discovery that pendulum number two is longer during C-D than it
was in A-B, while pendulum number one has remained the same
length, to explain why pendulum number two says that C-D is
shorter than A-B while pendulum number one says that these two
intervals are equal—that is, swings the same number of times in
the two intervals. That is, we can 'correct' pendulum number two
on the ground that it, and not pendulum number one, has suffered
a causally relevant change. Let us speak of a 'corrected clock' when

we are referring to the set of readings given by a clock after allowance has been made for all thus discoverable causes of inconstancy. We can then ask what happens when we apply to our two intervals *A-B* and *C-D* a large battery of corrected clocks. (The only question we are asking of them is whether they measure these two intervals as equal or not: the obviously arbitrary and trivial choice of units does not come into the matter.) Any one of three things might happen. They might all agree with one another in saying that these two intervals were equal, or, say, that *A-B* was longer than *C-D*; or they might all disagree in a chaotic way; or they might fall into two or more distinct families, with all the corrected clocks of one family agreeing with one another, but systematically disagreeing with the corrected clocks of another family. It is a thoroughly synthetic, empirical, question which of these three results emerges: I can show that the natural procedure for the causal correction of clocks does *not* prejudice this issue by counting as corrected clocks only ones which all agree with one another. Moreover, we can ask what happens when we apply our large battery of corrected clocks not just to a single pair of intervals *A-B* and *C-D*, but to a large number of such pairs of intervals. Now it seems to be an empirical fact that for clocks in this solar system the first of our three possibilities is realized: corrected clocks systematically agree with one another within the limits of observational accuracy in saying, for example, that *A-B* and *C-D* are equal, that of some other pair of intervals the first is greater than the second, and so on.

Now how is this empirical fact to be explained? How does it come about that so many and such different clocks keep on giving agreed answers to a long series of questions of this form? As I said, this result has not been faked up by 'correcting' the clocks in an *ad hoc* way to yield this result. Nor is there any sort of interaction between the various clocks by which they could, so to speak, keep in step with one another. But it is implausible to say that it is a mere coincidence—or rather a whole series of coincidences—that corrected clocks keep on agreeing with one another about the equality or inequality of each pair of intervals. The only plausible explanatory hypothesis is that there is some intrinsic equality between *A-B* and *C-D*, some intrinsic inequality between another pair of intervals, and so on. There are intrinsic metrical relations between such intervals, and that is why each separate clock (once any caused inconstancies have been eliminated) performs the same number of its characteristic performances, whatever they are, in *A–B* as in *C–D*, but systematically different numbers of these performances in other intervals, and so on. This is, in a new sense, the more economical hypothesis.

On these grounds there seems to be a strong case for the absolutist view about the issue numbered 6.2 [in Table 1]. But we can then go further. Once it is admitted that there are absolute relations of equality or inequality of time intervals, it is an easy further step to the conclusion that these absolute relations are themselves to be explained by the hypothesis that each interval on its own has an intrinsic metrical feature that we can call 'time-length' or 'duration', something that, as we may put it, interacts with the intrinsic features of each clock to determine just what performances it will go through in that interval. In other words, we can regard as well confirmed also the absolutist view on the issue numbered 5.2.

However, this triumph may be premature. This case collapses, this line of argument fails, when we relax our initial restriction and consider 'clocks' which are not all (approximately) in the same inertial frame of reference. When we consider particles, or clocks on space-ships, which are moving, relatively to the solar system, at speeds that are a fair proportion of the speed of light, we have to recognize and allow for the Fitzgerald–Lorentz 'retardation'. The Special Theory of Relativity seems to be empirically well confirmed, and it entails that corrected clocks will conform not to the first but to the third of the possibilities distinguished above. While all clocks which are roughly stationary with respect to the solar system form one family, clocks that are all moving together in a different frame of reference, even another inertial one—say clocks of many different sorts on a rapidly receding space-ship—form another family, and so on. This is dramatically illustrated by the Clock Paradox, for example that the interval which is measured by all corrected earth-related clocks as a hundred years will be measured as only sixty years by clocks on a pair of space-ships which have passed the earth, and one another, as in Figure 1, with four-fifths of the speed of light relatively to the earth. This result is a firm and unavoidable consequence of the Special Theory, and within that theory it has nothing to do with accelerations or decelerations: it depends purely on relative velocities.

The Clock Paradox is, however, very easily solved. We have merely to recognize that *clocks do not measure time*. What they

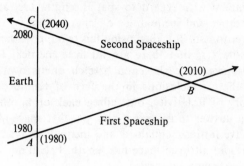

Figure 1

measure is something else, 'proper time', or the 'time-like length' of particular space-time paths—the path followed by each particular clock. Whereas our old-fashioned concept is of time as a single dimension, so that there is only one unique time interval between two specified events, such as *A* and *C* in Figure 1, the first space-ship's passing earth and the second space-ship's passing earth, once we introduce this new concept of proper time we can see that there can be one proper time interval along the earth's path from *A* to *C*, but a different—and, as it turns out, shorter— proper time interval along the joint path of the two space-ships *A*– *B*–*C*.

Once we have thus introduced proper time, we can see that the whole of the above argument for absolutism can be transferred to it. What explains the agreements about equality and inequality of intervals among all corrected earth-related clocks? Surely a real, objective, equality or inequality of each pair of slices of proper time along the earth's path. What explains the agreements among themselves of all the corrected clocks of another family, say those on one space-ship? Likewise a real, objective equality or inequality of each pair of slices of proper time along the space-ship's path. And these various equalities and inequalities are themselves explained in turn by the hypothesis that each slice of proper time on its own, each interval along a space-time path or 'world line', has an intrinsic metrical feature of time-like length. That is, we here abandon the absolutist answers to issues 6.2 and 5.2, but accept instead the corresponding absolutist answers to issues 6.3 and 5.3.

It would be only a technical exercise to construct a closely analogous argument with regard to spatial length, first arguing for intrinsic equalities and inequalities of lengths, that is, for the absolutist answer to issue 6.1, then using this to support the absolutist answer to issue 5.1, that there are intrinsic metrical features of length or distance for each spatial stretch on its own, but then abandoning these conclusions in the face of the success of the Special Theory of Relativity, but falling back on another part of the absolutist answer to issues 6.3 and 5.3, that space-like lines in space-time have intrinsic equalities and inequalities, and that each on its own has an intrinsic space-like length. I shall not waste time or space on this technical exercise.

We cannot, of course, appeal to our present *concept* of time as a single universal dimension against the recognition of an indefinite multiplicity of equally real proper times. That concept is exactly what we could have been expected to develop through being acquainted with one and only one proper time, that of things practically stationary with respect to the earth, and through having no experience until very recently of things moving at high speeds in relation to this frame.

The conclusion of this discussion, which I have given in only a condensed form, is that there is indeed an intrinsic metric of space-time. Though the choice of units is of course arbitrary, there are intrinsic absolute quantitative features that have the general character of lengths or distances, though what they are lengths of or distances along are something other than the purely temporal or purely spatial dimensions of Newtonian theory. And it is worth noting that this conclusion rests upon and accommodates and incorporates all the characteristic doctrines of what is called the Special Theory of Relativity. This name is misleading: the doctrines themselves are very far from constituting a pure relativism about space and time.

4 ABSOLUTE MOTION AND REST

In this final section I shall put forward an argument that is much more radical than those of Sections 2 and 3. Whereas Sections 2 and 3 were directed only against loose thinking in some philosophical views about scientific matters, Section 4 will challenge what has been an orthodox view for about seventy years within science itself. I shall argue that the Special Theory of Relativity, as ordinarily understood, and as intended by Einstein, destroys itself, and collapses back into the Newtonian picture that includes absolute spatial positions and absolute motion. I have little doubt that my argument in this section is correct. On the other hand, I am not optimistic enough to hope that so heretical a thesis will win widespread acceptance in the foreseeable future. Though, like Hume with respect to religion, I am endeavouring to open the eyes of the public, and look forward to the ultimate downfall of a prevailing system of superstition, I am as reconciled as he was to the reflection that this will not happen in my lifetime, though I need not assume, as he did, that the superstition would last 'these many hundred years'.[4] So I would stress that while the arguments of Sections 2 and 3 may prepare people's minds for that of Section 4, they in no way depend upon the acceptance of the latter. *The conclusions of Sections 2 and 3 will stand, as will the general argument in Section 1 against attempts to settle all the issues together in favour of relativisim, even if the more extreme speculations of Section 4 are not cogent.*

I shall restrict my discussion to a type of situation which seems to be adequately represented by the Special Theory of Relativity, not bringing in the complications of the General Theory: that is, situations which are to all intents and purposes free from 'gravitational' forces. My argument starts from the above-mentioned fact, that the Special Theory of Relativity is ill-named, since it is itself far from being a pure space-time relativism. This comes out strikingly in the fact that light paths in space-time, the 'world lines' of light and other electro-magnetic radiations, are physically determinate: *light does not overtake light.* These paths are independent of the source of the radiation. They are equally independent of any observers, and of any choice of frame of reference. If, for simplicity of representation, we neglect two of the three spatial dimensions and picture space-time as a two-dimensional manifold of spatio-temporal points (or possible point-events), possible light paths constitute a rigid grid as in Figure 2. That is, there are two physically determinate families of parallel light paths. (Of course, there are really infinitely many such paths in the two sets of parallels.) This is a very different grid from that presupposed in Newtonian mech-

---

[4] Letter from Adam Smith to William Strahan dated 9 November 1776, in *Hume's Dialogues concerning Natural Religion*, edited by Norman Kemp Smith (London, 1947), pp. 243-8.

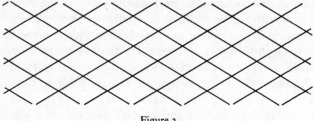

Figure 2

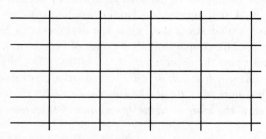

Figure 3

anics, shown in Figure 3, where the horizontal lines represent simultaneity at different places, and the vertical lines represent sameness of position at different times. But the Einsteinian grid is no less rigid than the Newtonian one, and it has the advantage of being experimentally detectable, which even Newton did not claim for his. We can tell directly whether two point-events lie on the same light path or not, by seeing whether light emitted at one reaches the other.

Now consider a single point-event 0, where a burst of radiation is sent out in all directions. Again, for simplicity, let us represent merely the light sent out in two diametrically opposite directions, represented as to the left and to the right in Figure 4. An equal group of photons, say, goes in each direction. Then the world lines of these two groups of photons are the determinate light paths in space-time 0*A* and 0*B*. Along such a light path there is neither a time-like length nor a space-like length other than zero. If, *per impossibile*, a set of clocks were to travel with the photons, they would all agree in measuring the proper time along any stretch of this path as zero, whether from 0 to *C*, say, or from 0 to *A*. Yet in the going of the photons from 0 through *C* to *A*, there is undoubtedly a causal process. If the radiation had not been emitted at 0, it would not have been received at *A*. Equally, if something had intercepted it at *C*, it would not have been received at *A*. The photons' being at *C* is causally intermediate between their being at 0 and their being at *A*. Also, the causal process represented by the line 0*A* is exactly like that represented by the line 0*B* in all respects other than the diametrically opposite directions in which the light travels. It follows that if we arbitrarily select a particular space-time point *C* on 0*A*, there is a unique corresponding space-time point—call it *D*—on 0*B*. That is, there is a part 0*D* of the 0*B* process which is, apart from direction, just like the 0*C* part of the 0*A* process. (See Figure 4.)

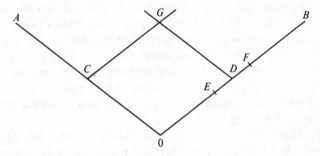

Figure 4

Here someone might object, asking 'How can you determine this corresponding point?' He might go on: 'Since anything that you could use to measure the "length" of 0*C* would yield the answer "zero", and anything you used to measure the "lengths" of 0*E*, 0*D*, 0*F*, and so on along 0*B* would also measure *each* of these as zero, you could not pick out *which* of 0*E*, 0*D*, and 0*F*, for example, corresponds exactly to 0*C*, and hence you could not decide that *D*, say, rather than *E* or *F*, corresponds to *C*.' I fully concede this. I do not claim that there is any way of *determining* the point that corresponds to *C*; I say only that *there is* one. And nothing but the sort of extreme verificationism which I mentioned, but set aside, in Section 1 would rule out this claim as meaningless. Verificationism apart, there may well *be* things which we cannot discover or identify; I persist, therefore, in the assertion that there is, on 0*B*, some point that corresponds, in the sense indicated, to *C*.

Now suppose that radiation is sent to the right from C just as the original group of photons reaches C, and to the left from D just as the original group of photons reaches D. (A mirror at each of these two space-time locations would do the trick.) Then these two new lots of radiation (or reflected photons) will also follow determinate space-time paths, as in Figure 4, and these paths will intersect at a unique, determinate, space-time point, which we can call G. The symmetry of the situation shows that, in the single spatial dimension represented in our diagrams, G is symmetrically placed with respect to $0A$ and $0B$. If we were to repeat the procedure, selecting a series of points C_1, C_2, ..., C_n, ... on $0A$, and identifying the corresponding points D_1, D_2, ..., D_n, ... on $0B$, and hence deriving a series of intersections G_1, G_2, ..., G_n, ..., then the line $0G_1G_2 \ldots G_n \ldots$ would be the one and only one world line in this plane which was thus symmetrically related to the physically determinate world lines, the light paths, $0A$ and $0B$. That is, $0G_1 G_2 \ldots G_n \ldots$ represents absolute rest, so far as this one spatial dimension is concerned. Similar constructions yield lines of absolute rest with respect to any two other spatial axes at right angles to this one, and putting them together we have a unique line of absolute rest through 0.

The same point can be made in a slightly different but equivalent way. If a single burst of radiation is sent out in all directions from a space-time point 0, and a space-time point C is arbitrarily chosen on one of the rays, then there is a sphere constituted by the corresponding points on all the other rays—in the sense of 'corresponding' indicated above. Secondary (or reflected) radiation from all over that sphere, coming inwards, will meet at a unique space-time point G; then the line $0G$ will be a line of absolute rest.

This conclusion can be related to what was said about the meaning and determination of absolute motion at the end of Section 2. Our present argument shows that *there is* a preferred frame of reference which is the only one to which all the causal processes constituted by the paths taken by radiation (with no 'gravitational' disturbance) are symmetrically related; though there is no *dynamically* preferred frame of reference there is a frame preferred on these other grounds.

This conclusion will, no doubt, seem shocking to anyone with even a slight acquaintance with Relativity Theory. A very natural reaction will be to object that the proposed construction is somehow circular, that the selection of the point D as that corresponding to C must be made from the point of view of some particular observer, or some particular frame of reference who, or which, has already implicitly taken $0G$ as a line of rest in that frame.* But I reply that the light paths $0A$ and $0B$ are observer-independent and frame-independent. They, above all else, are physically real and determinate. I concede that it is only from the point of view of a particular frame or observer that we can *specify* a point on $0B$ which we take to correspond to C, a point D' such that $0D'$ *looks* to this observer exactly like $0C$. But I maintain that as a frame-independent and observer-independent fact there must *be* some point D which really corresponds to C, which may well not be the D' which from some particular point of view seems to correspond to C, and I support this claim by an appeal to the concrete reality of the similar causal processes represented by $0A$ and $0B$.

How can this conclusion be reconciled with the empirical success of the Special Theory? Very easily. All that success involves is that there is no physical procedure that will pick out a uniquely preferred frame of reference from the set of inertial frames. My argument does not pretend to supply any such physical procedure. It is an abstract, philosophical, argument to show that there really is such a uniquely preferred frame, although we cannot identify it. In a sense my argument makes no difference to physics as a practical concern, as an applied theory. It would not matter at all to someone whose interest in science was purely technological or utilitarian. But it should matter to someone who is interested in the truth, in the question about what is the case.

Though shocking to those familiar with the scientific orthodoxy of the twentieth century, my conclusion should not really be surprising to anyone who reflects upon the way in which, as I said, possible light paths constitute a physically determinate space-time grid. We are simply using the admitted rigidity and symmetry of that grid to show that there must be a further, though concealed, symmetry, in fact to show that there is, though we cannot discover it, the Newtonian grid of Figure 3.

---

*At this point Mackie had added, for inclusion in the revised version of his paper, a parenthetical sentence referring to the additional note that was never written: '(This objection is developed further in the Additional Note at the end of this article.)'—Edd.

However, there is *something* surprising here. Why, and how, does it come about that although there really is such a thing as absolute rest, we cannot identify it? There must be something odd about the laws of nature that enables them to constitute such a conspiracy of silence. In effect, this means that although there is a unique line of absolute rest through 0 with respect to which the light paths 0A and 0B are symmetrically placed, they appear, to each observer, to be symmetrically placed with respect to the line of rest in the inertial frame, whichever it is, with which he is moving. But this is simply the fact that the *measured* velocity of light in both directions (along 0A and 0B) is equal in each inertial frame, when that velocity is measured by the means which it is natural for an observer at rest in that frame to use. In effect, we shall have to take the Fitzgerald–Lorentz 'contractions' and 'retardations' literally, as real effects of high-speed absolute movement, that is, as Fitzgerald and Lorentz themselves interpreted them. But this is only a hint; a rather long story would be needed to explain in detail how mere motion could have such effects.[5] And I agree that until such an explanation is given, this conspiracy of silence will provide the best available evidence for the existence and activity of Descartes's *malin génie*—though I would, for this purpose, translate '*malin*' not as 'malignant' but merely as 'mischievous'.

When we thus take the 'contractions' and 'retardations' literally, as effects of absolute motion, we are explicitly satisfying the definition of 'absolute motion' that was offered at the end of Section 2, at least to the extent that we are saying that there is a preferred frame of reference such that even uniform motions relative to it have systematic effects, quite independently of there being any things associated with that frame.

If the argument of this section is sound, and there is such a thing as absolute rest (and therefore also absolute spatial position), this not only settles the issues numbered 3 and 2.1 in favour of absolutism, it also reacts upon the decisions we reached at the end of Section 3. At that point I said that the belief in absolute durations—lengths of time rather than proper time—could be rejected as resulting from the fact that our experience, until recently, has been confined to the proper time of one particular inertial frame, which we have therefore mistaken for a single universally applicable

---

[5] I am indebted for some suggestions about how such a story might go to the late Geoffrey Builder, of the Sydney University Physics Department.

dimension. But it now appears that out of all the different proper times there will be a unique one with a special status, namely the proper time of things at absolute rest. This we can now call 'time' *simpliciter*, and we can call the determinate lengths of this time 'absolute durations'. Other proper time intervals will still be intrinsic features of the space-time paths, but as resultants of their spatial and temporal components, and their significance as measurements will be a consequence of the odd behaviour of clocks systematically affected by Fitzgerald–Lorentz retardation. These clocks can therefore be corrected (as in the early part of Section 3) for these causal disturbances to yield measurements of *time*, and then *all* corrected clocks will, after all, come into line with one another. However, this unification of all families of clocks is purely theoretical: we can make no practical use of absolute time. In particular, we have no right to assume (at least without some further argument) that the proper time of our solar system is time *simpliciter*. Though our old-fashioned belief in a unique time dimension will turn out to have been true, it will still have been, as I said at the end of Section 3, unjustified.

To conclude, then, there is a case for absolutism about each of the issues numbered 2.1, 3, 5.1, 5.2, 5.3, 6.1, 6.2, and 6.3. About that numbered 4, my specific conclusion in Section 2 was only that it is an empirical question whether there is absolute acceleration or not, but if Section 4 shows that there is absolute motion, this will carry absolute acceleration with it. I have said nothing specifically about issue 2.2, or about any of the issues concerning absolute or relative existence.

However, I am at least as much concerned about the methods used in this discussion as about the conclusions reached on particular issues. My general thesis is that items that are not directly observable, and terms and statements to which meaning cannot be given directly by methods of verification, can be legitimately introduced. To justify such introductions, we require only familiar methods for the sorting out of causally relevant factors, together with the principle that a hypothesis which would compel us to accept certain observed agreements as no more than a massive coincidence can be rejected in favour of a hypothesis which explains that apparent coincidence by resolving the agreements into consequences of some unitary state of affairs.

XV

LOCKE AND REPRESENTATIVE PERCEPTION

A NATURAL way to approach this topic would be first to enquire what view Locke held about perception, to go on to consider whether it counts as a representative theory, and finally whether it is defensible or not. But I prefer—and I believe it will be more economical—to reverse this order, and first outline what I think is a defensible theory of perception, then ask in what sense this is a representative theory, and only at the end discuss whether such a view can be plausibly ascribed to Locke.

In *Problems from Locke* I distinguished two variants of the picture-original theory, one which made the pictures physically real objects somewhere inside the perceiver's head, the other which made them merely intentional objects, existing as the contents of states of awareness, and therefore literally mind-dependent. I also made, but perhaps did not sufficiently stress, a further distinction within the first alternative. One view would be that the alleged physically real pictures are contemplated and made the objects of an initial class of perceptual judgements, and that judgements about the material or external world are inferred from these by some explicit process of reasoning. The other would be that though physically real intermediates occur and play some important role in perception, they are not themselves normally taken as objects of perception, let alone as pictures representing some originals distinct from them, from which the existence and characters of the originals are to be inferred; that on the contrary ordinary perception is judgementally direct, that we make claims and form beliefs non-inferentially about how things outside our heads are. Of these two possible views involving physically real pictures, the first is so evidently false that we need pay no further attention to it, while the second is almost uncontroversially true. In my book I devoted some space to this second view, mainly in order to get clearer what might be meant by the claim that we see ordinary outside things

Previously unpublished: typescript dated April 1977.

directly; but I said there, and I would still maintain, that the important sort of representationalist or picture-original view is that which takes the pictures (perhaps Locke's 'ideas') to be intentional objects. It is this account that I am concerned to defend.

In this defence, the first and vital step is to show that there are such intentional objects. But this is surely undeniable. At the moment a large number of birds are twittering outside my window. There is a perfectly sensible question, 'How does it sound to me?'. Of course, I can't answer this question adequately in words, but simply in hearing the birds I am aware of the answer: *that* is how it sounds to me. And this answer could hold unchanged even if there were in fact no birds, and I were hearing a tape-recording or having an hallucination. Or I put a bit of salt on my tongue: *that* is how it tastes to me. But the crucial case is that of visual perception; can I say equally lucidly, '*That* is how it looks to me'? One complication is that a more satisfactory verbal answer is now available: 'It looks to me as if there is a level floor covered with a grey carpet, several wooden chairs standing on it, and behind them bookshelves containing books of various shapes, sizes, colours, and so on.' This is, indeed, only a rough and far from adequate description: how it looks has far more detail in it than any verbal description can capture. Still, the important thing is that how it looks to me includes the recognition of persisting solid objects in a three-dimensional space. On the other hand, I can, with an effort, pick out 'how it looks to me' in another sense: I can concentrate on a purely visual presentation—a combination of variously coloured areas in a two-dimensional visual field. That is, I can distinguish an uninterpreted how-it-looks from an interpreted how-it-looks. But it is the interpreted how-it-looks that is really how it looks to me in all normal adult visual perception. Yet that it looks thus-and-so, even in the interpreted way, is one thing, that it is thus-and-so would be another. The intentional object is not an external object or state of affairs.

The second step in this defence is to insist that it is by virtue of my having these intentional objects that I perceive the outside world. But this, too, seems undeniable. Moreover, it is on the whole body of such perceptions that all my ordinary knowledge or belief about the material world rests, directly or indirectly.

This much, as I say, seems undeniable. But does it constitute or commit us to a representative theory in any interesting sense, to anything that direct realists have denied or would want to deny?

Does it entail that we do not see tables and chairs but only our ideas of tables and chairs? This unnatural way of speaking would be forced on us only if we assumed, quite unnecessarily, that to see X is to have a form of awareness that informs us infallibly and completely about X. Or does it entail that all we perceive directly or immediately is ideas or percepts or sense-data, and that we perceive tables and chairs only mediately or indirectly? I cannot answer this question, because I find both this claim and its opposite unclear: I am not sure what issues are being raised. We can and must still say that even when we allow for these intentional objects perception is ordinarily judgementally direct though causally mediated.

For this is in a way a causal theory. Its looking as it does to me now is a causal product of how things are: outside objects act upon my sense organs and so upon my brain; the antecedent condition of these is also causally relevant; how it looks (or sounds, or tastes, etc.) to me is a result of this interaction. To what extent causation enters into a correct analysis of our concept of perception, or into the meaning of perception statements, is more doubtful. It is plausible to take '*He* sees a chair' as implying that there is a chair which is giving rise to his visual perception. But if I simply say, while seeing it and because I see it, 'There is a chair over there', I may well not be making any causal claim, even an implicit one. And 'I see a chair' can be used as practically equivalent to this.

What is more important is that this account leaves room for the suggestion that our ideas, in the sense of these intentional objects, may either resemble or fail to resemble the outside things. It looks to me as if there is a level floor, chairs, shelves, books, that is to say, solid objects of certain three-dimensional shapes and sizes arranged at various distances from me in a three-dimensional and at least roughly Euclidean space. And perhaps there are things with pretty much these positions and sizes and shapes. But it also looks to me as if all these things had colours as intrinsic features of their surfaces. And perhaps they do not. I don't mean that I may be getting the colours a little bit wrong, as I may well be making small mistakes about the shapes and sizes: I mean that the things may have no colours as I see colours at all. No doubt, if one book looks red to me while another looks blue, under standard illumination and in good conditions for seeing, this will be because there is *some* intrinsic difference between their surfaces, and we could use the adjective 'red' (or 'blue') to mean 'such as to look red (or blue) to a standard observer in good conditions'. (Locke himself suggests something like this in *Essay* II xxxii 14–16.) But something which is red or blue in this sense may well not have, intrinsically, any colour-as-I-see-it. Thus the intentional object view leaves room for the question whether our ideas are or are not resemblances of objective qualities, and for Locke's distinction on this ground between primary and secondary qualities, his claim that our ideas of primary qualities resemble those qualities, while our ideas of secondary qualities do not resemble anything intrinsic to the objects. My account is enough of a representative theory to leave room for Locke's way of drawing the primary/secondary quality distinction, whereas direct realism would either exclude the distinction or allow it to be drawn only in some other way.

(Admittedly it is controversial whether, as Locke thinks, we ordinarily take our ideas of secondary qualities to be such resemblances. On the one hand I find in myself a strong tendency to ascribe colours-as-I-see-them to the surfaces of things. On the other hand it is hard not to realize that colours-as-I-see-them depend somehow on illumination. Again, just where do we naïvely locate sounds-as-we-hear-them? And do I, even in my most naïve moments, really want to ascribe saltiness-as-I-taste-it to that white powder, the salt? That is to say, we might consider offering the Lockean distinction between primary and secondary qualities as an analysis of the conceptual scheme of not very sophisticated people, rather than as a correction of it. But this is a minor matter.)

A still more important question is whether this is a representative theory in the sense of being one which leaves room for scepticism about the external world as a whole, one which has what Jonathan Bennett calls a veil-of-perception problem built into it. *Prima facie* it is. For once we have distinguished its looking, sounding, tasting, etc. thus-and-so from its being thus-and-so, we have made it at least logically and conceptually possible that there is nothing which is, in any respect at all, as things look and sound and taste. Summing up all these elements that consist in how it looks, how it sounds, and so on as the contents of my experience, I can ask coherently whether there is anything at all which these contents

resemble or even represent. In fact, several options are open here.*
There is the common-sense realist view which draws no distinction
between primary and secondary qualities, allowing not only shapes
but also colours-as-we-see-them and the like to be resemblances
of intrinsic qualities of things. There is the Lockean view which
allows this for shapes, etc., but denies it for colours and the like.
Again, there is a view which Bertrand Russell held at one time, in
effect that such spatial qualities as shape are secondary qualities,
that physical space is quite distinct from perceptual space; there is
something which gives rise to our percepts, but it corresponds
to them only structurally, not qualitatively in any respect. But also,
it seems, there is the sceptical possibility: perhaps there is just my experience with its contents, its intentional objects, and nothing else
at all.

It may be argued that this last suggestion is incoherent. 'Where
is there nothing else?' 'Outside us.' But 'outside' has meaning only
if we accept the very thing we are supposed to be doubting. Or if
we say, 'Perhaps there is just my experience with its contents' we
are using a set of concepts which involves the identification and
reidentification of myself as a subject of experience, and this makes
sense only along with the concepts of a spatio-temporal world of
persisting things which I can observe with some success, which
again is the very thing we are supposed to be doubting. However,
I do not find this argument cogent. From whatever source I have
derived them or however I have constructed them, I have these
concepts now. It is part of the contents of my experience that things
seem to be, objectively, thus-and-so. Once I have also introduced
the notion of the contents of my experience, of its looking thus-
and-so, I can raise the question whether things are like this in a
sense which is not automatically answered in the affirmative merely
because they look like this. It is true that I cannot report the
contents of my experience with any approach to adequacy except
in terms which relate to a supposed material world. But it does not
follow that I have to presuppose the objective existence of a
material world in order to ask whether these contents really represent any such world, and so undermine this question itself.

The account of perception which I am defending has, therefore,

---

* In a marginal note at this point Mackie suggests adding a reference to 'the very
naïve view which makes no distinction between content of experience and reality'.—
Edd.

some of the main characteristics of representative theories, including the one often thought to be fatal to them, that they leave room for sceptical doubts and a veil-of-perception problem, that they compel one to raise what is thought to be, once raised, the unanswerable question, 'How do we know that there is anything which our percepts resemble or represent?', or 'If all that we are directly acquainted with are ideas (or percepts, or contents of experience, or intentional objects), how can we ever break out of this circle so as to have even beliefs, let alone knowledge, of a real world?'.

However, this supposedly unanswerable question can be answered. But in order to answer it we must split it into its two components, a problem of meaning and a problem of justification. The first problem is, 'How can we make meaningful claims about a reality other than our ideas, percepts, etc.?' The second is, 'Given that we can make such claims, how can we support them?'

Now it is clear that for anyone who adopts a verificationist theory of meaning these questions are not separable: what justified any claim would be what gave it its meaning, and, what is more serious, would wholly determine and restrict the meaning given. Since the ultimate verification of any claims I make about the material world must consist in how things look or feel or sound or taste or smell to me, the real meaning of those claims would also be that I should have just such-and-such contents of experience. But this is only a further reason for not adopting a verificationist theory of meaning, which in any case has little initial plausibility. A plausible empiricist doctrine of meaning would say rather that the meanings of any claims we make must be built up somehow out of elements which figure within the contents of our experience, and this does not entail that what we meaningfully say must be wholly about actual or possible experiences.

It is obvious that if we think of the content of our experiences on the model of what I called an interpreted how-it-looks there is no real problem in the meaning part of the supposed veil of perception. If it looks to me as if there is a level floor, chairs, books, and so on, then this how-it-looks already includes the standard meanings of the material object language in which we make claims about the external world. But what if we attend rather to items of the form of an uninterpreted how-it-looks? This is important, because if we deny, as Locke denied, that we have innate ideas of space and time and substance and causation, we must suppose that at an early stage in our lives we started with experiences whose contents were only of the uninterpreted sort, and somehow developed the interpreted sort out of these. The plausible empiricist doctrine must be applicable also to these, though even if we deny innate ideas we need not deny that we have several innate perceptual propensities, tendencies to seek and pick out and concentrate on certain kinds of feature within the content of our experience. It would require detailed work in conceptual analysis to show how we might have built up the interpreted from the uninterpreted content, and it would require detailed work in genetic psychology to find how we have actually done so. But the main point, and the only one I can make here, is that there is no barrier in principle to this development. Even an uninterpreted how-it-looks is a cluster of features seen simply as being there. These features are not given *as* appearances, *as* mind-dependent, so there is no danger that claims given meaning in terms of them will be limited to what is purely phenomenal. The meaning part of the veil-of-perception problem is therefore soluble in principle, and there is no reason to doubt that by detailed work it can be solved in full.

The disposal of the problem of meaning brings the problem of justification into focus. If we can meaningfully claim that there is an objective material world which the contents of our experience represent, we can also meaningfully frame the suggestion that there may be no such world. Of course, this problem arises only in retrospect. We did not raise it in infancy and then construct a rational argument for the material spatio-temporal world. We just came automatically to have our ordinary view of the world by processes in which what we can roughly call imagination and innate propensities played a large part: no question of justification arose at that time. But when it does arise, in retrospect, we can surely give and defend the well known answer that the broad outline hypothesis of the existence of material things is well confirmed, by the success with which it explains our having experiences with just such contents as our experiences do have. Though we can find coherent formulations of, for example, Descartes's suggestion that it may all be a dream, or of Berkeley's thesis that a more powerful mind, rather than a material world, is responsible for those of our experiences that we mark off as perceptions of real things, no such rival hypotheses yield nearly so good an explanation of all the details of our experience. An important part of these details is the way in which we can develop, within our outline hypothesis, causal accounts of our perceptual processes themselves.

If there is a defensible view of this sort, and it is in some interesting ways a representative theory, we can turn to the question whether Locke held any such view—in particular whether we can identify his 'ideas', in contexts where he is writing about perception, with intentional objects. I would concede that this question does not admit of a conclusive answer. Locke is too careless in his terminology and, perhaps surprisingly, too little concerned to describe exactly what goes on when we perceive something, to have committed himself firmly to any one view. Yet there are several things that at least favour the proposed identification.

There was repeated controversy, in the century or so after Descartes, on the question whether ideas should be taken as internal real objects of perception and judgement or whether having ideas should be taken merely as a synonym for perceiving. A key figure in this controversy is Arnauld. Malebranche had argued that 'in order to the mind's perceiving any object, it is absolutely necessary that the idea of that object be actually present to it'; 'the immediate object of the mind, when it sees the sun, for example, is not the sun, but something which is intimately united to the soul'. And then, rejecting various other possible ways in which ideas can be actually present to our minds, he concludes that it must be God's ideas that achieve this. That is why 'we see all things in God'. But Arnauld criticizes this whole approach, saying that ideas are not objects whose existence is distinct from their being perceived. They are rather modifications of our minds, namely acts of perception: 'I take the *idea* of an object, and the perception of an object, to be the same thing'.

Now John Yolton has pointed out, in a paper which he read recently in Oxford, that Locke not only had Arnauld's criticism of Malebranche in his library, but marked his copy of it extensively and apparently with approval. Locke seems both to have known Arnauld's arguments and to have been inclined to agree with them. (Yolton mentions this also in his introduction to the Everyman abridged edition of Locke's *Essay*, pp. xxi–xxii.) And there are quite a number of passages in the *Essay* which seem to endorse Arnauld's view, especially if we read them in the light of this controversy. For example:

I iv 20: 'Whatever *Idea* is in the mind, is either an actual perception, or else, having been an actual perception, is so in the mind, that by the memory it can be made an actual perception again.'

II i 5: '*External Objects furnish the Mind with the* Ideas *of sensible qualities*, which are all those different perceptions they produce in us.'

II i 9: 'To ask, *at what time a Man has first any Ideas*, is to ask, when he begins to perceive; having *Ideas*, and Perception being the same thing.'

II i 23: 'I conceive that *Ideas* in the Understanding, are coeval with *Sensation*; which is such an Impression or Motion, made in some part of the Body, as produces some Perception in the Understanding.'

II viii 12: 'If then external Objects be not united to our Minds, when they produce *Ideas* in it; and yet we perceive *these original Qualities* in such of them as singly fall under our Senses, 'tis evident, that some motion must be there continued by our Nerves, or animal Spirits, by some parts of our Bodies, to our Brains or the seat of Sensation, there to *produce in our Minds the particular* Ideas *we have of them*.'

That is, Locke assumes that in sensory perception there will be some bodily modification, but the function of this is to produce a perception in the understanding (and this is the idea), not to be itself inspected or contemplated.

IIx2: 'But our *Ideas* being nothing, but actual Perceptions in the Mind, which cease to be any thing, when there is no perception of them, this *laying up* of our *Ideas* in the Repository of the Memory, signifies no more but this, that the Mind has a Power, in many cases, to revive Perceptions, which it has once had, with this additional Perception annexed to them, that it had had them before.'

This insistence that ideas do not actually exist as ideas in our memories except when they are being consciously recalled comes closer than any other passage I know of to committing Locke to denying that his ideas are physically real intermediates, say images, and hence to identifying them either with acts of perceiving or with the intentional objects of such acts.

II xxxii 1: '... our *Ideas*, being nothing but bare Appearances or Perceptions in our Minds ...'

It is true that these considerations might be taken to point in a different direction from that which I want. They might make us identify having an idea of a table, as this occurs when we are actually seeing a table, simply with perceiving the table, while the latter is itself construed in a direct realist way, with no representative factor present at all. But this is surely ruled out by all of Locke's talk about ideas sometimes resembling and sometimes failing to resemble something in the objects. The intentional object interpretation is the one which best accommodates both this way of speaking and the denial that ideas have any existence distinct from that of the act or process of perceiving.

There is at least one passage in which Locke tries explicitly to deal with the contrast between what I have called the interpreted how-it-looks and the uninterpreted how-it-looks. This is II ix 8–10, where he discusses Molyneux's problem. The way he puts it is that '... *the Ideas we receive by sensation, are often* in grown People *alter'd by the Judgment*, without our taking notice of it'. When we have before us a globe of uniform colour, he says ''tis certain, that the *Idea* thereby imprinted in our Mind, is of a flat Circle variously shadow'd', but 'the Judgment presently'—that is, immediately—'alters the Appearances into their Causes' and 'frames to it self the perception of a convex Figure and an uniform Colour'. This remark seems to equate 'idea' with the uninterpreted how-it-looks, or perhaps even with some physical intermediate which is literally received, and to contrast this with the 'perception' produced by the judgement. But a page later Locke reverses this terminology, saying of the same sort of example that 'we take that for the Perception of our Sensation which is an *Idea* formed by our Judgment'. And a little later again he says ''tis not so strange, that our Mind should often change the *Idea* of its Sensation, into that of its Judgment, and make one serve only to excite the other, without our taking notice of it'.

This passage illustrates what is in any case abundantly shown elsewhere, that Locke has no precise terminology, and that it is therefore pointless to ask exactly what he means by, say, 'idea'. But what is more important is that it shows also that he was well aware of the threefold contrast between what is there, how it looks in the uninterpreted sense, and how it looks in the interpreted sense. Moreover, he knew that in ordinary sophisticated adult perception we are often not consciously aware of the second at all. We have the third not by explicit and time-taking inference from the second, but by unconscious automatic and immediate interpretation. Yet this interpretation, he holds, results from past experience of, for example, 'what kind of appearance convex Bodies are wont to make in us; what alterations are made in the reflections of Light, by the difference of the sensible Figures of Bodies'. Also, these matters can be deliberately taken into account, and are so used by painters.

I would, therefore, defend the intentional object variant of the representative theory of perception, both in itself and as the account which can best do justice to the various points on which Locke insisted, and was right to insist.

XVI

ANTI-REALISMS

A GOOD deal has been said and written recently about realism and anti-realism, but I find the variety and mixtures of views that come under these two headings bewildering. I can hardly hope to say anything new about these topics. This paper is rather an attempt to sort out part of the tangle, and at least to indicate some things that I still find obscure.

Michael Dummett (in his 1963 paper 'Realism', in *Truth and Other Enigmas*, pp. 145-65) points out that there are quite a number of different 'realisms'—that is, we can have realism about each of a number of subject-matters: for example, about universals, the material world, mental states, character, theoretical scientific entities, mathematics, the past and the future. Some of the anti-realisms opposed to these have recognized names—nominalism, phenomenalism, behaviourism, scientific positivism, constructivism (or intuitionism). In many cases the issue can be stated by asking whether there really exist entities of a certain type, or whether such entities are 'among the ultimate constituents of reality', or again linguistically by asking whether certain terms genuinely refer, or—and this is Dummett's preferred formulation—whether statements of a certain class 'possess an objective truth-value, independently of our means of knowing it: and are true or false in virtue of a reality existing independently of us' (p. 146). Anti-realism, he says, often takes a reductionist form—for example, mental states or characters may be reduced to behaviour, and phenomenalism says that material objects are 'reducible to (constructions out of) sense-data'; or a statement of the disputed class is held to be true only if some suitable statement of the reductive class is true.

But Dummett argues that reductionism is neither necessary nor sufficient for anti-realism. He identifies the conflict between realism and anti-realism with 'a conflict about the kind of meaning possessed by statements of the disputed class' and about what their

Previously unpublished: first (and longer) part read in Oxford on 13 November 1980 as a paper to the Philosophical Society. Typescript dated two weeks earlier. All page numbers refer to Dummett's *Truth and Other Enigmas* (London, 1978) except where Mackie clearly indicates otherwise.

truth consists in: 'For the anti-realist, an understanding of such a statement consists in knowing what counts as evidence adequate for the assertion of the statement, and the truth of the statement can consist only in the existence of such evidence', but the realist holds that we 'have a conception of the statement's being true even in the absence of such evidence'. In consequence, 'The anti-realist cannot allow that the law of excluded middle is generally valid: the realist may, and characteristically will' (p. 155). However, in the Preface to *Truth and Other Enigmas* (1978) he corrects this, saying that only the principle of bivalence is the touchstone for realism, not the law of excluded middle (p. xxx).

In 'Common Sense and Physics' (in *Perception and Identity*, edited by G.F. Macdonald, [1979],) Dummett again recommends the characterization of realism in terms of our possession of 'a notion of truth for statements of the given class relative to which they satisfy the principle of bivalence' (p. 4). The reason which he actually gives there for this recommendation is circular—namely, that we should not characterize realism in terms of non-reduction, because reduction need not lead to a failure of bivalence, that is, it need not yield non-realism as here characterized. However, it is plain that his real reason is that by making bivalence or the failure of it the touchstone we arrive at a more significant classification of philosophical views. Let me, then, try to illustrate the relations between different ways of formulating the realist/anti-realist issue, reductionism, and bivalence, by examining some particular disputes.

I want to start with a variety of anti-realism about the past; not, however, either of the forms that Dummett discusses in 'The Reality of the Past'* (in *Truth and Other Enigmas*, pp. 358–74), but rather a set of views which I shall ascribe to Philip Henry Gosse, whose opinions inspired Russell's formulation of scepticism about the past; but I am not claiming that what I offer is a historically correct account of the views of the nineteenth-century naturalist.

Gosse held that the Bible, being the word of God, is literally true, and therefore that the world was created in 4004 B.C. (give or take a year or so). But I assume that he did not find any obscurity or indeterminacy in the meaning of sentences of the form 'Such-and-such happened three thousand years ago', or of the form 'This happened a thousand years before that'. Using a suitable number of iterations of the latter construction, he would have had no dif-

---

* Originally published (Aristotelian Society) 1969.—Edd.

ficulty in giving a determinate literal meaning to such a sentence as 'There were trilobites swimming in the sea five hundred million years ago'; but all such statements, with time references to dates before 4004 B.C., were, he held, false. However, he knew well that there are geological strata which look as if they were laid down over millions of years, and fossils in them which look like traces of prehistoric animals and plants, and that these appearances are such that they can be interpreted as a coherent (though incomplete) record of a prehistory of the earth going back for millions of years. He knew also that some of his contemporaries who were not convinced of the literal truth of the Bible did so interpret them. In order to be able to discuss particular points of science with men like Lyell and Darwin, and perhaps also in order to formulate his own discoveries, queries, and arguments more economically, Gosse (I assume) introduced new meanings for his own use of sentences that on the surface seem to refer to dates before the Creation. For example, our one about trilobites simply means 'There are geological strata, and fossils in them, which are *as if* there were trilobites swimming around five hundred million years ago', where this 'as if' can be spelled out further in terms of indications that emerge when we try to put together all the various geological data and interpret them as a record of prehistory. Whereas with their previous, literal, meanings all prehistorical statements were, in Gosse's view, false, with these introduced meanings some would be true. And if the introduced meanings also involved the rule that the statement about trilobites, for example, would be false only if there were geological data which similarly 'indicated' that there were not trilobites at that time, there would be some prehistorical statements which were neither true nor false, namely those for which there are no 'indications' either way. And whereas Lyell and Darwin would assume that prehistorical statements (if sufficiently precise) obey classical logic and have truth-values quite independently of our having any evidence for or against them, Gosse is in a more complex position. With what he might call their literal meaning they do indeed have such an evidence-independent truth-value: they are all false. But with the new meanings that he introduces in order to be able to make a worthwhile use of them they may be true, may be false, but again may be indeterminate, and so, presumably, obey some non-classical logic.

As a second example I shall take a certain interpretation of Berkeley's views. Dummett, by the way, has complained that Berkeley's argument for the existence of God 'is usually caricatured and always sneered at' (p. xxxix). I have been discussing the argument elsewhere; I hope I have not caricatured it and I have certainly not sneered at it; but here I shall not discuss it but merely look at some of its implications. I shall follow what I believe to be the best interpretation both in the sense that it agrees better than any other with most of what Berkeley says and also in the sense that it gives him a more defensible position than any alternative interpretation. But for my present purposes I need not defend either of these claims: we can regard this simply as a position that some-one, whom we can arbitrarily call 'Berkeley', might conceivably hold.

There is, on this view, a reality which exists quite independently of my mind and of my knowledge. The only ultimate constituents of that reality are minds or spirits, including both finite minds and the mind of God. But each mind has ideas which, in a less ultimate sense, 'exist' in and by being perceived by that mind. Some of God's ideas are, as we may put it, *as of* material things—trees, houses, stars, planets, and so on—in somewhat the same way in which most of my ideas are as of material things, though God's ideas are much clearer and more detailed than mine. I have an indication of some of these ideas in God's mind because God puts copies of them into my mind. But there is 'an opinion strangely prevailing amongst men, that houses, mountains, rivers and in a word all sensible objects have an existence natural and real ...' (*Principles* § 4). If this is an opinion, presumably the statement that expresses it must be meaningful, and Berkeley must allow that particular material object sentences used in accordance with this opinion, asserting the 'natural and real' existence of, say, a tree in the middle of the Gobi desert, independent of my mind, or of any mind, are also meaningful. But all such material object statements, embodying this opinion, will be false. However, Berkeley, and anyone persuaded of the correctness of his philosophy, can and naturally will use material object sentences with a different meaning— for example, 'God has a set of ideas as of a tree in the middle of the Gobi desert'. Of material object statements with this interpretation, some are true and some are false, and they have truth-values quite independently of my access to them. All that is needed to determine a truth-value is that God should have ideas as of the existence or as of the lack of a material object of that kind at that place. But again these statements may fail to obey the principle of bivalence. If we think, for simplicity, of the whole of space-time as being divided into numbered cells, there might be some cells with regard to which God did not have ideas as of their containing objects of certain sorts, nor yet ideas as of their being empty. Thus a statement of the form 'There is an object of kind X in cell number N', with this Berkeleian interpretation, might fail to be either true or false—where it counts as false only if God has a contrary idea, either as of that cell's being empty, or as of its being occupied by something not of kind X. Material object statements, thus interpreted, would again presumably obey not classical logic, but some logic that allows them to be neither true nor false.

On the other hand, since his mind is infinite, it might be that God has thought one way or another about every possibility, that he has thought as of some description of the apparent contents of every one of those numbered cells, so that every material object statement will, as it happens, be either true or false. But there is no necessity about this.

As I said, material object statements thus understood have truth-values quite independently of my access to them. They likewise have meanings that are quite independent of any ways that I have of determining their truth-value. If it is asked how they acquire such meanings, the answer must be that I know what it is myself to have a set of tree-ideas, and I have some 'notion' of my own mind as having those ideas; from these materials I can construct the notion of another mind having somewhat similar ideas. So although my initial grasp of the relevant meanings is acquired in circumstances in which I am sure that the statements in question are true, I am subsequently able to use statements about God's having ideas, or Berkeleian material object statements which are equivalent to these, irrespectively of any means that I have for determining their truth-value.

It seems to me that Philip Henry Gosse is an anti-realist, of a certain sort, about prehistorical statements or about events before 4004 B.C., and that Berkeley is an anti-realist, of a certain sort, about the material world or about material object statements. But in neither case does the anti-realism originate from any problem about meaning or from any general theory about meaning or truth-conditions. Rather, Gosse has biblical grounds for saying that there were no prehistorical events, and Berkeley has several reasons for saying that there are no material things with a 'natural or real' existence as ultimate constituents of the universe. In either case the statements have non-problematic meanings with which they are all false.

(In Berkeley's case, these meanings may be somewhat problematic. For, first, he lays great stress on the argument of § 23 which, if it were valid, would show that I cannot conceive the existence of anything apart from my own mind; it is fortunate that it is not valid, since, if it were, it would make it impossible for Berkeley to assert that God exists independently. Secondly, Berkeley thinks that I cannot abstract the existence of any sensible thing from its being perceived, which suggests that I cannot meaningfully assert such existence. But this is incompatible with his report of the opinion strangely prevailing amongst men.)

However, the statements of both these 'disputed classes' are then given other meanings such that they may be true, false, or indeterminate. For Berkeley, such indeterminacy has nothing to do with *my* having no way of deciding their truth-value, for there are other statements of the class whose truth-value is completely cut off from me, and yet which, on this Berkeleian view, still have a definite truth-value. For Gosse, the indeterminacy goes along more closely with our inability to decide, since if there were rocks of the right sort anywhere we might in principle be able to inspect them; but still the important thing is that what would constitute a truth-value is lacking, quite objectively, rather than that we cannot get at it.

Each of these is plainly a local anti-realism, not a global one. Gosse is a realist about rocks and fossils, as well as many other post-Creation events and things. Berkeley is a realist about minds and about the fact that minds, others as well as his own, have ideas. Also, each of these views is reductionist: the new meanings given to statements of the disputed class are given in terms of statements about things with regard to which the thinker in question is a realist: prehistory is reduced to rocks and fossils, material things to a mind having ideas.

I borrow a third example from Hilary Putnam's 'What is "Realism"?' (in *Aristotelian Society Proceedings*, 76 (1975-6)). Putnam contrasts two sorts of history that a scientific theoretical term may have. 'Phlogiston', for example, was used for a time and then disappeared without trace. There is nothing recognized by nineteenth or twentieth century science that we can say that eighteenth century chemists were talking about when they used this term. On the other hand, we can still say, from the point of view of the physics of the second half of the twentieth century, that when Bohr and Rutherford used the word 'electron' in the early 1900s they were talking about electrons, the very same particles that we still talk about, even though they misdescribed them to some extent. Let us think of the history of science as a sequence of theories, T_1, T_2, T_3, etc. In one sort of history the terms used in T_1 are dropped from T_2, those used in T_2 are dropped from T_3, and so on. In the other sort of history the old terms are still used, though new ones are added, in the newer theory, and the newer theory allows that the old one was dealing, somewhat inaccurately, with the same theoretical entities as it now recognizes. If the history of science were wholly of the first sort, it would be reasonable to perform a meta-induction and conclude that the terms of the currently accepted theory, T_3 say, will also sink without trace before long, and so on with all theoretical terms, and consequently to refuse to interpret any theoretical science realistically, since a realistic interpretation would make all its statements false, and not even approximations to truth. Rather we should adopt the positivist view that any scientific theory merely says that macroscopic, fairly directly observable, things behave *as if* there were such-and-such a microstructure, or, in general, such-and-such not directly observed entities. If, on the other hand, the history of science is predominantly of the second sort, it will be reasonable to take a realist view of theoretical entities, and say that there really are electrons and so on, and that we are acquiring progressively more, and more correct, information about the same things. The choice between realism and anti-realism about theoretical scientific entities is thus an empirical one, to be settled by seeing just how the history of science goes. (It is not, of course, that the realist view here is just the view that there is 'convergence'; rather it is that such 'convergence' is evidence for the real existence of entities which are fairly correctly described by the meanings of our theoretical terms, and to a correct description of which our theories approach more closely as time goes on.)

Now suppose that someone believes, and has good reason to believe, that the history of science is of the first sort, supporting the positivist view. But suppose that he is also a scientist, and, like most scientists, goes in mainly for what Kuhn calls 'normal science': he is largely doing detailed work that fits pretty well into the framework of the currently accepted theory T_3. Naturally he uses the language of T_3 in talking and thinking about his experimental and theoretical work. Yet, being a positivist, he thinks that every statement of T_3, taken literally, purporting to refer to certain real entities, is either false or, if it has a subject term that lacks reference, neither true nor false, and yet not just undecided either. In this predicament, he will naturally give the statements of T_3 a different meaning, taking a statement S to be true whenever the macroscopic, fairly directly observable, objects either do or would behave in ways which someone who accepted T_3 unreservedly would take as establishing S in its literal meaning, and taking S to be false whenever things do or would behave in ways which would similarly be taken as establishing not-S. And then, since the ways in which fairly directly observable things either do or would behave might be such as neither to establish S nor establish not-S (in their original meaning), S in its new meaning might be neither true nor false.

(Putnam seems to say that the statements of T_3, thus interpreted, would obey intuitionist logic. However, he adds an epicycle. It is possible to define what we can then call classical logical connectives within intuitionist logic, so that statements built with the help of these connectives will (on the surface) obey classical logic after all, even though the underlying logic in terms of which these connectives are defined is intuitionistic. Putnam speculates that if scientists found themselves in the predicament of our positivist, they would do just this. As a result, the formal logic and also, he claims, the formal semantics of this science would still be classical, giving an appearance of realism. To detect the anti-realism, we should have to look beyond these formal features, presumably to some informal explanation of the statements of this theoretical science, or of the conditions which were taken as justifying their being described as true or false. No doubt Putnam is right about this technical possibility, and he may be right also in his speculation that it would be utilized if the occasion arose. But, if it were, this would surely be what Russell called, in another context, a 'pitiful and paltry evasion'. The statements of T_3, as understood by the positivist, would really be obeying some non-classical logic.)

I borrow a fourth example from Dummett's article 'The Reality of the Past'. Someone who has no sympathy with constructivist philosophies of mathematics, he points out (p. 366), may hold that the continuum hypothesis, having been proved consistent with but independent of the standard axioms of set theory, is neither true nor false. His reason could be the belief that when we do set theory 'we do not have in mind any one definite structure, but only a class of structures sharing certain common features described in our set-theoretical axioms', and that the hypothesis is true of some of these structures but false of others. If this thinker adds the rule that 'true' as applied to statements of set theory is to mean 'true of (Dummett: 'in') all such structures', and 'false' to mean 'false of (Dummett: 'in') all such structures', then if the continuum hypothesis is true of some such structures but false of others, it will count as neither true nor false as a statement of set theory. But for any one determinate structure it will be either true or false. Has this thinker adopted any sort of anti-realism? His position is analogous to that of someone setting out to write a short encyclopaedia article on 'Grasses' and deciding to count as true all and only those statements that are true of all grasses, such as 'Grasses are monocotyledons', and as false all and only those that are false of all grasses, and who must therefore regard many statements with 'grasses' as subject as being neither true nor false. We might say that this writer is recognizing the non-existence of a certain supposed entity, an imaginary completely uniform class of grasses, and therefore giving to sentences that might have been taken as describing this supposed class new meanings in terms of the real but highly diverse species of the order *Gramineae*. And similarly our mathematician could be called an anti-realist about a supposedly unitary structure identified by set theory, but a realist about the many diverse structures.

It is obvious in what sense each of the four views introduced in these examples is anti-realist. The thinker in question denies the existence of certain supposed entities: events before 4004 B.C., extra-mental material objects, all theoretical entities such as electrons and phlogiston, or a unitary structure of sets. Correspondingly, he says that a class of terms that look like referring terms do not really refer. Again, he says that there is a class of sentences which can have either of two sorts of meaning. With one sort of meaning they always either are false or are neither true nor false because their subjects lack reference. With the other sort of meaning, they may be true, may be false, but may be neither true nor false. In each case the meanings of this second sort are given to statements of the disputed class in terms of statements of another class (ones about rocks, or God's ideas, or observable objects, or specific set structures); and in this sense each of the four views is reductionist. Finally, in each case there is a specific motive for the particular anti-realism: reliance on the word of God; belief that we are initially acquainted only with mind-dependent ideas, and that nothing of a radically different sort can be inferred or reasonably postulated; a meta-induction from the history of science; or the proofs of the non-determination of the continuum hypothesis (either way) by the standard axioms of set theory.

I want to relate these anti-realisms to what Dummett calls 'The general form of the argument employed by the anti-realist', and which, he says, 'is a very strong one'. This runs as follows:

> He [the anti-realist] maintains that the process by which we came to grasp the sense of statements of the disputed class, and the use which is subsequently made of these statements, are such that we could not derive from it any notion of what it would be for such a statement to be true independently of the sort of thing we have learned to recognise as establishing the truth of such statements. What we learn to do is to accept the truth of certain statements of the reductive class, or, in the case that there is no reductive class, the occurrence of certain conditions that we have been trained to recognise, as conclusively justifying the assertion of a given statement of the disputed class, and the truth of certain other statements, or the occurrence of certain other conditions, as conclusively justifying its denial. In the very nature of the case, we could not possibly have come to understand what it would be for the statement to be true independently of that which we have learned to treat as establishing its truth: there simply was no means by which we could be shown this ... (*Truth and Other Enigmas*, p. 362)

As Dummett indicates, this general form of argument can be interpreted, or could be applied, in either of two ways.

One interpretation would link closely with what we have noted about the above-mentioned four kinds of anti-realism. The 'process by which we came to grasp the sense of statements of the disputed class' would be, for example, the move which I have attributed to Philip Henry Gosse by which he deliberately gave a new meaning to sentences describing occurrences before 4004 B.C., or the move by which Dummett's non-constructivist mathematician gives a new meaning to statements of set theory with reference to the class of structures which share the common features described in the axioms. If this is the sort of process in question, then indeed the argument goes through. But, as Dummett makes clear, any analogue of this non-constructivist anti-realism about set theory will be a local rather than a global anti-realism. With regard to the past, there will be a set of possible past histories of the world each of which is compatible with everything that is now the case, and anything that is true in *all* these possible past histories will count as being true absolutely.

(Since any statement of the form $p \lor \sim p$ will be true in each such possible history, it will be true absolutely; hence the logic required for statements about the past with this meaning, though not two-valued, will not be intuitionist.)

Something that Dummett does not stress, however, is that for an anti-realism of this sort—about the past, for example—we require some further specific motivation, such as Gosse had with regard to prehistorical statements, or such as the mathematician has in the proofs about the consistency and independence of the continuum hypothesis. What motivation could there be for this local anti-realism about the *whole* of the past—about events, among others, in 1969, when Dummett's paper purports to have been published?

The alternative interpretation goes along with a global anti-realism. Here the suggestion is that *any* process by which we could have come to grasp the sense of statements of *whatever* class is, for the moment, the disputed class, and *any* use that we subsequently make of them, must be such that we could not derive from them any notion of what it would be for such a statement to be true independently of the sort of thing we have learned to recognize as establishing the truth of such statements.

The differences between this approach and our previous anti-realisms are evident. Here there is no original meaning which makes statements of the disputed class all either false or subjectless. Instead of a new meaning being introduced to give these statements a worthwhile use, it is alleged that the anti-realist meaning is forced on us, that it is the only one by which we could grasp what it would be for such a statement to be true. The anti-realism is now closely linked with limitations on *our* access to the truth of the statements in question, whereas Berkeley, for example, could be a realist even about parts of God's thinking to which *we* have no access. It is hard to see how the global anti-realist could even say 'There aren't any so-and-sos'. Perhaps he could use this as an equivalent of 'Terms of such-and-such a class do not really refer', where this is itself explained by the kind of meaning that is allegedly forced on us. Indeed, writing about intuitionism in mathematics, Dummett suggests that any such non-existence claims would be beside the point (pp. 231, xxv-xxviii). In any case any non-existence assertion would now follow the anti-realist account of the meanings of statements and terms, whereas in each of our four anti-realisms the non-existence assertion preceded the corresponding account of meanings. Also, with this interpretation, no further specific motivation is needed for anti-realism about, for example, the whole of the past. For any statement about the past is such that what we can treat as establishing its truth is something about the present, that is, something other than the past fact which the statement appears to report.

But though no such further specific motivation would be needed, we now have a problem in a different place. Why should we be convinced by this general argument, or even be swayed by it in the slightest degree? Indeed, it seems not to be an *argument*, but just a dogmatic *assertion* of a general theory of meaning which, as Dummett says (p. 370), is 'a generalisation of the intuitionist account of the meaning of mathematical statements'. Such phrases as 'In the very nature of the case ...' and 'we could not possibly have come to understand ...' and 'there simply was no means ...' made good sense within the previous interpretation of the argument, where there was a specific nature of the case for them to refer to—namely the deliberate giving, to statements of the disputed class, of a new meaning which carried the limitation in question with it; but in this second interpretation these phrases lack any such specific reference, and degenerate into mere table-thumping.

Perhaps this 'argument' can be understood at least as stating a challenge, as asking the realist about whatever subject is at issue to explain how we might come to an understanding of what it is for a statement of the class in question to be true independently of that which we have learned to treat as establishing its truth.

But, as Dummett goes on to show, the realist about the past can take up this challenge.

The realist's answer is: Just as you can grasp that the statement B, made in a year's time, will be true in virtue of the evidence that now exists for the truth of the present-tense statement A, even though in a year's time all trace of that evidence may have vanished, so you can conceive of the possibility that, a year ago, there was evidence justifying the assertion then of a present-tense statement 'P', even though there is now no evidence to justify the assertion now of the statement 'It was the case a year ago that P'; in forming this conception you have come to grasp precisely the sort of condition under which, on my account, the statement 'It was the case a year ago that P' is true, and under which it would not be true on your account. (p. 370)

In other words, if we can conceive the possibility that, a year hence, all evidence about a state of affairs which now obtains will have vanished, we can by analogy understand the possibility that there was a state of affairs a year ago all evidence of which has vanished now. Or can we put the central point even more simply? We know what it is for some present-tense statement 'P' to be true now. We know what it is for time to pass, for it to come to be, not (as it is now) November 13, but November 14. We have only to put these together to form the conception of a time when the past-tense statement 'It was the case yesterday that P' will be true. And since this procedure makes no use of evidence that may or may not be available on November 14, it gives us the required understanding of what it is for a statement about the past to be true-independently-of-present-evidence.

As far as I can see, Dummett does not criticize this suggestion *as a way of taking up the global anti-realist's challenge*. What he argues in the following pages is that both the global anti-realist and the local anti-realist about the past can go on saying something without being forced into incoherence. That is, their respective theses cannot be conclusively disproved by the realist's appeal to the 'truth-value link'. This may be so; but if the debating position is as I have supposed it to be, this is not good enough. The global anti-realist has issued a challenge; the realist about the past has taken it up; and the global anti-realist has said nothing to show that this answer is not an adequate reply to his challenge. For all that has been said, there *is* a way in which we can understand a past-tense statement's being simply true, that is, true independently of there being evidence for it, and the supposedly strong argument for (global) anti-realism no longer stands even as a challenge.

There is, perhaps, a way in which the anti-realist could resist the realist's suggestion. He might deny that he has now, on November 13, any grasp of the notion of its coming to be November 14, that is, any understanding of the term 'tomorrow'. Or perhaps he might say that he does understand the term 'tomorrow', but not the term 'yesterday'; or again that though he has some tenuous grasp of each of these terms he has no grasp of any analogy between the way in which tomorrow will be related to today and that in which today is related to yesterday. By making any of these moves he could deny that he can use the realist's suggestion in order to build up an understanding of what it is for a statement about the past to be simply true (true-independently-of-present-evidence). But this is a desperate remedy: if anyone says any of these things, I see no reason why we should believe him. Further, anyone who does say one of these things cannot be the anti-realist about whom Dummett says (p. 370), 'It is the anti-realist who takes time seriously, who thinks in the way McTaggart described as believing in time': one cannot believe in time and have so weak a grasp of 'yesterday', 'today', and 'tomorrow', and the analogies between them as this person pretends to have.

It seems, then, that while we can agree with Dummett that neither the global anti-realist nor the anti-realist solely about the past has been entrapped in incoherence, there is still nothing positively in favour of either of their views. The local anti-realist needs a further specific reason, perhaps analogous to Gosse's, for rejecting all statements about the past in their original meaning; but no such reason seems to be available. The global anti-realist, having no plausible reply to the way in which the realist takes up his challenge to explain our grasp of simple truth for statements about the past, is left with a merely dogmatic adherence to a theory of meaning which is a generalization of the intuitionist theory of the meaning of mathematical statements.

Perhaps it will be argued that the intuitionist theory is itself so powerful that it lends colour to this generalization. But it seems to me that whatever plausibility intuitionism has as a philosophy of mathematics is due to the elusiveness of what might count as mathematical objects, or at least of some of them, and to the associated peculiarities of mathematical thinking. Because they differ from Platonists 'over the kind of thing that [mathematical statements] are about', taking them to be 'about the free products of human thought' (Dummett, *op. cit.*, p. xxv), because they 'do not attribute an existence independent of our thought to the integers or to any other mathematical objects' (Heyting, in *Philosophy of Mathematics: Selected Readings*, edited by Benacerraf and Putnam (Oxford, 1964)), they are led to assign a special sort of meaning to mathematical statements: the peculiar status of products or objects of thought carries a peculiar logic with it, as we saw with the Berkeleian view that replaced material things with the objects of God's thought. If this is the order of argument, then intuitionism is just another local anti-realism, with a specific motivation not utterly unlike those of the four kinds of anti-realism with which I began. If so, whatever support there is for intuitionism will not carry over to a generalization of its theory of meaning. However, I am very conscious of the fact that in ascribing this order of argument to intuitionism I am going directly against what Dummett argues both in the Preface to *Truth and Other Enigmas* and in 'The Philosophical Basis of Intuitionistic Logic' (reprinted in the same volume, pp. 215–47).

... the alternative metaphysical views about mathematical objects do not serve as *premisses* for the rival interpretations of the meanings of mathematical statements ... It is more tempting to suppose that there is a dependence in the opposite direction ... If ... one believes, with the intuitionists, that the content of a mathematical statement resides entirely in our ability to recognise what constitutes a proof of it and what a disproof ... one will prefer a picture according to which mathematical reality is constructed by us, or, at least, comes into existence only as we become aware of it ... (Preface, p. xxviii)

Indeed, Dummett rebukes Strawson for assuming that the order of argument is what I have suggested that it is. It is quite consistent with his claim that 'the fundamental case for the intuitionistic position rested on quite general considerations about the way in which we give meaning to our sentences, rather than to any features peculiar to mathematical statements' that Dummett should expect that 'the reasoning could be applied to other areas of discourse' (p. xxix)

Since I have no authority and little confidence in this area, I must leave it to others to dispute, if they will, Dummett's interpretation of the order of argument in intuitionist theory. I can, however, state a dilemma. If the order is what I have suggested, then there is no good reason for generalizing from intuitionism to give support to a general theory of meaning which would lead in turn to a global anti-realism. If, on the other hand, the order is what Dummett maintains that it is, then this general theory of meaning precedes the intuitionist philosophy of mathematics and is not supported by it, and we are still in need of an *argument* to support it: we are back where we were before, where the allegedly strong general form of argument for anti-realism had turned out to be sheer unsupported assertion.

*

It is obvious that much more needs to be said, especially since Dummett indicates, for example in 'The Philosophical Basis of Intuitionistic Logic', how he would argue for the general theory of meaning in question. But as this paper is already too long, I must break off at this unsatisfactory point. However, the conclusion which I would hope in the end to defend is now plain enough. There may well be defensible special anti-realisms, each with its own special motivation, special grounds for adopting the meanings for a certain class of a statements which then lead to failures of bivalence and to some non-classical logic. If there is indeed more than one of these, it is very likely that there will be formal analogies between them, which make it illuminating to class such theories together as anti-realisms. But there is no warrant for a global anti-realism or for the generalization of the intuitionist theory of meaning that appears to lead to it.

ANTI-REALISMS: A CONTINUATION

In 'The Philosophical Basis of Intuitionistic Logic' Dummett's central thesis is that intuitionism in mathematics must be based on a general theory of meaning, not on anything peculiar to mathematics. This thesis is developed by arguing that the question of the sort of meaning that statements (in mathematics or elsewhere) have is prior to the question whether there are or are not objects of some category: the assertions or denials of the existence of objects of a certain category have to be taken as metaphors whose literal counterparts are the statements about meaning.

This claim is implausible when we consider the examples I have offered, of Gosse on prehistory, Berkeley on the material world, Putnam's positivist's view of theoretical entities in science, and Dummett's own example in set theory.

The claim is supported, however, by two specific arguments. First, that even if someone took a platonist view of the natural numbers he might still take an intuitionist view of meaning and so reject a classical logic for number-theoretic statements in general. Secondly, that even if someone took the view that natural numbers are creations of human thought he might still think that there is a conception of truth that makes every number-theoretic statement determinately either true or false, so that the meaning of such statements could be explained in terms of truth-conditions (p. 231).

The first of these two arguments presupposes that there is a plausible general theory of meaning of an intuitionist sort; since this is the ultimate question at issue, it will be circular to use this argument here. The second argument is developed at length, in details which I cannot follow. On general grounds it seems likely that it could apply only where the method by which human thought is supposed to create numbers is of a very systematic sort—which perhaps holds for the natural numbers, but not so obviously for other parts of mathematics: the analogy of the four examples mentioned above shows that it will not hold for 'creations' in general.

2 Before developing the thesis stated in 1 above, Dummett has argued that intuitionism *can* be defended by reference to this general theory of meaning, which is itself supported by the Wittgensteinian thesis that 'use exhaustively determines meaning' (pp. 216, 218, 220, 224). This thesis in turn is both interpreted in the light of and supported by the view that meaning must be totally communicable between individuals, and that 'An individual cannot communicate what he cannot be observed to communicate' (p. 216).

In the Preface to *Truth and Other Enigmas* Dummett rebukes Strawson for 'unblushingly reject[ing] that whole polemic of Wittgenstein's that has come to be known as "the private-language argument"' (p. xxxii). Since I think that that argument, so interpreted as to tell against the account that Strawson gives of the meaning of, for example, 'pain', is unsound, I don't think that Strawson had any need to blush about this. Blushes might be more becoming in those who simply reiterate their conviction that Wittgenstein's case against 'private ostensive definition' is 'incontrovertible' (p. xxxiii). But this is too big an issue to reopen here. I merely record my view that it cannot be assumed to have been settled in favour of the necessary publicity, and public checkability, of all aspects of meaning. If the case for the intuitionistic general

theory of meaning has to assume that meaning is wholly determined by publicly checkable use, then it is built on sand.

However, one need not query this foundation in order to be
rationally dissatisfied with that case as a whole. Dummett says,
rightly, that there are sentences (in mathematics as elsewhere)
whose truth-value we are not capable of effectively deciding (p. 223),
and that 'on the theory of meaning that underlies platonism'—a
realist one—'an individual's grasp of the meaning of such a sentence consists in his knowledge of what the condition is which has
to obtain for the sentence to be true, even though the condition is
one which he cannot, in general, recognise as obtaining when it
does obtain' (p. 224). But he then argues that this conception 'violates the principle that use exhaustively determines meaning'. 'For',
he says, 'if the knowledge that constitutes a grasp of the meaning
of a sentence has to be capable of being manifested in actual linguistic practice, it is quite obscure in what the knowledge of the
condition under which a sentence is true can consist, when that
condition is not one which is always capable of being recognised
as obtaining' (p. 224). But I suggest that this is obscure only
because the issue has been stated in such utterly general terms. Let
us take an example. Tom and Dick have succeeded in establishing
a communicated, public, meaning for the present-tense sentence 'It
is raining now'. On Monday, Tom says 'It is raining now, on
Monday; and it will rain tomorrow, on Tuesday'. Dick says that
he understands the first half of Tom's sentence but not the second
half. Tom says 'All right, just wait'. On Tuesday Tom says 'You
see, it's raining now, on Tuesday; that is the condition that makes
true the second half of the statement I made on Monday'. And if
Tom goes on to say 'And it will rain tomorrow, on Wednesday',
will not Dick have to be excessively stupid to fail to understand
this? Although the condition under which this sentence is true 'is
not one which is always capable of being recognised as obtaining',
and indeed cannot be recognized on Tuesday as obtaining, it is by
no means 'obscure in what the knowledge of the condition under
which [the] sentence is true can consist'. Dick knows on Tuesday,
by employing the analogy 'Monday is to Tuesday as Tuesday is to
Wednesday' along with what has been communicated as the
truth-condition for the statement made on Monday about rain on
Tuesday, what the truth-condition for the statement made on Tuesday about rain on Wednesday is, despite the fact that he cannot

on Tuesday recognize whether that condition obtains or not. I agree that this would fail if Dick were very slow in the uptake; but even if there are reasons for thinking that meaning has to be communicable, it would not follow that it has to be communicable among morons.

This is, of course, only a variant of what I said previously about how the realist about the past can take up the challenge of the global anti-realist. Unless the latter can show that there is something wrong with such responses to his challenge, he cannot simply go on appealing to a 'principle' which may sound plausible when it is stated only in general terms, but which becomes utterly implausible when implemented in particular cases. And since it is meant to be a general principle justifying a general theory of meaning which leads to global anti-realism, a single good counter-example is enough to refute it once and for all. Also, the situation is not that the anti-realist has an already-established position, and merely needs to *defend* it against attack. We are still in search of any argument at all for global anti-realism and the general theory of meaning associated with it. We therefore need positive reasons for saying that the apparent counter-examples to the alleged principle are not counter-examples, not merely some device by which they might be explained away if we already had independent reasons for accepting the principle.

3 There seems to be a special difficulty about Dummett's derivation of intuitionism in mathematics from the proposed general theory of meaning. If that theory led us to reject a realist view of truth-conditions for mathematical statements and of truth-conditions as constituting the meaning of those statements, it might be plausible to turn to proof, instead, as what determines meaning (p. 225). But what are the grounds on which we could then criticize the conventional 'canons of proof'? (p. 226) If we were to decide that some alleged proofs are not really proofs, would we not have to be relying on something other than proof as constituting the meaning of the statements in question? Dummett seems to be saying that what we first fix, in this line of argument, is a construal of the logical constants in terms of the conception of meaning; but *what* conception of meaning, if it is prior to the determination of what counts as proof? At least this needs some further explanation.

4 Essentially the same argument is appealed to in 'What is a Theory of Meaning? (II)' in *Truth and Meaning*, edited by Evans and McDowell (Oxford, 1976), pp. 67–137, especially at pp. 81–2. Natural language, Dummett rightly says, is 'full of sentences which are not effectively decidable'. He goes on:

But, for such a sentence, we cannot equate a capacity to recognize [a] the satisfaction or non-satisfaction of the condition for the sentence to be true with a knowledge of what that condition is. We cannot make such an equation/because, by hypothesis, either the condition is one which may obtain in some cases in which we are incapable of [b] recognizing the fact, or it is one which may fail to obtain in some cases in which we are incapable of recognizing that fact, or both:/ hence a knowledge of what it is for that condition to hold or not to hold, while it may demand an ability to recognize one or other state [c] of affairs whenever we are in a position to do so, cannot be exhaustively explained in terms of that ability./In fact, whenever the condition for the truth of a sentence is one that we have no way of [d] bringing ourselves to recognize as obtaining whenever it obtains, it seems plain that there is no content to an ascription of an *implicit* knowledge of what that condition is,/since there is no practical abil- [e] ity by means of which such knowledge may be manifested.

In this passage I have marked off and labelled the five statements (a) to (e). It is supposed to present a difficulty for 'the attempt to construct a theory of meaning which uses the notion of truth as its central notion'. However, while (b) is clearly true, the inference of (a) and (c)—which are practically equivalent to one another—from (b) is dubious, and similarly while (e) is true, the inference of (d) from it is questionable: what it alleges is not at all plain.

Against (a) and (c), I would suggest that if someone has the capacity to recognize that a certain condition is satisfied whenever he is in a position to do the recognizing, he has the knowledge of what it is for that condition to be satisfied as long as he retains that capacity, even in circumstances where he is not at the moment in a position to do such recognizing. To deny this would seem to deprive the notion of having a capacity of all use or content. For exactly the same reason, we can say, against (d), that there is content available for the ascription of an implicit—that is, not at the moment being manifested—knowledge of a condition, despite the fact that at the moment there is no practical ability by means of which it may be manifested—that is, that the knower is not at the moment able to manifest his knowledge. This could be denied only by someone who rejected altogether the concept of someone's having at t a capacity that circumstances prevent him from manifesting at t, saying, for example, that someone who loses his tennis racquet thereby loses the capacity to play tennis. To do this is to reject the very concept of a capacity; is Dummett prepared to go so far?

INDEX OF NAMES